With the Master On Our Knees

By
Susan J. Heck

With the Master On Our Knees
By Susan J. Heck

Focus Publishing, Bemidji, Minnesota

Cover design by Barb Van Thomma

Cover portrait, *He Shall Hear My Voice*, painted by Michael Dudash—www.cmdudash.com

ISBN 978-1-885904-78-2

Printed in the United States of America

To my praying friend

Helen Ruth

who has inspired me
to be more faithful
With the Master On Our Knees

Table of Contents

Chapter 1

An Introduction to Prayer

Selected Scriptures

If I were to ask you, "what is one of the greatest struggles you have in your spiritual walk?" I would venture to say that the primary answer I would receive would be "prayer." Elizabeth Elliot once said at a conference that I attended, "Prayer is irksome. We are reluctant to start and delighted to end." Why is that? Why is it that the greatest need in our Christian life is an effective prayer life, and yet we are reluctant to pray? As we introduce this topic of prayer, I'd like to suggest some answers to that question, but first I want to give a definition of prayer as well as some interesting facts regarding prayer.

What is Prayer?

Prayer is the desire, opportunity and privilege of talking to God. Prayer is the expression of man's dependence upon God for all things. Prayer is an absolute transfer of my will to God. Prayer requires sincerity, repentance or contrition, purpose of amendment and a good life, the spirit of consecration, faith, and submission to the will of God.

Terms for Prayer

There are numerous Hebrew and Greek terms for prayer in the Bible, and as we study we will see some of these terms in their context, and I trust they will give these passages new meaning for each of you. We have terms for prayer that include supplication to God and supplication for others. Another term is a quiet whispering prayer because of a consciousness of sin which crushes so completely that a man does not dare to address God aloud. There is another word for prayer which speaks of praying in general, another which expresses personal need, and yet another which expresses childlike confidence. In their original meaning these words will add much to our understanding of the prayers we'll study in the coming chapters.

The Origin of Prayer

Where did prayer originate? How did it get started? Have you ever wondered what the first prayer was that man prayed to God? How did he approach God? What were the first words he said? Since prayer is talking to God, then we must look at Genesis 3, where we find our first glimpse of prayer. Consider the following:

> Now the serpent was more cunning than any beast of the field which the LORD God had made. And he said to the woman, "Has God indeed said, 'You shall not eat of every tree of the garden'?" And the woman said to the serpent, "We may eat the fruit of the trees of the garden; but of the fruit of the tree which is in the midst of the garden, God has said, 'You shall not eat it, nor shall you touch it, lest you die.' "Then the serpent said to the woman, "You will not surely die. For God knows that in the day you eat of it your eyes will be opened, and you will be like God, knowing good and evil." So when the woman saw that the tree was good for food, that it was pleasant to the eyes, and a tree desirable to make one wise, she took of its fruit and ate. She also gave to her husband with her, and he ate. Then the eyes of both of them were opened, and they knew that they were naked; and they sewed fig leaves together and made themselves coverings. And they heard the sound of the LORD God walking in the garden in the cool of the day, and Adam

> and his wife hid themselves from the presence of the LORD God among the trees of the garden. Then the LORD God called to Adam and said to him, "Where are you?" So he said, "I heard Your voice in the garden, and I was afraid because I was naked; and I hid myself.' And He said, "Who told you that you were naked? Have you eaten from the tree of which I commanded you that you should not eat?" Then the man said, "The woman whom You gave to be with me, she gave me of the tree, and I ate." (Genesis 3:1-12)

If prayer is talking to God, then we cannot ignore Genesis 3:10 where Adam spoke to God. Adam's words to the Lord fit in the category of prayer. He's not asking God for anything, or confessing sin, but just talking to God. So we could say this was the first prayer. Though it is not recorded in the Word, it is likely Adam and Eve had talked to God even before this account here in Genesis 3.

We must next consider the next account in Genesis 4:26b: "Then men began to call on the name of the LORD." This appears to be the first time that men began to actually call out to God. Why? Because of the broken fellowship which was a result of the sin of Adam and Eve. Mankind became very aware of their sin and their separation from God, their Creator. They desired to seek Him, to fear Him and to do his will. They became conscious of their own weakness, and so men began to call upon the name of the Lord. By the way, these are excellent reasons to approach God in prayer. Prayer is a privilege that we should never take for granted. God did not have to communicate with man after Adam and Eve sinned, but He did, because He loves us and desires to have fellowship with us. So these two accounts are the first prayers recorded in the Word of God. Obviously, we cannot make mention of all the other accounts of prayer in the Scriptures, but let's at least consider the last account of prayer that is recorded for us.

What is the last prayer that is mentioned for our benefit? Where is it located in the Scriptures? The last prayer recorded for us in the Bible is in Revelation 22:20b which also happens to be the last words in the Bible: "Even so, come, Lord Jesus!" The writer of Revelation, the Apostle John, is the one who prays this prayer. It is fitting that the last prayer recorded for us pertains to the blessed hope which is the coming of our Lord Jesus. This is the hope of all saints from ages past, present and future. The reason men began calling on the name of the Lord in Genesis 4:26, which was because of sin and broken fellowship, will no longer be a need when we see Him face to face when He comes. Prayer, as we now know it to be will no longer be necessary. We will be praising Him throughout eternity—yes, but praying—no! "Even so, come, Lord Jesus!"

Prayer in the Old Testament

So, we have considered the first prayer and the last prayer mentioned in the Word of God, but what else do we know about prayer from the Bible? Let's take a look first at the Old Testament. Prayer is evidently associated with sacrifice as seen in Genesis 12:8, 13:4, and 26:25. Genesis 12:8 reads, "And he moved from there to the mountain east of Bethel, and he pitched his tent with Bethel on the west and Ai on the east; there he built an altar to the LORD and called on the name of the LORD." In Genesis 13:4 we read, "to the place of the altar which he had made there at first. And there Abram called on the name of the LORD." And Genesis 26:25 tells us, "So he built an altar there and called on the name of the LORD, and he pitched his tent there; and there Isaac's servants dug a well." This is interesting due to the fact that Hebrews 13:15

indicates that prayer is associated with sacrifice: "Therefore by Him let us continually offer the sacrifice of praise to God, that is, the fruit of our lips, giving thanks to His name."

As we continue on in the Old Testament, it is interesting to note that the Old Testament Law has remarkably little to say on the subject of prayer. The access of the private individual to God is viewed more as mediation of the priest as seen in Deuteronomy 21:5. In Exodus 32:11-13 we have the intercession of the prophet Moses as he is communicating with God, as well as the example of Samuel in 1 Samuel 7:5-13 and 12:25. Prayer in the Old Testament was also associated with the ordered approach of tabernacle and temple services as evidenced by the passages in Exodus 40 and 1 Kings 8. Things began to change drastically after Israel went through the experience of being chastened by God and then exiled. Chastisement drove the nation to seek God more earnestly than before. Of course, there is nothing new under the sun, as many times chastisement has a way of bringing us to our knees. The devotional habits of Ezra, Nehemiah, and Daniel (3 times a day) seem to show how important prayer had become to these dear saints. We not only learn from these men how devoted they truly were in prayer, but also that they gave great importance to confession of sin in their prayers. Nehemiah 9:3 records for us that a quarter of the day was spent in confession of sin. What a revival that must have been as the people confessed and turned from their sin!

We can't leave a survey of the Old Testament without mentioning the 150 Psalms—they have been left for our benefit. Each of the 150 Psalms is a prayer in itself. The Psalms are some of the loftiest prayers which have ever been written, and we would do well to incorporate them into our daily communication with our Lord. The Psalmists had intense craving for pardon, purity and immense spiritual blessings.

They had something our day and age is missing, which is a heartfelt longing for a living communion with God Himself to the point that nothing else seemed to matter to them. The Psalmist pens it well in Psalm 42:1 “As the deer pants for the water brooks, so pants my soul for You, O God.”

The Old Testament Jew practiced prayer in some interesting ways, far different from our practices today. The beginning of the day and the end of the day were celebrated by special prayers. The end of the week would also be celebrated with special Sabbath services which would include prayer. In the Jewish home there was daily prayer, especially grace after meals (interesting that we do it before), and then there would be frequent prayers of the individual. As early as David’s time we hear of private prayer being offered three times a day, which became an established practice, the hours being at the time of the morning sacrifice—about the third hour, at midday—about the sixth hour, and at the time of the evening sacrifice—about the ninth hour (Daniel 9:21). That would be at 9:00 a.m., 12:00 noon, and 3:00 p.m., respectively. As a rule, the Israelites prayed in a solitary room, especially the upper chamber, or in elevated places and mountains with the view of being alone. If they were near the sanctuary, they offered their prayers in the court, with their faces turned toward the Holy of Holies. Prayer was generally made standing, but sometimes, expressing deeper devotion, they would kneel or bow their head to the ground. In both cases the hands were uplifted and spread toward heaven or in the direction of the Holy of Holies. In cases of deep, penitential prayer it was usual for them to strike the breast with the hand and to bend the head toward the bosom. The prayers of the Old Testament saints were unshakable, unusual and daring, yet they were heard in that they feared (something we have lost sight of in our age). These Old Testament saints knew little of the philosophy of prayer that many of us are taught, i.e., the ACTS method of prayer (Adoration, Confession, Thanksgiving, and Supplication). What they did know was the God to whom they prayed, and they knew there was power in prayer. Now let's shift from the Old Testament to take a look at what we know about prayer from the New Testament.

Prayer in the New Testament

The role model we have of Christian prayer in the New Testament comes to us from Christ in the Gospels. We would do well to take notice of His habits which have been left for us to emulate. He spent all night in prayer (Luke 6:12); He got up very early to pray (Mark 1:35); He prayed at the feeding of the 5000 (Luke 9:16) at the transfiguration (Luke 9:28). He prayed at His own baptism (Luke 3:21), at the garden before His crucifixion (Luke 22:40), and even while dying He prayed to His Father (Luke 23:34). He taught us to approach God as our Father in the Lord's Prayer, which serves as a model of prayer (Luke 11:2-4). But according to John's Gospel, this was not His final word on the subject. On the night of His betrayal, knowing that He would soon die, He told His disciples that prayer was to be addressed to the Father in the name of the Son, and that prayer offered in this manner was sure to be granted (John 16:23-24, 26). He then left the disciples and us with an awesome prayer known as the High Priestly Prayer in John 17. We see a contrast between Old Testament praying and New Testament praying in that prayer was to be offered in the New Testament in the name of Christ.

In Acts and the Epistles we see the early church giving heed to Christ's teaching on prayer. It was in a praying atmosphere that the church was born as seen in Acts 1:14 and

Acts 2:1, and even throughout its early history prayer continued to be vital to the church. The Epistles abound with references to prayer. Paul, in particular, alludes frequently to his own personal practice in the matter (Romans 1:9; Ephesians 1:16; Philippians 1:9; 1 Thessalonians 1:2). He also includes many exhortations to his readers to cultivate a habit of prayer (Romans 12:12; Ephesians 6:18; Philippians 4:6; 1 Thessalonians 5:17). But the new thing about Christian prayer that we see in the Epistles is that it is connected with the Spirit. As Paul wrote in Romans 8:26 and 27, "Likewise the Spirit also helps in our weaknesses. For we do not know what we should pray for as we ought, but the Spirit Himself makes intercession for us with groanings which cannot be uttered. Now He who searches the hearts knows what the mind of the Spirit is, because He makes intercession for the saints according to the will of God." The apostles were known as men of prayer and they record much for us on the subject. In fact, James, who wrote the Epistle of James, was known to have knees like camels because he was on his knees so much in prayer.

Some Interesting Facts Regarding Prayer

Now we have mentioned something regarding prayer in the Old Testament and the New Testament, but do you know how many prayers there are in the Bible, not including the Psalms? There are over 650 prayers in the Word of God, and out of those 650 prayers there are at least 450 that have recorded answers. Now obviously, there is not time or space in this book to mention all of these, and to exposit them. But, there are prayers about obedience; prayer for a bride; prayer for a wicked city; prayer for the needy; prayer for protection; prayer of a discouraged heart; prayer of a meek man; prayer for a new leader; prayer as a blessing, as thanksgiving, as a song; prayer God does not answer (this is one most of us don't like); prayer for direction; prayer for an unborn child; prayer in the face of death; prayer without words; prayer of a grieved heart; prayer for a sick child; prayer for a wise heart; prayer for a withered hand; prayer for longer life; prayer in emergency; prayer for a prosperous journey; prayer for false friends; prayer for a perfect life; prayer for Christian stability; and prayer of the martyred host. This is just a small fraction of some of the things which are prayed for according to what is in the Holy Scriptures.

Saints of Old and Their Prayer Habits

Now as we leave the New Testament church and enter into the distant past, we do find men and women who were devoted to prayer. Jonathan Edwards once spent three days and nights praying (that's no food and no sleep) before he preached the sermon entitled *Sinners in the Hands of an Angry God*, which touched the lives of many and still does to this day. Susannah Wesley, who in spite of the fact that she had nineteen children, found time to shut herself in her room for a full hour every day to be alone with God. George Mueller once stated that once he felt a thing was right he would pray until the answer came. John Knox fasted regularly and history tells us that the Queen of Scotland feared his prayers more than the armies of England. Andrew Bonar said he would not be content until he prayed at least two hours every day. Samuel Chadwick went apart three times a day for prayer. He said it wasn't easy, the dinner hour short, the family was large and the house small, but he managed. Charles Wesley would leave company at 9:00 p.m., in order that he might collect his thoughts before God before going to bed. But he was up at 4:00 a.m.

so that he might have uninterrupted time with God in prayer. These are just a few of the saints of old who left us a legacy to follow. Oh, how we need to follow their example in the 21st century, as we are a Christianized people who fall far short.

Prayers of the 21st Century

As we come to our day we stand ashamed, as our prayers fall far short of the examples of the saints who have gone before us. Unfortunately, some of our praying might sound like this: "Lord bless this mess, amen!" "Lord, give me this and give me that. Amen!" When many of us pray, we offer "popcorn" calls to heaven and few are serious in prayer, and some of us don't pray at all. We don't make time for prayer because we do not see it as a vital part of our relationship with God. We make time to sleep, eat, read the newspaper and novels, watch television, surf the internet, visit our friends, have endless lunches, phone calls, meetings and more meetings, but no time for prayer. By our constant activity and self-absorption, we force Christ away from our thoughts and prayers. May I say that living a holy life would not be such a rarity in our day if our devotions were not so short and hurried? The songwriter put it well when he wrote that we must "take *time* to be holy"[1] (emphasis mine). Where are the women and men who will devote time to pray? Who will go down in history in our age as men and women of prayer? Or will there be any? Are you a woman of prayer? Do you pray? D.L. Moody once said that "Next to the wonder of seeing his Savior would be the wonder that he made so little use of the power of prayer."

1 Words by William D. Longstaff. 1882.

Attitudes in Prayer

Now I have given you a lot of facts regarding prayer and I hope that they have whetted your appetite for this study, but in the remaining part of the introduction to this book, I want to say a few words about prayer itself. Prayer is hard work, but it is a holy work. There must be certain attitudes that accompany our praying. Have you ever thought about what your attitudes should be when you pray? I would like to give you six attitudes that should be present when we come to God in prayer.

1. *Awe.* In Revelation 1:17, when John saw the glorified Christ, he fell at his feet as though dead. When Isaiah saw the Lord he said, "Woe is me, for I am undone! Because I am a man of unclean lips, And I dwell in the midst of a people of unclean lips; For my eyes have seen the King, The LORD of hosts" (Isaiah 6:5). We should show respect when we talk to a Holy God. He is not the man upstairs or our best bud, or a genie waiting to grant all our selfish desires.

2. *Helplessness.* In 1 Peter 5:5, Peter records for us that God is against the proud, but gives grace to the humble. Nothing will probably hinder your prayers more than the attitude that says "I don't need God's help; I can fix this, thank you very much." But for the soul who says, as Jehoshaphat said, "Lord, I don't know what to do but my eyes are on you" (II Chronicles 20:12), to that soul, God pours out His grace and mercy and gives aid in our time of need.

3. *Faith.* Hebrews 11:6 says, "But without faith it is impossible to please Him, for he who comes to God must believe that He is, and that He is a rewarder of those who diligently seek Him." Do we really believe that He is all powerful and that there is nothing too hard for Him? Or do we come with an unexpectant attitude, which says, "yeah right,

He won't answer this prayer"? Without faith, there can be no prayer, no matter how great our helplessness may be.

4. *Persistence.* Jesus Himself said in Matthew 7:7, "Ask, and it will be given to you; seek, and you will find; knock, and it will be opened to you." The Greek literally reads, ask and keep on asking, seek and keep on seeking, knock and keep on knocking. In the parable of the unjust judge, Jesus uses a persistent widow and an unjust judge to teach us that "men ought always to pray and not to lose heart" (Luke 18:1). Most of us give up after praying about something once. There are things that I have been praying for years, as I am sure there are for you also.

5. *Earnestness.* James says in his Epistle, in 5:16b, "The effective, fervent prayer of a righteous man avails much." Our prayers should have energy and zeal, and should not be lethargic and half-hearted. We should pray like Jacob when he wrestled with God, and prayed, "I will not let You go unless You bless me!" (Genesis 32:26b).

6. *Boldness.* Hebrews 4:16 says: "Let us therefore come boldly to the throne of grace, that we may obtain mercy and find grace to help in time of need." We should come with confidence and freedom of speech. We should tell God what He already knows, and we should talk to Him as if He were our dearest friend, pouring out our heart with all sincerity.

Hindrances to Answered Prayer

Having examined the attitudes that should be present when we pray, let's consider some things that might hinder our prayers from being answered. Perhaps you pray often, even daily, or many times a day, and yet God doesn't answer your prayers. Have you ever wondered why? There are many hindrances to prayer, but we will list the three main ones that Scripture gives us.

1. *Unconfessed sin.* Psalm 66:18 says, "If I regard iniquity in my heart, the Lord will not hear." Isaiah 59:2 tells us, "But your iniquities have separated you from your God; and your sins have hidden His face from you, so that He will not hear." These passages are very clear to point out the fact that it is impossible for God to even hear our prayers if we have sin in our lives and in our hearts. For example, if you come to God in prayer while harboring an unforgiving spirit toward another person or if you have just lashed out in anger at your mate and not made it right, or if you are involved in sexual immorality, you cannot expect the ear of the Lord to bend to your prayers. This is a huge hindrance to prayer and in our day and age when sin has been minimized in the life of believers, it goes without saying, God may not be answering your prayers due to ongoing, unrepentant sin.

2. *Wrong motives.* James 4:3 says, "You ask and do not receive, because you ask amiss, that you may spend it on your pleasures." In the context here, James tells us that we might be praying, but if our prayers are for selfish motives God is not going to answer them. For example, if you are asking God for a new car or a new home so that you can impress some one or look good, then that is a selfish motive. If you are asking for a new car or home for the glory of God and to be used for ministry and hospitality, then if it is His will you might receive it. I would encourage you to examine your prayers as you pray and ask yourself, "What is the motive behind this request?" You might be surprised as to what you discover about your prayer life.

3. *Not praying according to God's will.* The aged apostle John tells us in his first Epistle: "Now this is the confidence that we have in Him, that if we ask anything according to His will, He hears us" (I John 5:14). As we pray, we must always keep in mind that God has a perfect plan for each of us and our

thoughts are not His thoughts and our ways are not His ways. So if he doesn't answer our prayers or give us what we want when we think we need it, it often is due to the fact that it might not be His will. I remember having a conversation with an individual asking why they divorced their mate, to which they replied, "I prayed that God would stop me if it wasn't His will, and He did not stop me." I remember being shocked, as this person did not have Biblical grounds for divorce. I shared that with them regarding their error, but it fell on deaf ears. If God has already revealed His will to you through His Word, then there is no reason to waste time praying about it. But if He hasn't specifically done so, then we can certainly plead before the throne, but always keeping in mind that it may not be His will.

Dear friends, God does answer prayer. Sometimes He says yes. Sometimes He says wait. Sometimes the answer is no. Sometimes He answers, but not in the way perhaps we would like to see Him answer, but He does answer prayer.

When Should We Pray?

Many times women find it difficult with busy schedules at home with family to find time to pray. When does one pray? Some women I know have scheduled times with the Lord and that is good, and some pray all day and that is even better. Paul says in I Thessalonians 5:17 that we are to pray without ceasing. As mentioned previously, the Jews prayed morning, noon and night. Remember, our Lord got up a great while before day and prayed, and even spent all night in prayer. We can pray anywhere: in the car, in the shower, on your bed, outside, inside, on the sea, on land, anywhere (Jonah prayed in the belly of a fish). We can pray privately or publicly. It is good to have a set time to pray each day, but don't get into such a legalistic routine of praying, that it becomes dry and mundane.

The Method of Prayer

You might be wondering what your prayers should consist of. Before I answer this, let me say that we should be careful with *methods* of prayer, as they are not inspired by God. They can, however, be helpful. Samuel Chadwick said "Methods are nothing apart from inspiration, and the most faulty tools are better with Him then the most approved without Him." The one that is probably the most familiar to each of us is the ACTS method: Adoration, Confession, Thanksgiving, and Supplication. *Adoration* is where we begin with who God is. We acknowledge His attributes and worship Him. This might include praying His names back to Him. Prayers about Him from the Word are good to use as you adore Him. *Confession* deals with agreeing with God that you have sinned and then confessing what those sins are. May I also say that we should be confessing our sins with a desire to also turn away from them in repentance? *Thanksgiving* is when we offer our gratitude for all God has done for us. This will remind of us the goodness of God and less of our own needs. We have so much to be thankful for. In fact, sometime spend all your time in prayer just thanking God. It will be a rich time! *Supplication* is the area most of us spend most of our time in when we pray. Supplication is where we bring our needs and other's needs to God. If this is all you do in prayer, then as AW Tozer says, "We go to God as we send a boy to a grocery store with a long written list." One of the greatest blessings I have found when supplicating for others and for myself is to use Scripture. It is powerful! For example, "Lord I pray that I will remember that you will never leave me or forsake me." "Lord, please give my child the ability to flee youthful lusts and follow after righteousness." "Father, give me the grace to be submissive to my husband as unto You, and help him to live with me in an understanding way." When we pray the Word of God we will avoid praying aimlessly and outside of the will of God.

As we conclude this introductory chapter, let me say that my goal for you is not just to inform you of what the Bible says about prayer, even though we will do that, or to inform you of how the saints who have gone before prayed, even though we will do that as well. More than these, my goal is that each of us will become a woman of prayer. May we each echo with the disciples who said, "Lord teach us to pray," because "a day without prayer is a day without blessing and a life without prayer is a life without power."[2] Will you journey with me as we walk *With the Master On Our Knees*?

2 Harvey, Edwin.

Questions to Consider

An Introduction to Prayer

Selected Scriptures

1. How would you define prayer?

2. (a) What do you know about prayer from the Bible? (b) What do you know about prayer from your own life or from the lives of others?

3. (a) Do you have a favorite prayer in the Bible? (b) If so, what is it?

4. (a) What is the most difficult thing about prayer for you personally? (b) Why do you think we should pray? (c) How have you taught your children or grandchildren or others you mentor to pray?

5. What do you hope to gain from this study? Put your hope in the form of a prayer request to God.

Chapter 2

The Prayer of Jehoshaphat:
What to Do When You Don't Know What to Do!
2 Chronicles 20

In the past few years the Lord allowed me to go through the most difficult trial of my life. At times the grief was so deep that I did not know if I would ever recover. I wept; I was depressed, which is not normal for me; and I wanted to go home to heaven. Life seemed to have lost its purpose, and most days I walked around in a fog. I wondered if my joy would ever return. When I thought about which prayer should begin this book, *With the Master On Our Knees*, there was really no other option for me.

On more than one occasion in the midst of this trial, Jehoshaphat's prayer struck clear in my mind. I would say, "Lord we don't know what to do, but our eyes are on you." I know that many of you could say the very same thing, that is, there are those times in your life when life seems impossible. The battle is raging, the trials of life seem overwhelming, and quite frankly you don't know what to do. What *do* we do during those difficult times in our life? Where *do* we turn? To *whom* do we turn?

I am excited about our first chapter, since we can learn eleven practical principles from King Jehoshaphat when facing what seems to be the impossible. Let's look together at 2 Chronicles 20, where we find the story of Jehoshaphat and what prompted this prayer of his. Here is the outline for this lesson: *Jehoshaphat's problem* (vv. 1-2); *Jehoshaphat's response* (vv. 3-4); *Jehoshaphat's prayer* (vv. 5-13); *the Lord's response* (vv. 14-19); *the victory* (vv. 20-30); and *the rest of the story* (vv. 31-37).

Before we get into the text, I would like to begin by giving you some preliminary information about Jehoshaphat. First of all, he was the son of King Asa. He received an excellent heritage from his father, who in the earlier years of his reign showed a desire to seek God. Jehoshaphat's faith in God led him to "delight in the ways of the Lord." *Jehoshaphat* means "the Lord is judge." He was 35 years old when he became king, and he reigned 25 years in Jerusalem. He attacked pagan idolatry and sent teachers to the people so they could learn more about God. The reign of Jehoshaphat appears to have been one of unusual religious activity. I say this because it appears that Jehoshaphat sought the Lord in almost every detail of his life. The character of Jehoshaphat is summarized in 2 Chronicles 22:9: "…Jehoshaphat, who sought the Lord with all his heart." When you look at his life, especially compared with the lives of the other kings mentioned in the Old Testament, no trace of the pride that dishonored and ruined the other kings who preceded and succeeded him can be found.

As we leave Jehoshaphat enjoying peace and prosperity in chapter 19, all seemed to be going well with this young king, until he received the startling news that a "great multitude" was coming against him (2 Chronicles 20:1-2.) Isn't this when the biggest battles come? Life seems to be going oh so well. We are enjoying the abundant life of peace and joy and then WHAM—a test—which is what we have here. I remember basking in how good God had been to me before the onset of this overwhelming trial, thinking that life could not have been any better. God was blessing me in so many ways that I could hardly count them.

Jehoshaphat's Problem
2 Chronicles 20:1-2

> It happened after this that the people of Moab with the people of Ammon, and others with them besides the Ammonites, came to battle against Jehoshaphat. [2]Then some came and told Jehoshaphat, saying, "A great multitude is coming against you from beyond the sea, from Syria; and they are in Hazazon Tamar" (which is En Gedi). (2 Chronicles 20:1, 2)

Here we see that everything is going well for Jehoshaphat and the kingdom of Judah, until the threat of an invasion by the Moabites and the Ammonites. Now put yourself in Jehoshaphat's shoes. How would you feel about now? You would probably feel the same way that he felt. So, what did Jehoshaphat do? Let's see in verse 3.

Jehoshaphat's Response
2 Chronicles 20:3-4

> And Jehoshaphat feared, and set himself to seek the LORD, and proclaimed a fast throughout all Judah. [4]So Judah gathered together to ask help from the LORD; and from all the cities of Judah they came to seek the LORD. (2 Chronicles 20:3, 4)

Notice that Jehoshaphat feared. Yes, he feared. Jehoshaphat was afraid? That seems strange, doesn't it? After all, he was the King of Judah! You wouldn't think such an important person would be afraid, and yet he was. Ladies, fear is an emotion that God has given us, and yet we must not let fear overtake us. We must not allow our fear to be a temptation to sin. Notice that Jehoshaphat did not allow himself to wallow in that fear. He did not have a panic attack, nor did he take drugs for his anxiety; instead he set himself to seek the Lord. "The surprise added to the fright. Holy fear is a spur to prayer and preparation."[3]

Jehoshaphat knew that he was totally unable to do anything in and of himself, so he turned to the Lord. What would have been involved here in seeking the Lord? It actually means that Jehoshaphat worshipped the Lord. In the midst of his fear Jehoshaphat worshipped the Lord. Is that what *we* do when *we* are afraid? Do *we* worship the Lord?

Principle #1: *Worship the Lord.* Notice that Jehoshaphat proclaimed a fast throughout all of Judah. This would indicate that not only did Jehoshaphat fast, but he also enlisted others to do the same. Jehoshaphat knew that he could not possibly stand against such a vast army; therefore, he could not expect to be delivered except by the strong arm of God. To get this assistance, it was necessary to seek it, and so he proclaimed a universal fast. This event is interesting because up until now in the Old Testament, there is no mention of any authority proclaiming a fast. Jehoshaphat appears to be the first king to do so. This particular fast would have also been extended to children and infants (see v. 13; see also Joel 2:15-16 and Jonah 3:7).

Principle #2: *Ask others to assist you in prayer and fasting.* I have seen the Lord work in some very unusual ways when someone seeks His face through fasting. The day I was working on this lesson—and fasting, I asked the Lord to encourage someone who was very discouraged. By two o'clock that afternoon, three sources of encouragement had come to this person. It is unfortunate that in our American Christianity we don't fast more often. We miss out on such a blessing! The text goes on to say that *Judah gathered together to ask help from the LORD;*

3 Henry, Matthew-(*Matthew Henry's Commentary on the Whole Bible*-MacDonald Publishing Co.-Volume II-Joshua to Esther) -page 966.

and from all the cities of Judah they came to seek the LORD. Now I don't know how many people were actually there since the text does not indicate, but what a prayer meeting that must have been! And so we come to the actual prayer of Jehoshaphat.

Jehoshaphat's Prayer
2 Chronicles 20:5-13

> Then Jehoshaphat stood in the assembly of Judah and Jerusalem, in the house of the LORD, before the new court, [6]and said: "O LORD God of our fathers, are You not God in heaven, and do You not rule over all the kingdoms of the nations, and in Your hand is there not power and might, so that no one is able to withstand You? [7]"Are You not our God, who drove out the inhabitants of this land before Your people Israel, and gave it to the descendants of Abraham Your friend forever? [8]"And they dwell in it, and have built You a sanctuary in it for Your name, saying, [9]'If disaster comes upon us—sword, judgment, pestilence, or famine—we will stand before this temple and in Your presence (for Your name is in this temple), and cry out to You in our affliction, and You will hear and save.' [10]"And now, here are the people of Ammon, Moab, and Mount Seir-- whom You would not let Israel invade when they came out of the land of Egypt, but they turned from them and did not destroy them-- [11]"here they are, rewarding us by coming to throw us out of Your possession which You have given us to inherit. [12]"O our God, will You not judge them? For we have no power against this great multitude that is coming against us; nor do we know what to do, but our eyes are upon You." [13]Now all Judah, with their little ones, their wives, and their children, stood before the LORD. (2 Chronicles 20:5-13)

First of all, notice in verse 5 that Jehoshaphat was standing. There are many postures of prayer mentioned in the Bible, this being one of them. We have examples of kneeling in prayer, lifting up one's eyes in prayer, lifting up holy hands in prayer, lying prostrate in prayer, and even praying on one's bed. God is not looking at the posture of your body but the posture of your heart.

Also notice in verse 5 that the prayer takes place *in the house of the Lord, before the new court*. What is the new court? In Solomon's Temple there were two courts. One of these had probably been renovated by Jehoshaphat or by his father, Asa, and was known as "the new court." And so we have the beginning of the prayer in verse 6.

Jehoshaphat began his prayer acknowledging God's greatness. Like many Old Testament prayers, his began with reverence for the Lord. Jehoshaphat acknowledged that God is in heaven, that He is all powerful, and that He is ruler over these heathen nations that were threatening Judah.

Principle #3: *Acknowledge God's greatness.* He is bigger than any problem you are facing, and nothing is impossible for Him. I remember saying often during my trial, "If God can part the Red Sea, then He can take care of this!"

Next, Jehoshaphat acknowledged God's goodness by affirming that He gave this land to Abraham His friend forever. In essence, he was saying, "Lord, you gave this land to us, now don't let it be invaded and taken from us."

Principle #4: *Acknowledge God's goodness.* There is nothing better for one's soul than to remind ourselves of how good God is and what He has already done for us in the past.

As we look at verses 8 and 9, we see yet another great aspect of this prayer. Jehoshaphat's appeal here is based on Solomon's prayer, which God had already heard (see 2 Chronicles 7:12-16). Jehoshaphat reminded God of his promises to Solomon.

Principle #5: *Remind God of his promises*—promises like, "Lord, you have said, 'I will never leave thee or forsake thee.' You also have said that nothing is impossible for you, and yet this situation seems impossible. And then, Lord, there is that promise that your grace is sufficient for me. Lord, help me to draw upon your grace in this situation." After Jehoshaphat reminded God of His promise, He told God the problem that he was facing in verses 10 and 11. Next time you don't know what to do, apply principle #6.

Principle #6: *Tell God your problem.* Maybe you are saying, "He already knows, so why should I tell Him?" You tell Him because He is your dearest friend and the One who allowed the situation to come up. He is also the only One who knows how it is going to turn out, so why not discuss it with Him? Many times we run to other sources to share our problems, but we should instead do as the songwriter says, "I must tell Jesus all of my problems, I cannot bear these burdens alone."[4] And so Jehoshaphat did.

In verse 12 he continues his communion with God by saying, "O our God, will You not judge them? For we have no power against this great multitude that is coming against us; nor do we know what to do, but our eyes are upon You." Verse 12 stands alone as his petition. God, *judge them.* That is his entire petition. Judge them, Lord. Inflict deserved punishment on them. The reason Jehoshaphat asked for God's intervention was because of their weakness against the *great multitude* of an army that was coming against them. In fact, Jehoshaphat expressed his weakness in the next part of his prayer: *nor do we know what to do, but are eyes are upon You.* Jehoshaphat was saying, Lord, we rely upon You, and from You is all our expectation, which leads us to our next principle.

4 Words by Elisha Hoffman, 1839-1929.

Principle #7: *Look to Him.* Turn your eyes to Him; focus on God for the answers and not on your own circumstances. This is why so many of us get all worked up and allow fear to paralyze us—we keep our eyes on people and circumstances instead of fixing our eyes on Jesus, the author and finisher of our faith! (Hebrews 12:2) The Psalmist said, "My eyes *are* ever toward the LORD, for He shall pluck my feet out of the net" (Psalm 25:15).

So the prayer ends, and we read in verse 13: "Now all Judah, with their little ones, their wives, and their children, stood before the LORD." What a sight that must have been as the whole congregation looked to the Lord for its help. So now we ask, "How does the Lord respond to this prayer?" We find the answer in the next portion of Scripture.

The Lord's Response
2 Chronicles 20:14-19

> Then the Spirit of the LORD came upon Jahaziel the son
> of Zechariah, the son of Benaiah, the son of Jeiel, the
> son of Mattaniah, a Levite of the sons of Asaph, in the
> midst of the assembly. 15And he said, "Listen, all you of
> Judah and you inhabitants of Jerusalem, and you, King
> Jehoshaphat! Thus says the LORD to you: 'Do not be
> afraid nor dismayed because of this great multitude, for
> the battle is not yours, but God's. 16'Tomorrow go down
> against them. They will surely come up by the Ascent
> of Ziz, and you will find them at the end of the brook
> before the Wilderness of Jeruel. 17'You will not need to
> fight in this battle. Position yourselves, stand still and
> see the salvation of the LORD, who is with you, O Judah
> and Jerusalem!' Do not fear or be dismayed; tomorrow
> go out against them, for the LORD is with you." 18And
> Jehoshaphat bowed his head with his face to the ground,
> and all Judah and the inhabitants of Jerusalem bowed
> before the LORD, worshiping the LORD. 19Then the

> Levites of the children of the Kohathites and of the children of the Korahites stood up to praise the LORD God of Israel with voices loud and high.

Notice in verse 14 that the Spirit of the Lord came upon the prophet Jahaziel. He is not mentioned anywhere else in the Bible, but evidently the Lord wanted to use him to encourage Jehoshaphat and the kingdom of Judah. Here in this verse we have God's gracious answer to Jehoshaphat's prayer, and it was a speedy answer. While he was yet speaking, God heard; and before the congregation was dismissed they had been given assurance that they should be victorious. This reminds me of Isaiah 65:24 where it says, "It shall come to pass that before they call, I will answer; and while they are still speaking, I will hear." What an encouragement to them, as well as to you and me, that God knows what we are going to say before we say it, and that He hears and answers. And so this prophet, Jahaziel, sent by God, said, *Do not be afraid nor dismayed.* Why? *For the battle is not yours, but God's.* We try and fight our own battles, and yet they are not ours to fight—they are God's. Similar words were spoken by David to Goliath: "the battle is the Lord's and He will give you into our hands" (1 Samuel 17:47).

Principle #8: *Never fear, for the battle is the Lord's.* In verse 17 we see that the prophet Jahaziel went on to tell Jehoshaphat and his people that they weren't even going to have to fight in the battle. What a deal! Just stand still and know that I am God. That is exactly what we need to do when we're going through difficult times. We need to get out of God's way and let Him fight for us. We try to fight the battle ourselves and usually end up losing. How much better things would go if we would let Him fight for us. *Stand still and see the salvation of the Lord. Stand still* does not mean inactivity; it does not mean "let go and let God." But because of the power of prayer, we can face *any* issue in our lives with confidence. It is this attitude that Paul wrote about in Hebrews 11:1, of faith being the substance of things hoped for, the evidence of things not seen, which leads us to our next principle.

Principle #9: *Have faith.* This is probably where most of us give a foothold to Satan, because we shake in our faith and wonder whether God can really work in our situation, whatever it may be. We are like the double-minded man who, while going through a trial, is like a wave of the sea driven and tossed by the wind. James says that that man should not suppose that he will receive anything of the Lord. James tells us instead that when going through a trial we are to ask in faith, *with no doubting* (James 1:6-7).[5]

Have faith in God, dear friend. Hasn't He been faithful in the past, and won't He be faithful in the future? *Do not fear, or be dismayed.* This is the second time the prophet Jahaziel said this (the first being in verse 15). He went on to say, *tomorrow go out against them, for the LORD is with you.* These are very similar to the words that God spoke to Joshua, "Have I not commanded you? Be strong and of good courage; do not be afraid, nor be dismayed, for the LORD your God is with you wherever you go" (Joshua 1:9).

After these words of encouragement from Jahaziel, we see the response from Jehoshaphat and the people in verse 18. "And Jehoshaphat bowed his head with his face to the ground, and all Judah and the inhabitants of Jerusalem bowed before the LORD, worshiping the LORD. Then the Levites of the children of the Kohathites and of the children of the Korahites stood up to praise the LORD God of Israel with voices loud and high." Observe here that Jehoshaphat bowed with his face to the ground worshipping the LORD, which illustrates our next principle.

5 See *With the Master in the School of Tested Faith: A Ladies' Bible Study of the Epistle of James*, by the author of this volume; pages 33-36.

Principle #10: *Allow your circumstances to humble you.* The apostle Peter wrote, "Therefore humble yourselves under the mighty hand of God, that He may exalt you in due time" (1 Peter 5:6). What Peter was really saying is that we have two choices: we can either allow ourselves to be humbled by the circumstances that God allows in our lives, or we can fight against Him and watch Him humble us. Jehoshaphat allowed himself to be humbled by his circumstances. He bowed his face to the ground in humble adoration. He did not shake his fist at God. Instead, his attitude expressed reverence for God and His Word, confidence in His promise, and thankfulness for His favor. Once again, we see this attitude of worship in the midst of a trial. Not only did Jehoshaphat worship God, but notice in verse 19 that the people praised *the LORD God of Israel with voices loud and high.* This leads us to our next principle.

Principle #11: *Praise the Lord.* It's amazing what praise will do. And part of that praising can be with song, as we will see in verses 21 and 22. Try it next time you are in a fix—you'll like it! They lifted up their voices in praise to God, showing their faith was active. An active faith can give thanks for a promise even though it has not yet been fulfilled. What He says, He will do! And in the next passage of our study, we see that victory.

The Victory
2 Chronicles 20:20-30

> So they rose early in the morning and went out into the Wilderness of Tekoa; and as they went out, Jehoshaphat stood and said, "Hear me, O Judah and you inhabitants of Jerusalem: Believe in the LORD your God, and you shall be established; believe His prophets, and you shall
> prosper." [21]And when he had consulted with the people,
> he appointed those who should sing to the LORD, and

> who should praise the beauty of holiness, as they went out before the army and were saying: "Praise the LORD, for His mercy endures forever." [22]Now when they began to sing and to praise, the LORD set ambushes against the people of Ammon, Moab, and Mount Seir, who had come against Judah; and they were defeated. [23]For the people of Ammon and Moab stood up against the inhabitants of Mount Seir to utterly kill and destroy them. And when they had made an end of the inhabitants of Seir, they helped to destroy one another. [24]So when Judah came to a place overlooking the wilderness, they looked toward the multitude; and there were their dead bodies, fallen on the earth. No one had escaped. [25]When Jehoshaphat and his people came to take away their spoil, they found among them an abundance of valuables on the dead bodies, and precious jewelry, which they stripped off for themselves, more than they could carry away; and they were three days gathering the spoil because there was so much. [26]And on the fourth day they assembled in the Valley of Berachah, for there they blessed the LORD; therefore the name of that place was called The Valley of Berachah until this day. [27]Then they returned, every man of Judah and Jerusalem, with Jehoshaphat in front of them, to go back to Jerusalem with joy, for the LORD had made them rejoice over their enemies. [28]So they came to Jerusalem, with stringed instruments and harps and trumpets, to the house of the LORD. [29]And the fear of God was on all the kingdoms of those countries when they heard that the LORD had fought against the enemies of Israel. [30]Then the realm of Jehoshaphat was quiet, for his God gave him rest all around. (2 Chronicles 20:20-30)

Notice in verse 20 that King Jehoshaphat encouraged them twice to believe. Faith was their armor. Faith is the Victory! As they went forth, instead of calling them to take up their swords for battle, Jehoshaphat called them to believe in the Lord God and what his prophet had said. I cannot think of anything else that will so establish one's heart in shaking times than a firm belief in the power, mercy, and promises of God. "The heart is fixed, trusts in the Lord, and is kept in perfect peace. In our spiritual conflicts, this is the victory; this is the prosperity, even our faith."[6]

In verse 22 we see that *when* they began to sing and to praise *then* the Lord acted. Not when they worried and fretted, but when they did exactly what Jehoshaphat said they were going to do, which was to keep their eyes on Him. "Nor do we know what to do, but our eyes are upon you" (2 Chronicles 20:12). Now you might ask how this ambush was actually an ambush. Some think that this was done by angels in human form whose sudden appearance began an uncontrollable panic. Others suppose that jealousies and animosities had sprung up, which led to widespread dissensions and fierce feuds in which they drew their swords against each other. Regardless of what happened, God allowed these wicked men to destroy each other, and the work of destruction was completed even before Jehoshaphat and his people arrived at the battlefield. These wicked people were used as instruments of God to destroy each other. The march of the troops of Judah from Jerusalem would have taken five to six hours, and by the time they reached the watch-towers in the wilderness of Jeruel, all was over. None escaped! (Verse 24) The Lord does His job thoroughly and completely. I think this is a good point to note here. I have noticed over the years, when people are intent on doing me harm, that as I trust in the Lord and try not to defend or vindicate myself, the Lord vindicates me. It is amazing to just sit back and watch His handiwork. "'Ven-

6 Henry, Matthew-*Matthew Henry's Commentary on the Whole Bible*-MacDonald Publishing Co.-Volume II-Joshua to Esther; page 969.

geance is mine, I will repay,' says the Lord" (Romans 12:19)

Notice in verse 25 that there was more spoil than they could carry away. In fact, it took three days to remove everything. This reminds me of what Paul wrote to the Ephesians: "Now to Him who is able to do exceedingly abundantly above all that we ask or think, according to the power that works in us" (Ephesians 3:20). I am sure that the people of Judah stood in awe at God's greatness as He fought this great battle for them, and then to top it off with so much stuff that it took three days to gather! And doesn't He do that in our lives at times? Not only does He answer our petition for help, but then He also surprises us many times with those extra blessings! And so as God blessed them, they turned around and blessed Him, spending a day thanking God for His mercy and answered prayer (verse 26). They returned to Jerusalem with *joy*, which means blithesomeness or glee, for the LORD had made them rejoice over their enemies (verse 27).

What an example for you and me to follow! This is probably where many of us fall short. God hears our prayers and answers them, but we are like the nine out of ten lepers cleansed by Jesus who did not bother to return to Him and give thanks (Luke 7:12-19). But here we see the nation of Judah spending a day in thanksgiving to God. After the battle was over and thanks were given, then *the fear of God was on all the kingdoms of those countries when they heard that the LORD had fought against the enemies of Israel. Then the realm of Jehoshaphat was quiet, for his God gave him rest all around* (verses 29, 30).

Notice the result: the fear of the Lord was on *all* the kingdoms (emphasis mine). So the realm of Jehoshaphat was quiet—for his God gave him rest round about. When we put our eyes on Him and allow Him to fight for us, we too are quiet and can bask in the rest that God has promised. If God can give us rest, who can give us disturbance? If He is for us, who can be against us? Now I want to end this lesson with the rest of the story.

The Rest of the Story
2 Chronicles 20:31-37

> So Jehoshaphat was king over Judah. He was thirty-five
> years old when he became king, and he reigned twenty-
> five years in Jerusalem. His mother's name was Azubah
> the daughter of Shilhi. [32]And he walked in the way of his
> father Asa, and did not turn aside from it, doing what was
> right in the sight of the LORD. [33]Nevertheless the high
> places were not taken away, for as yet the people had not
> directed their hearts to the God of their fathers. [34]Now
> the rest of the acts of Jehoshaphat, first and last, indeed
> they are written in the book of Jehu the son of Hanani,
> which is mentioned in the book of the kings of Israel.
> [35]After this Jehoshaphat king of Judah allied himself
> with Ahaziah king of Israel, who acted very wickedly.
> [36]And he allied himself with him to make ships to go to
> Tarshish, and they made the ships in Ezion Geber. [37]But
> Eliezer the son of Dodavah of Mareshah prophesied
> against Jehoshaphat, saying, "Because you have allied
> yourself with Ahaziah, the LORD has destroyed your
> works." Then the ships were wrecked, so that they were
> not able to go to Tarshish. (2 Chronicles 20:31-37)

In verse 35 there is an emphasis laid upon the time frame—*after this*—*after* God had done such great things for him, *after* God had given him not only victory, but wealth. *After this*, Jehoshaphat joined himself with a wicked king. *After* God had given him such deliverance as this he should break God's commandments and join with such wicked men! This is a warning to us all that we should take heed lest we fall (1 Corinthians 10:12). It goes without saying that just when we have experienced the mountain-tops of our lives, just when God has done great things for us, that is when we must be on the alert. We must be careful *that* our hearts are not lifted up to think that we can dabble just a little with sin. After all, God has shown his favor toward us. We cannot for a moment let our spiritual guard down, lest Satan come and attack. Yet God was merciful and did not allow Jehoshaphat to sin but brought him to repentance by two means: first by a prophet who foretold the destruction of his project; and then by a storm, which broke the ships in the port before they set sail (verse 37). The destruction of the ships was a judgment of God on Jehoshaphat for entering into an alliance with Ahaziah. This event was also referred to in the Psalms: "As when You break the ships of Tarshish with an east wind" (Psalm 48:7, 1 Kings 22:47-49). Jehoshaphat wasn't strong enough to flee the temptation, so in His mercy God intervened on his behalf. And so the account of Jehoshaphat concludes in Chapter 21. "And Jehoshaphat rested with his fathers, and was buried with his fathers in the City of David. Then Jehoram his son reigned in his place" (2 Chronicles 21:1).

Summary

What a great story! What a merciful ending! So what can we learn from this godly king during tough times? What should you do the next time you don't know what to do?

I just imagine that if King Jehoshaphat were still alive today, he would identify with the Helen Lemmel song, *Turn Your Eyes Upon Jesus*. As I thought about these words, they reminded me of the text we have been studying.

O soul, are you weary and troubled? No light in the darkness you see? There's light for a look at the Saviour, and life more abundant and free. Turn your eyes upon Jesus, look full in His wonderful face, and the things of earth will grow strangely dim, in the light of His glory and grace.[7]

7 Words by Helen Lemmel, 1864-1961

Questions to Consider

The Prayer of Jehoshaphat

2 Chronicles 20

1. Read 2 Chronicles 17, 18 and 19. (a) Make note of the ways that Jehoshaphat "walked in the ways of the Lord." (b) Would you say Jehoshaphat was a good king or a bad king?

2. Read 2 Chronicles 20:1-2. What were the events surrounding Jehoshaphat and his kingdom at this time?

3. In 2 Chronicles 20:3-19, what things does Jehoshaphat do to seek the Lord in the midst of his trial?

4. (a) How did God answer Jehoshaphat's prayer? (b) How did Jehoshaphat and his people react?

5. (a) What is the "rest of the story?" See vv. 31-37. (b) What does this teach you about letting down your guard after spiritually victorious times?

6. Psalm 48 was written after the events of 2 Chronicles 20. Read Psalm 48 and list those things that coincide with 2 Chronicles 20.

7. (a) Recall a time when you "did not know what to do." (b) What did you do? (c) What principles can you learn from Jehoshaphat the next time that "you don't know what to do?"

8. Are you in a situation today where you don't know what to do? Please write down your prayer request.

Chapter 3
Solomon's Prayer for Wisdom
1 Kings

"Age has nothing to do with wisdom," said Simple. "I know a man 52 years old who never goes home *except* to take a bath and change his underwear." This indeed is a true statement about wisdom. Age really has nothing to do with wisdom. I have seen men and women who are much older than I who seem to lack wisdom; however, I also have been around those who are much younger than I who seem to be endowed with much wisdom from God.

Solomon was the wisest man in all of history, yet he was not *even close to the age of 52* when God graciously answered his prayer for wisdom. (You might even be surprised to know how young he was when God answered His prayer. We will learn that a little later in the lesson.) As a believer in Jesus Christ, I am sure you can echo the same thing I am going to say, which is this: I think I pray for wisdom more than for anything. I pray for wisdom for what to do, wisdom for when to do it, wisdom for what to say, wisdom for when to say it, and wisdom for how to say it. On and on go my prayers for wisdom. Wisdom is a wonderful thing to possess. As wise Solomon said in Proverbs 4:7, "Getting wisdom is the most important thing you can do! And with your wisdom, develop common sense and good judgment" (The Living Bible).

Solomon's prayer for wisdom is an appropriate prayer to study after Jehoshaphat's prayer from the last chapter. Why? Because both of these men needed wisdom from God.

Jehoshaphat was in the midst of a great battle which seemed overwhelming, and even though Jehoshaphat's words were not specifically, "Lord I need wisdom," they were directed to the only One who could give him wisdom and help. Solomon and Jehoshaphat both had something in common—both were kings and both were in desperate need of wisdom.

Now as we examine this prayer of King Solomon for wisdom, I want us to look at the place, the time, the offer, the prayer, the answer, the reality of the answer, the fall, and the lessons to be learned from this portion of Scripture.

The Place
1 Kings 3:1-4

> Now Solomon made a treaty with Pharaoh King of Egypt, and married Pharaoh's daughter; then he brought her to the City of David until he had finished building his own house, and the house of the LORD, and the wall all around Jerusalem. [2]Meanwhile the people sacrificed at the high places, because there was no house built for the name of the LORD until those days. [3]And Solomon loved the LORD, walking in the statutes of his father David, except that he sacrificed and burned incense at the high places. [4]Now the king went to Gibeon to sacrifice there, for that was the great high place: Solomon offered a thousand burnt offerings on that altar. (1 Kings 3:1-4)

Notice in verse 3 that Solomon loved the Lord. The Holy Spirit put a very important statement here, since one who loves the Lord will obey the Lord. As it is written, "For this is the love of God that we keep his commandments. And His commandments are not burdensome" (1 John 5:3 NKJ). Solomon loved God, which in turn resulted in his obedience to the One he loved so much. By the way, here is an interesting fact: the name *Sol-*

omon means *beloved of the Lord.* Verse three also records that Solomon walked in the statutes of David his father. We know that Solomon's father David was a man after God's own heart.

Now in verse 4 we see that Gibeon was the place from where his request for wisdom was made. Five miles north of Jerusalem, it was the location of the great high place. According to 2 Chronicles 1:3, it was there that the tabernacle and the bronze altar were present. Gibeon was the most popular high place for sacrifices at this time. It was at Gibeon that Solomon offered his great sacrifices—a thousand to be exact. A good principle found here is: the nearer we come to the heart of God in our worship, the more reason we have to expect the blessings of God's presence. Solomon was actively worshipping His God; therefore he had no problem in making such a bold request for wisdom, as we shall see later on. As 1 John 3:22 says "And whatever we ask we receive from Him, because we keep His commandments and do those things that are pleasing in His sight" (NKJ). When you and I are walking with God and worshipping Him with all of our being, then we can boldly come to His throne of grace to obtain mercy and find grace to help in our time of need (Hebrews 4:16). So the place of the request was Gibeon.

What time was it when Solomon made this request for wisdom? Verse 5 records the time for us.

The Time
1 Kings 3:5

> At Gibeon the LORD appeared to Solomon in a dream by night; and God said, "Ask! What shall I give you?" (1 Kings 3:5)

The time of the request was at night, the night after Solomon had offered a generous sacrifice of a thousand burnt offerings. Now we don't know exactly how long it took Solomon to offer a thousand burnt offerings, but I imagine it was a full day's work. The type of offering mentioned here is important. When a burnt offering was made, the entire offering was burned up, and so it symbolized one's entire surrender to God or an entire congregation's surrender to God. Even though it had been a very busy day for King Solomon with worship and sacrifices to the Lord, the Lord continued to visit him in the night.

This reminds me of an account in Luke chapter six. Recorded there for us is one of our Lord's busiest days in ministry, and yet Luke tells us in verse 12 of chapter 6 that the Lord spent all night in prayer. I am sure we all could testify that some of God's kindest visits are often in the night, even after a busy day. I thought it was rather interesting that the Lord awoke me on a Saturday night at 1:30—after a busy day and before the Lord's Day—to work on this lesson. The Psalmist often speaks of the Lord and his communication with Him at night. Psalm 16:7 says, "I will bless the LORD who has given me counsel; my heart also instructs me in the night seasons." I am sure that many of us can testify to the fact that when we can't sleep at night, some of our best times are just lying in bed communing with God.

Now 1 Kings 3:5 says that God appeared to Solomon in a dream. Speaking to the Old Testament prophets in dreams was a normal way in which God communicated with them. For example, Numbers 12:6 states, "Then He said, 'Hear now My words: If there is a prophet among you, I, the LORD, make Myself known to him in a vision; I speak to him in a dream.'" So the Lord speaks to Solomon in a dream, and next we have the offer from God to Solomon.

The Offer
1 Kings 3:5

> At Gibeon the LORD appeared to Solomon in a dream by night; and God said, "Ask! What shall I give you?" (1 Kings 3:5)

Ask what you want! What do you want Solomon? I will give it to you! Wow! Now the Lord was in no way indebted to Solomon, but because God is gracious He made Solomon this offer. Now ladies, what would you say to God if he asked you that question? What is the one thing you would ask for? A new dress, a new house, a boat, a million dollars? Worldly things were obviously not on Solomon's mind. He had a much loftier and eternal perspective. Solomon had the glory of God in mind, and His name was of utmost importance. As Jesus said so well in John 14:13, "And whatever you ask in My name, that I will do, that the Father may be glorified in the Son." In 1 John 5:14 the apostle John wrote, "Now this is the confidence that we have in Him, that if we ask anything according to His will, He hears us." So God made the offer to Solomon—*ask what you will*—then in verses 6-9, Solomon submitted his request in the form of a prayer.

The Prayer
1 Kings 3:6-9

> And Solomon said: "You have shown great mercy to Your servant David my father, because he walked before You in truth, in righteousness, and in uprightness of heart with You; You have continued this great kindness for him, and You have given him a son to sit on his throne, as *it is* this day. [7]"Now, O LORD my God, You have made Your servant king instead of my father David, but I

> am a little child; I do not know how to go out or come in. [8]"And Your servant is in the midst of Your people whom You have chosen, a great people, too numerous to be numbered or counted. [9]"Therefore give to Your servant an understanding heart to judge Your people, that I may discern between good and evil. For who is able to judge this great people of Yours?" (1 Kings 3:6-9)

Observe that Solomon spent time praising God *before* he petitioned Him. This is a good principle that we can all learn from King Solomon. Most of us start our prayers with petitions, thinking that God is a genie waiting to grant us our every wish—*give me this and give me that*. We would be wise to first acknowledge who He is and ask ourselves "Just who is this Awesome Being with whom we are talking?" It would be most wise of us to enter into His presence with adoration and thanksgiving for His goodness to us. Solomon knew that God was kind to him because of his father David's faithfulness to God, and so he expressed that first. In verse seven notice Solomon's humility: "but I am a little child, and I do not know how to go out or come in." Solomon recognized his own insufficiency and well knew what Paul echoed in 2 Corinthians 3:5: "Not that we are sufficient of ourselves to think of anything as being from ourselves, but our sufficiency is from God." When Solomon said that he did not know how to go out or come in, he was saying that he was just like an infant learning to walk alone and could not come or go without help.

Josephus has recorded that Solomon's age at this time was 14; however, most scholars think he was actually around the age of 20. Regardless of whether he was 14 years old or 20 years old, he was very young to be leading such an enormous number of people. In fact, verse eight tells us that it was so great that they could not even be numbered or counted. In verse nine he follows with the question: "For who is able to judge this great people?" And so we come to Solomon's petition.

The Petition
1 Kings 3:9

> "Therefore give to Your servant an understanding heart to judge Your people, that I may discern between good and evil. For who is able to judge this great people of Yours?" (1 Kings 3:9)

Solomon was praying, "Because You are merciful, because my father David walked in truth and righteousness, because of my insufficiency, then therefore give Your servant an understanding heart to judge Your people, that I may discern between good and bad." Now what exactly was Solomon asking for here? An understanding heart literally means a hearing heart. Solomon wanted a heart that was so tuned in to the voice of God that he would lead Israel the way God would lead Israel. And why did Solomon desire such a thing? Was it so he could succeed by being famous? No, he desired this request in order to be able to discern good and evil and to judge the people. Solomon didn't ask for an understanding heart to please his own curiosity or impress his neighbors or even to have his name recorded in a history book, but he desired wisdom so that he might judge God's people.

Now what is wisdom? *Chokmah* (Hebrew word for *wisdom*) is the knowledge and the ability to make the right choices at the opportune time. The prerequisite for wisdom is the fear of the Lord. According to Proverbs 1:7, "The fear of the LORD is the beginning of knowledge, but fools despise wisdom and instruction." Solomon knew that, and he knew that he must pray for wisdom. As James 1:5 states, "If any of you lacks wisdom, let him ask of God, who gives to all liberally and without reproach, and it will be given to him." His ability to judge the people would be essential in King Solomon's position, since one of the chief functions of the King was to hear and decide cases. So did God answer Solomon's request for wisdom? Let us read verses 10-15 for the Lord's answer to Solomon's request.

The Answer
1 Kings 3:10-15

> The speech pleased the LORD, that Solomon had asked this thing. [11]Then God said to him: "Because you have asked this thing, and have not asked long life for yourself, nor have asked riches for yourself, nor have asked the life of your enemies, but have asked for yourself understanding to discern justice, [12]"behold, I have done according to your words; see, I have given you a wise and understanding heart, so that there has not been anyone like you before you, nor shall any like you arise after you. [13]"And I have also given you what you have not asked: both riches and honor, so that there shall not be anyone like you among the kings all your days. [14]"So if you walk in My ways, to keep My statutes and My commandments, as your father David walked, then I will lengthen your days." [15]Then Solomon awoke; and indeed it had been a dream. And he came to Jerusalem and stood before the ark of the covenant of the LORD, offered up burnt offerings, offered peace offerings, and made a feast for all his servants. (1 Kings 3:10-15)

Notice in verse 10 that Solomon's prayer request pleased the Lord. Have you asked yourself lately, "Self, do my prayer requests please the Lord?" It pleased the Lord that His beloved asked for wisdom. And so God said, Solomon, because you have asked for wisdom, and not for wealth or health, or that I destroy your enemies, then I will grant your request. In fact, Solomon, not only will I give you a wise and understanding heart, but you will be the wisest man ever—none before you will be wiser and none after you. And more than that, beloved one of mine, I will give you things you have not even asked for—things like riches, and honor, and even a long life.

But notice the condition stipulated by the Lord in verse 14—*if.* "If you walk in My ways, to keep My statutes and My commandments, as your father David walked." The Lord was telling Solomon that he must do his part, that he must continue to walk in obedience if he wanted to live a long life. The promise here was conditional. We will see in a moment that Solomon did not observe this condition (1 Kings 11:1-8), and so his right to a long life was forfeited and God's answer was not fulfilled. In fact, it is said that Solomon could not have been more than fifty-nine or sixty at the time of his death. Before we get into the sad ending, let us look at the reality of the answer.

The Reality of the Answer
1 Kings 3:16-28

> Now two women who were harlots came to the king, and stood before him. [17]And one woman said, "O my lord, this woman and I dwell in the same house; and I gave birth while she was in the house. [18]"Then it happened, the third day after I had given birth, that this woman also gave birth. And we were together; no one was with us in the house, except the two of us in the house. [19]"And this woman's son died in the night, because she lay on him. [20]"So she arose in the middle of the night and took my son from my side, while your maidservant slept, and laid him in her bosom, and laid her dead child in my bosom. [21]"And when I rose in the morning to nurse my son, there he was, dead. But when I had examined him

> in the morning, indeed, he was not my son whom I had
> borne." [22]Then the other woman said, "No! But the living
> one is my son, and the dead one is your son." And the
> first woman said, "No! But the dead one is your son, and
> the living one is my son." Thus they spoke before the
> king. [23]And the king said, "The one says, 'This is my
> son, who lives, and your son is the dead one'; and the
> other says, 'No! But your son is the dead one, and my
> son is the living one.'" [24]Then the king said, "Bring me a
> sword." So they brought a sword before the king. [25]And
> the king said, "Divide the living child in two, and give
> half to one, and half to the other." [26]Then the woman
> whose son was living spoke to the king, for she yearned
> with compassion for her son; and she said, "O my lord,
> give her the living child, and by no means kill him!" But
> the other said, "Let him be neither mine nor yours, but
> divide him." [27]So the king answered and said, "Give the
> first woman the living child, and by no means kill him;
> she is his mother." [28]And all Israel heard of the judgment
> which the king had rendered; and they feared the king,
> for they saw that the wisdom of God was in him to
> administer justice. (1 Kings 3:16-28)

Almost every time I read this portion of the Word of God, I am amazed at Solomon's wisdom. It was truly incredible. I don't think I would have ever thought of such a solution to this problem; I probably would have set up visitation rights for both women. But Solomon, being filled with wisdom, knew that the real mother would have such a deep love and compassion for her child that she would die for her child; and so Solomon commands the child to be cut in two, knowing that the real mother would give up her right to the child in order that the child would live. The result of this kind of wisdom was that all of Israel feared King Solomon (1 Kings 4:29-34). Today Solomon would be described as a man of encyclopedic knowledge. Godly wisdom can be intimidating.

For another instance of an answer to this prayer read 1 Kings 10:1-13. When the Queen of Sheba came to test Solomon's wisdom, he answered all her questions with ease. After she witnessed the extent of his empire and the immensity of his knowledge, she confessed that she had underestimated him. In fact, in verse 7 she said, "indeed the half was not told me," and the whole experience left her breathless. She observed the happiness of those who were around Solomon, even the servants.

Solomon wrote about this truth in Proverb 3:13: "Happy is the man who finds wisdom." Proverb 3:17 says that wisdom is pleasant and peaceful. James 3:17 tells us that God's wisdom is peaceful. As you and I walk with God, as we seek His face in every aspect of our life, it is pleasant, and it is peaceful. So God answered his prayer for wisdom, and it really goes without saying that King Solomon is usually remembered as a wise man. If you have forgotten how wise he was, read his writings in Proverbs, Ecclesiastes, and the Song of Solomon. The word *wisdom* appears 318 times in the Old Testament with over half of them found in Proverbs, Job, and Ecclesiastes, two of which were written by Solomon.

He had a deep knowledge of plants and animals. He also had a profound knowledge of human nature, as demonstrated by the two women who claimed the same child. Solomon also had a concern about the ethics of everyday life, evidenced by his Proverbs. Solomon's writings show his love of wisdom and his desire to teach others. He was a wise observer who could learn from the mistakes of others. During his lifetime, Solomon's fame as a man of wisdom spread to surrounding lands, and leaders came from afar to hear him speak. He seemed to have it all: wisdom, riches, and honor. It looked like he was heading for a long life—until *the fall*. Man has responsibility, and somewhere along the way Solomon forgot that.

The Fall
1 Kings 11:1-13

But King Solomon loved many foreign women, as well as the daughter of Pharaoh: women of the Moabites, Ammonites, Edomites, Sidonians, *and* Hittites— [2]from the nations of whom the LORD had said to the children of Israel, "You shall not intermarry with them, nor they with you. Surely they will turn away your hearts after their gods." Solomon clung to these in love. [3]And he had seven hundred wives, princesses, and three hundred concubines; and his wives turned away his heart. [4]For it was so, when Solomon was old, that his wives turned his heart after other gods; and his heart was not loyal to the LORD his God, as was the heart of his father David. [5]For Solomon went after Ashtoreth the goddess of the Sidonians, and after Milcom the abomination of the Ammonites. [6]Solomon did evil in the sight of the LORD, and did not fully follow the LORD, as did his father David. [7]Then Solomon built a high place for Chemosh the abomination of Moab, on the hill that is east of Jerusalem, and for Molech the abomination of the people of Ammon. [8]And he did likewise for all his foreign wives, who burned incense and sacrificed to their gods. [9]So the LORD became angry with Solomon, because his heart had turned from the LORD God of Israel, who had appeared to him twice, [10]and had commanded him concerning this thing, that he should not go after other gods; but he did not keep what the LORD had commanded. [11]Therefore the LORD said to Solomon, "Because you have done this, and have not kept My covenant and My statutes, which I have commanded you, I will surely tear the kingdom away from you and give it to your servant. [12]"Nevertheless I will not do it in your days, for the sake of your father David; I will tear it out of the hand of your son. [13]"However I will not tear away the whole kingdom; I will give one tribe to your

> son for the sake of my servant David, and for the sake of Jerusalem which I have chosen." (1 Kings 11:1-13)

Solomon failed in following the command of God and therefore forfeited the wisdom and understanding that God so graciously gave him. He disobeyed the law that had been given to Moses back in Deuteronomy 17:14-17. "When you come to the land which the LORD your God is giving you, and possess it and dwell in it, and say, 'I will set a king over me like all the nations that are around me,' "you shall surely set a king over you whom the LORD your God chooses; one from among your brethren you shall set as king over you; you may not set a foreigner over you, who is not your brother." But he shall not multiply horses for himself, nor cause the people to return to Egypt to multiply horses, for the LORD has said to you, 'You shall not return that way again.' "Neither shall he multiply wives for himself, lest his heart turn away; nor shall he greatly multiply silver and gold for himself."

When confronting the men of his day for the same sin of marrying foreign women, Nehemiah referred back to Solomon. "Did not Solomon king of Israel sin by these things? Yet among many nations there was no king like him, who was beloved of his God; and God made him king over all Israel. Nevertheless pagan women caused even him to sin" (Nehemiah 13:26). By marrying many foreign women—a thousand altogether—Solomon's spiritual life declined, and he became involved in gross idolatry. These foreign women worshipped goddesses of fertility, sex, love, and war. They had degraded moral characters. And so Solomon had begun to flirt with disaster.

In verse 14 we learn that the Lord was so angry with Solomon that He began to stir up enemies to come against him: Hadad, then later Rezon and Jeroboam. He died disillusioned and spiritually insensible at about the young age of 59, but the result of his foolish choices did not end with his death, as his arrogant and foolish son Rehoboam became the next king. You can read about him in chapters 12 and following when you have time. Rehoboam did not follow the pattern of David; instead he was an evil king. During his 17-year reign, the people of Judah built "high places, sacred pillars, and wooden images" and permitted "perverted persons" to prosper in the land.

Summary

What started out as a godly man with a godly prayer and godly motives ended as an ungodly man involved in ungodly idolatry with ungodly motives. So what are the lessons to be learned about wisdom from Solomon's life and Solomon's prayer for wisdom? I have six for you, which are listed in the form of an acrostic spelled *W-I-S-D-O-M.* If you desire wisdom, then…

W*alk in obedience.* If you want to be wise, then the way to obtain wisdom is to be obedient to God. As the Lord says in Deuteronomy 4:6, "Therefore be careful to observe *them*; for this is your wisdom and your understanding in the sight of the peoples who will hear all these statutes, and say, 'Surely this great nation is a wise and understanding people.'" I have lived long enough to notice that the most spiritually wise people are also the most obedient—they walk with God. The opposite is also true: if you show me a foolish person or one who cannot make wise decisions, then more than likely you are showing me someone who is walking in disobedience. Many times an unwise person will manifest their lack of wisdom by confused thinking and living. If you desire wisdom, then be…

I*ndifferent to temporal blessings*. Solomon was given wisdom because he asked for it; and wealth was given to him, because he did not ask for it. We get so wrapped up in asking God for health, long life, peace, and prosperity; but we can learn much from Solomon, as all he wanted was a wise heart. It was not for himself but for the glory of God in order to serve Him better. If you desire wisdom, then…

S*tay humble.* Solomon started with the attitude of a child—*I don't know what to do*—and ended up with the attitude—*I am going to do it my way.* He did evil, quit following the Lord, and clung to his pagan wives. Solomon started out by offering a thousand sacrifices as an act of worship and ended up with a thousand women as a gross act of idolatry. What a different ending Solomon's life would have had if only he had maintained the level of his great and lofty prayer! Somehow and somewhere he forgot his request for an understanding heart and for discernment. He forgot to take heed lest he fall. If you desire wisdom, then…

***D**on't stray from the narrow path.* What happened to Solomon? Why did he fall? For one thing, women were a part of his downfall. In Proverbs 7 Solomon devotes an entire chapter to warn his son about adulterous women. In verse 27 he said that "Her house is the way to hell." Don't go there my son, he was saying. But it was not only women; it was also wealth that caused him to go downhill. In Proverbs 30 Agur wrote, "Remove falsehood and lies far from me; Give me neither poverty nor riches—Feed me with the food allotted to me; Lest I be full and deny You, And say, "Who is the LORD?" Or lest I be poor and steal, and profane the name of my God" (Proverbs 30:8-9). Women and money may not be your downfall, but you know what your weak areas are. Find someone with whom you can be transparent, someone who will help you make wise choices and hold you accountable. If you desire wisdom, then…

***O**ne thing is needed—the fear of God.* "The fear of the LORD is the beginning of knowledge, *But* fools despise wisdom and instruction" (Proverb 1:7). True wisdom comes only from fearing God. If you desire wisdom, then…

***M**ake wise choices.* The fault with Solomon was not God's but Solomon's. He had much, but to whom much is given much is required. Solomon forgot that he had a responsibility. God gave him the wonderful gift of wisdom, but Solomon set his affections on the gifts and not the Giver. God is not impressed with our wisdom and knowledge but is concerned with our application of wisdom to everyday life. Your spiritual success will depend not only on insight, but also on making the right choices.

Do you desire wisdom this day? Have you asked God for wisdom? He promises to grant it, but to continue walking in wisdom you must: ***W****alk in obedience*; be ***I****ndifferent to temporal blessings*; ***S****tay humble*; ***D****on't stray from the narrow path*; remember the ***O****ne thing that is needed—the fear of God*; and ***M****ake wise choices*.

Questions to Consider

Solomon's Prayer for Wisdom

Selected Passages from 1 Kings

1. (a) As you read Solomon's prayer from 1 Kings 3:5-9, what aspects of prayer do you notice? (Example: praise in verse 6; humility in verse 7) (b) What does Solomon ask God for? (c) Does God answer Solomon's prayer? See verses 10-14. (d) What does God promise to give Solomon besides wisdom?

2. What happened in verses 16-28 indicating that God answered Solomon's prayer for wisdom?

3. Read 1 Kings 10:1-13 and answer the following questions. (a) Who came to visit Solomon and what was her motive? (b) What was her response as she observed the wisdom of Solomon? c) What other quality seems to come with wisdom? See verse 8. See also Proverbs 3:13. (d) Why is this true?

4. (a) From 1 Kings 11:1-8, what things did Solomon do that were unwise? (b) What was the Lord's response to this? See verses 9-43. (c) What does this teach you about man's responsibility when God answers prayer?

5. (a) How do you know if wisdom is from God or from the world? See James 3:13-18. (b) Would you say that your life manifests godly wisdom or earthly wisdom? How? (c) Recall a time when you know that God answered your request for wisdom.

6. (a) Why do you think it is important for believers to pray for wisdom? (b) What happens when we don't possess wisdom?

7. Define wisdom in your own words.

8. If God were to grant you one request, what would you ask Him for and why?

9. Is there a situation that you are facing today in which you need wisdom? Put your need in the form of a request to God. Why not ask Him for the "Wisdom of Solomon?"

Chapter 4

How to Pray for a Sick Child

Selected Passages from 2 Samuel and 2 Kings 4

Several summers ago, during the month of July, I was checking my e-mail on my computer. My eye immediately noticed an e-mail from my daughter who was on a 6-week mission trip to South Africa. We had not heard from her in 24 days except for the previous day in an e-mail in which she had given a glowing report of God's goodness to her while on her mission trip to South Africa. So of course, I was eager to hear from her, as any mother would be. I noticed the subject on her e-mail was: "Hi guys, I need your prayers." The following is what her email said. "Hi guys! I have a few minutes to email you because God is gracious. God is doing amazing things, which I will tell you about when I have more time. I would like you all to be praying for me please. I am very sick right now, the sickest I have been in a long time and I'm in a lot of pain and am shedding a lot of tears. I think that I may be going to the doctor tomorrow. Please pray that the Lord would heal me. Thank you all so much. I look forward to seeing you all. I love you guys—Cindi" And that was it. So you know as a Mother, even of grown children, numerous questions and thoughts ran through my mind. What kind of pain is she in? How sick is she? What kind of doctors are in South Africa? We need to get her home now; I knew we shouldn't have let her go there. Then I stopped this useless thinking, had a good cry, and called out to God in prayer.

Next I called our church prayer chain and asked for prayer.

What does one do when facing sickness and disease, and especially what does a parent do when a child is sick, or dying? When God chooses to heal our child, what should our response be? If He chooses not to heal, what should our response be?

In this chapter, we'll be looking at two prayers regarding two children who are sick. One prayer is offered by a father and the other by a prophet. We will see the love of a father and the love of a mother. What can we learn from these prayers and the stories surrounding them that God the Holy Spirit has left for us? Paul says in Romans 15:4 "For whatever things were written before were written for our learning, that we through the patience and comfort of the Scriptures might have hope." We will look at each of these prayers individually, making note of certain observations and principles as we go through them.

Let's first consider 2 Samuel 12:13-23. When he should have been out fighting in battle, King David instead had chosen to remain at home. One evening, while walking on the roof, he sees a beautiful woman named Bathsheba bathing and sends for her and commits adultery with her. A child is conceived by this adulterous relationship and David tries to cover it up by having her husband killed in the front lines of battle. But God did not let David get by with such wickedness; He sent Nathan the prophet to confront David with his sin. And this is where we begin.

2 Samuel 12:13-23

> So David said to Nathan, "I have sinned against the LORD." And Nathan said to David, "The LORD also has put away your sin; you shall not die. [14]"However, because by this deed you have given great occasion to the enemies of the LORD to blaspheme, the child also who is born to you shall surely die." (2 Samuel 12:13-14)

David's sin of adultery with Bathsheba was punishable by death according to the Law. However, God was merciful to David. Instead of dying for his own sin, Nathan tells David in verse 14, that his child would die for his sin. There is something very interesting in the words of Nathan in verse 13: The Lord has *put away* your sin. In other words, Yahweh has caused your sin to pass over, or transferred your sin. God has transferred the legal punishment of this sin to the child. He shall die; you shall not die. Now stop for a minute and think about how David must have felt at this point. *My child is going to die because of my sin*! What tremendous guilt must have come over David as he considered this. We must stop and think about the consequences of sin, not only in our own lives, but also in the lives of our children. Exodus 20:5 is clear—God visits the iniquity of the fathers upon the children.

Principle #1: *Sometimes our children suffer because of our sin.* I would like to encourage you to read Deuteronomy 28 sometime and look at the blessings of obeying the Lord as well as the curses of disobeying the Lord. They are a great motivation to keep one from sinning. Sin has its consequences, and unfortunately, many times innocent children bear those consequences. Now I am not saying that if you are sinning today that your child will die. But we must not mock the Lord by continuing in our sin, whatever it is. So God immediately struck David's child, and he became very ill:

> Then Nathan departed to his house. And the LORD struck the child that Uriah's wife bore to David, and it became ill. [16]David therefore pleaded with God for the child, and David fasted and went in and lay all night on the ground. [17]So the elders of his house arose and went to him, to raise him up from the ground. But he would not, nor did he eat food with them. (2 Samuel 12:15-17)

You might be asking, "Why does David pray? Didn't Nathan say the child would die?" Evidently, David wasn't willing to sit back and do nothing; he went immediately to prayer. The Hebrew word for *pleaded with God*, means to beg, to strive after. This was an earnest prayer. He went into his most private chamber. Fasting also was involved in this prayer, as well as lying on the ground. What did David actually say in this prayer? We don't know, as the Holy Spirit does not record even one word that David prays. Perhaps this is the time he prays Psalm 51, "Have mercy on me O God—I have sinned." Perhaps he asks God for healing for the child as mentioned in verse 22. We don't know, but we do know David prayed and fasted and that he did this for seven days, according to verse 18. David was very serious about his praying.

David would not get up, and he would not eat. Nothing would tear David away from fasting and praying. He almost has the tenacity of Jacob, who wrestled with God and would not let Him go until God blessed him. (Genesis 32) However, instead of a blessing from God, David received a curse.

> Then on the seventh day it came to pass that the child died. And the servants of David were afraid to tell him that the child was dead. For they said, "Indeed, while the child was alive, we spoke to him, and he would not heed our voice. How can we tell him that the child is dead? He may do some harm!" 19When David saw that his servants were whispering, David perceived that the child was dead. Therefore David said to his servants, "Is the child dead?" And they said, "He is dead." (2 Samuel 12:18-19)

> So David arose from the ground, washed and anointed himself, and changed his clothes; and he went into the house of the LORD and worshiped. Then he went to his own house; and when he requested, they set food before him, and he ate. (2 Samuel 12:20)

Bathing, anointing the body and changing one's clothes were all signs in Old Testament times that someone was coming out of a state of mourning or sickness. Having done these things, David then goes to the house of the Lord and worships. David went to the Lord's house first, before he went to his own house. He falls prostrate before the Lord in humility and worships the One who has just taken his child. Amazing! We can learn from King David's example that, in the face of a crisis, we must not shake our fists at God! We must worship the One who knows best. David was able to trust God's providential dealings without coddling himself with wasted hurting. It is sad to see believers allowing the simplest things to keep them from the house of God. Here we see David not even allowing the death of his child to keep him from worship. This reminds me of Job when he heard that all ten of his children died; he fell upon the ground and worshipped (Job 1:20).

Principle #2: *Our weeping must never hinder our worship.* And after David worships the Lord, he returns home and eats:

> Then his servants said to him, "What is this that you have done? You fasted and wept for the child while he was alive, but when the child died, you arose and ate food." [22]And he said, "While the child was alive, I fasted and wept; for I said, 'Who can tell whether the LORD will be gracious to me, that the child may live?' [23]"But now he is dead; why should I fast? Can I bring him back

> again? I shall go to him, but he shall not return to me."
> 24Then David comforted Bathsheba his wife, and went in to her and lay with her. So she bore a son, and he called his name Solomon. Now the LORD loved him,
> 25and He sent word by the hand of Nathan the prophet: So he called his name Jedidiah, because of the LORD. (2 Samuel 12:21-25)

God was merciful to David in that He gave him another son, Solomon.

Principle #3: *God is always merciful, even in the face of death!* Now obviously this does not mean that when we lose a loved one that loved one will always be replaced. But God is good: there are always manifestations of His goodness in our lives, even in death.

Now before we go on to the second story and prayer, I want to leave you with two keys to dealing with the death of a child or loved one. (1) *Trust in God's sovereignty.* Job, upon losing all ten of his children said, "The Lord gave, and the Lord has taken away, blessed be the name of the Lord" (Job 1:21). We don't always have the big picture. We don't know the end of the story. But God does. (2) *Trust in the resurrection.* Job did. Job 19:25,26 says, "For I know that my Redeemer lives, and He shall stand at last on the earth; And after my skin is destroyed, this I know, that in my flesh I shall see God." David, also, says in verse 23, "I shall go to him, but he shall not return to me." This was an indication that David believed in the resurrection, and that he knew he would see his child again. In eternity God will remove all crying and tears. Life's trials will seem so small when we see Christ.

Now let's turn from the death of David's child, to the death of another child. However, this child, by the prayers of a righteous man, was raised to life. We find the story in

2 Kings 4:18-37. Again, let me give a quick summary of the background to this story. Elisha meets a Shunammite woman as a result of traveling by her house regularly. She wanted to be a blessing to Elisha so she requested of her husband that they add on a room so that he would have a place to stay when he traveled by their way. As a result of her kindness, Elisha wanted to do something for her, so he asks his servant Gehazi what he could do. Gehazi tells him this woman does not have a child, and Elisha prophesies that she would have a child in approximately one year. The woman responds with doubt, as her husband was old. Nonetheless, she conceives and gives birth to a son. This brings us to the rest of the story:

2 Kings 4:18-37

> And the child grew. Now it happened one day that he went out to his father, to the reapers. (2 Kings 4:18)

Now we don't know for sure how old this boy was, but he was probably between four and six years old. He goes out to the field where he knows his father is, and notice what he says:

> And he said to his father, "My head, my head!" So he said to a servant, "Carry him to his mother." (2 Kings 4:19)

More than likely the boy was suffering from sunstroke. It was probably very hot, and many Palestinians would suffer from this while reaping the fields. Sunstroke often showed itself by pain, stupor, and fever. It was often fatal, as in this case. And so his dad said what most dads would say, "Go see your mother." Of course, I am sure that the father had no idea that his son's life was in danger, he only had a headache, or so it seemed.

> When he had taken him and brought him to his mother, he sat on her knees till noon, and then died. (2 Kings 4:20)

The child was well in the morning, and dead at noon.

Principle #1: *Don't take your children (or others) for granted.* Life is fragile, and we do not know what a day will bring forth. All of us could probably tell stories of people we loved or knew who were taken suddenly, without warning. Our words should be chosen carefully when speaking to others, as they may be our last.

> And she went up and laid him on the bed of the man of God, shut the door upon him, and went out. (2 Kings 4:21)

Now why would this woman lay her child on the bed of Elisha and not on the child's own bed? Perhaps the answer is found in I Kings 17:17-24 and II Kings 2:12-15. (Please take the time to read these accounts.) The woman, no doubt, had heard that Elijah had raised the widow of Zarephath's son to life, and that the spirit of Elijah had been passed on to Elisha. She believed that Elisha had the power to raise her son from the dead. It is very possible that she is one of the women referred to in Hebrews 11, the great faith chapter, where we read in verse 35 that "women received their dead raised to life again…"

> Then she called to her husband, and said, "Please send me one of the young men and one of the donkeys, that I may run to the man of God and come back." [23]So he said, "Why are you going to him today? It is neither the

> New Moon nor the Sabbath." And she said, "It is well." (2 Kings 4:22-23)

Now why this woman does not tell her husband that their child has died is certainly a mystery to me. Perhaps she knew he would not let her go to seek Elisha. Perhaps his faith was not as strong as hers, to think the child might be raised to life. We don't know with any certainty, but we know that she says she must see him today. The husband questions her, saying that it is not the New Moon or the Sabbath, but he does let her go. Notice the last words of verse 23, "It is well." With these words, this woman continues to manifest great faith.

> Then she saddled a donkey, and said to her servant, "Drive, and go forward; do not slacken the pace for me unless I tell you." (2 Kings 4:24)

The love of this woman for her child is evidenced by her willingness to ride a donkey to the top of Mount Carmel. The trip was about 16-17 miles and would have taken about five to six hours.

Principle #2: *Agape love goes the extra mile—always.* Women are commanded in Titus 2 to love their children with a phileo love, a tender affection. We not only see this mother's tender affection, but her agape love, which dies to herself.

> And so she departed, and went to the man of God at Mount Carmel. So it was, when the man of God saw her afar off, that he said to his servant Gehazi, "Look, the Shunammite woman! [26]"Please run now to meet her, and say to her, 'Is it well with you? Is it well with your husband? Is it well with the child?'" And she answered, "It is well." (2 Kings 4:25-26)

The woman tells the servant; it is well with me, with my husband, and with the child. "All is well," she says, and yet the child is dead in the house! Matthew Henry once said: "Note, when God calls away our dearest relations by death it becomes us quietly to say, It is well both with us and them-it is well, for all is well that God does."[8] This reminds me of a song that we all probably know well—*It Is Well With My Soul.* This song was written by a man who lost a son suddenly to death, and if that was not enough to deal with, he then lost all four of his daughters in a shipwreck. He wrote the song, *It Is Well With My Soul* when passing by the approximate place where his daughters had drowned. He could write "Whatever my lot thou hast taught me to say, it is well, it is well with my soul." The Shunammite woman could say "It is well." She had perfect peace that all indeed would be well.

> Now when she came to the man of God at the hill, she caught him by the feet, but Gehazi came near to push her away. But the man of God said, "Let her alone; for her soul is in deep distress, and the LORD has hidden it from me, and has not told me." (2 Kings 4:27)

Notice that the woman catches Elisha by his feet. This was a gesture which would have indicated humility, need, and desperation. The servant obviously thought this behavior was wrong as he tries to push her away, but Elisha recognizes that there must be a problem. And indeed there was, as we see in verse 28.

> So she said, "Did I ask a son of my lord? Did I not say, 'Do not deceive me'?" (2 Kings 4:28)

---

8 Henry, Matthew-*Matthew Henry Commentary*-MacDonald Publishing Co.-page 729.

The Shunammite woman says: "Did I ask a son of my lord?" I expressed no such wish to you. I was content and happy and you promised me a son; did I not say do not deceive me? Do not mock me with a child, which I will only then be deprived of by his death. I was not like Hannah or Rachel who said, "Give me children or I die." Take note of what Elisha says to his servant in verse 29.

> Then he said to Gehazi, "Get yourself ready, and take my staff in your hand, and be on your way. If you meet anyone, do not greet him; and if anyone greets you, do not answer him; but lay my staff on the face of the child." (2 Kings 4:29)

There was a sense of urgency in Elisha's voice as he tells his servant to go quickly and not to talk to anyone on the way. It would not be uncommon for a traveler to lose a great deal of time when traveling as they would stop and visit with others traveling the same roads. Elisha also gives his servant specific instructions: Take my staff and lay it upon the face of the child. You might ask, why did Elisha send the servant instead of himself? A few answers have been suggested. First, perhaps Elisha thought that God would honor the method—the staff—and that it did not matter who went. A second possibility suggests that perhaps Elisha wanted to teach the Shunammite woman to not place her dependence on him, but, rather, to look to God. The third possible answer may be that the servant was younger than Elisha and therefore could run faster and get to the child more quickly. But the woman would not settle for this as seen in verse 30.

> And the mother of the child said, "As the LORD lives, and as your soul lives, I will not leave you." So he arose and followed her. (2 Kings 4:30)

She was not going anywhere without Elisha. So while she objected to Elisha's plan, the servant Gehazi hurried on to perform the task his master had given him.

> Now Gehazi went on ahead of them, and laid the staff on the face of the child; but there was neither voice nor hearing. Therefore he went back to meet him, and told him, saying, "The child has not awakened." (2 Kings 4:31)

The plan did not work. You might be asking, why was the act of Gehazi allowed to fail? Is it possible that Gehazi had a different spirit? (See question # 2 in "Questions to Consider" at the end of the chapter.) His heart was evidently not in the right place. According to 2 Kings 5, he had a problem with money and specifically with coveting. This reminds me of what Paul says in I Timothy 6:10, "For the love of money is a root of all kinds of evil, for which some have strayed from the faith in their greediness, and pierced themselves through with many sorrows."

Principle #3: *If you regard iniquity in your heart, God will not hear you.* Psalm 66:18 states: "If I regard iniquity in my heart, the Lord will not hear." God is not impressed with any of our religious duties when our heart is far from Him. That is hypocrisy. Another possible reason why Gehazi was not able to raise the boy is perhaps to show the woman and Elisha that it would not be a rod or some magic formula that would raise the child, but only earnest prayer and faith in the power of God. This reminds me of something in Matthew 17, where the disciples of Jesus tried to cast a demon out of a child, but they could not. Jesus replies to this situation by saying, "This kind does not go out except by prayer and fasting" (verse 21). There aren't any magic formulas, only sincere earnest prayer in some cases. Man is always looking for the easy, instant way to solve problems, but God is calling for us to earnestly seek His face. So Gehazi is ineffective, but Elisha arrives on the scene.

> When Elisha came into the house, there was the child, lying dead on his bed. [33]He went in therefore, shut the door behind the two of them, and prayed to the LORD. (2 Kings 4:32-33)

Elisha prayed. Prayer was the only remedy in such a case as this. He had no power of his own to raise the child to life. The Hebrew word here for *prayer* means to entreat or make supplication, and it is a different Hebrew word for prayer than the one used in the story of David. David's prayer seemed to be more intense.

> And he went up and lay on the child, and put his mouth on his mouth, his eyes on his eyes, and his hands on his hands; and he stretched himself out on the child, and the flesh of the child became warm. (2 Kings 4:34)

After Elisha prays, he lays on the child. It is probable that Elisha was endeavoring to transfer a portion of his own natural warmth to the body of the child, and by blowing into the child's mouth, to inflate the lungs and restore respiration. This would be somewhat similar to our CPR. Elisha uses every natural means in his power to restore life, while praying to God to perform a miracle. There is a good lesson for all of us here: use the natural means that God has placed within our power, and trust God for the supernatural.

> He returned and walked back and forth in the house, and again went up and stretched himself out on him; then the child sneezed seven times, and the child opened his eyes. (2 Kings 4:35)

Principle #4: *We should always do our own work, and beg God to do His.* Along with prayer and stretching himself upon the child, Elisha also walks back and forth in the house. Perhaps he was pacing in prayer to God. And after the child had sneezed seven times, he opened his eyes. It is interesting to note that physicians tell us sneezing is beneficial for the removal of obstructions in the head, and that sneezing actually relieves disorders of the head. So God answers the prayer of this prophet: the boy is raised to life.

> And he called Gehazi and said, "Call this Shunammite woman." So he called her. And when she came in to him, he said, "Pick up your son." [37]So she went in, fell at his feet, and bowed to the ground; then she picked up her son and went out. (2 Kings 4:36-37)

Elisha sends his servant after the boy's mother. Perhaps the Shunammite woman was off praying somewhere; we are not told. But she comes to the place where Elisha and her son are, and before she picks up her son, she does something much more important—she worships God. This is the same Hebrew word for worship used in the story of David. She worships the One who raised her son from the dead. Isn't it interesting that in both stories we find the parents worshipping? One who loses his son in death and the other whose son is raised to life. But neither death nor life should separate us from the love and worship of our Lord. Our last principle is:

Principle #5: *Love never gives up. It always believes.* This woman's faith was evident—see verses 8-10, 21-23, 26, 30, 37. She had tremendous faith. She certainly exhibited the type of faith mentioned in Hebrews 11:1, 6. "Now faith is the substance of things hoped for, the evidence of things not seen. But without faith it is impossible to please Him, for he who comes to God must believe that He is, and that He is a rewarder of those who diligently seek Him." Faith is a key element in our praying that is stressed repeatedly in the Word of God.

Take note, if you will, of some things I would like to call to your attention before we finish our look at these two stories:

1. In the story of David, the parent prays; in the story of the Shunammite woman, she calls on another to pray. Sometimes I have found in my own life, that I can pray and find strength in unusual circumstances, and at other times, I need the support and prayers of others. In these two stories we see both.

2. David's child is sick because of his own sin, but the Shunammite's child just got sick because of the fallen world we live in. When facing illness, it is always wise to examine our hearts for sin as mentioned earlier, and yet we must realize that we live in a fallen world, and sometimes we just get sick. In John 9 we have an account of a man who was born blind, and the disciples ask Jesus who had sinned, the man or his parents. Jesus replied that neither one of them had, but this man was born blind so that the works of God might be made manifest in him. Some sickness is for the glory of God.

3. The actual prayer is not recorded in either one of these stories. It just states that they prayed. In most prayers we study, we actually read the prayers that were prayed. These prayers are not of any less importance. Sometimes we might tell people we are praying for them, and sometimes we tell them what prayers we actually pray for them. The important thing is that we pray.

4. God is gracious. In both stories these families were given a child. The Shunammite woman was childless and God graciously gave her a child. David's child died; yet God gave him another one.

5. The child's name is not mentioned in either story.

6. Another lesson we can learn in both of these stories

is to hold our children loosely. Remember Abraham and Isaac? We as mothers do not own our children; they are on loan to us for a very short time. The more intensely we hold on to our children, the more intense the pain will be when it is time to let go. Our children are a gift from God, but they are on loan. We don't own them, and God would have us hold them loosely so that there is no competition for our worship of Him and Him alone.

I remember when we got word that Cindi was so ill in South Africa. At the same time, my neighbor's young daughter had ovarian cancer. Cindi returned home and the other girl died. Why did God take one and not the other? I don't know the answer to that question, but I do know we can trust in God's sovereignty whatever the problem may be—in sickness, and yes, even in death.

Questions to Consider

How to Pray for a Sick Child

Selected Passages in 2 Samuel and 2 Kings 4

1. Read 2 Samuel 12:13-25 and answer the following questions. (a) Whose child is sick in this story and why? (b) What sin had David committed? (Skim chapter 11) (c) How long did David pray, and how would you characterize his praying? (d) After the child died, what things did David do?

2. Read 2 Kings 4:18-37. (a) Whose child is sick in this story? (Skim verses 8-17, especially noting v. 14) (b) What happens to the child? (c) Who does the woman call upon for help? (d) Why do you think Gehazi could not raise him? (The answer might be found in 5:1-26) (e) Who prayed for the raising of this child? (f) Did God answer his prayer? (g) What verses in this story prove that this woman had immense faith?

3. As you read over both of these stories answer the following questions. (a) What was the difference in the response of each parent to the death of their child? (b) What similarities are there between David's and Elisha's prayer? (c) Write down any other observations you see as you compare and contrast these two stories.

4. Jot down any verses that you can recall in which praying in faith is a key element. (Example: Matthew 17:20) (b) How can you use these verses in your own life and the lives of others? (c) How would you counsel someone who says they have faith to believe that God will answer their prayers and yet some of their prayers are not answered?

5. (a)What do you do (or what did you do) when your children are (were) sick? (b) When you, or your child, are sick, do you examine yourself to see if the sickness is a result of sin?

6. (a) How would you encourage someone who has lost a child? (b) How would you help them specifically in seeing the goodness of God in their tragedy?

7. Do you know anyone who is sick? How do you think the Lord would have you pray for them? Write your request and pray!

Chapter 5

A Prayer of a Young Man

Psalm 8

The story of David and Goliath is one of the most exciting stories in the Old Testament. I remember as a little girl, I used to love to sing a song about David. The lyrics and hand motions were thrilling for a small child. The song went like this: "Only a boy named David, only a little sling, only a boy named David, and he could pray and sing. Only a boy named David, only a rippling brook, only a boy name David, but five little stones he took. And one little stone went in the sling and the sling went round and round, and one little stone went in the sling and the sling went round and round. And round and round and round and round and round and round and round. And one little stone went up in the air and the giant came tumbling down." It is a miraculously story when you consider how God used such a young boy and a tiny stone to kill Goliath, the giant. But He did. It was perhaps that very night after his victory over Goliath and the Philistines that David sits on a hill in the darkness and looks up and writes:

Psalm 8

O LORD, our Lord,
How excellent is Your name in all the earth,
Who have set Your glory above the heavens!
2 Out of the mouth of babes and nursing infants
You have ordained strength,

Because of Your enemies,
That You may silence the enemy and the avenger.
3When I consider Your heavens, the work of Your fingers,
The moon and the stars, which You have ordained,
4What is man that You are mindful of him,
And the son of man that You visit him?
5For You have made him a little lower than the angels,
And You have crowned him with glory and honor.
6You have made him to have dominion over the works of Your hands;
You have put all things under his feet,
7All sheep and oxen—
Even the beasts of the field,
8The birds of the air,
And the fish of the sea
That pass through the paths of the seas.
9O LORD, our Lord,
How excellent is Your name in all the earth!
(Psalm 8:1-9)

In this prayer of praise we will see the following: *praise for the Lord's excellent name* (vv. 1, 9); *praise for the Lord's enemies' defeat* (v. 2); and *praise for the Lord's evaluation of man* (vv. 3-8).

Before we get into this wonderful prayer, let's ask and answer some questions which will help us to better understand this prayer of praise. First of all, who wrote this Psalm of praise? Well, we know David wrote it. What kind of Psalm is it? You could call it a nature Psalm because of the reference to God's handiwork in creation, but mainly it is a hymn or psalm of praise. It is also a messianic psalm by type—which means it refers to the work of Christ, as the writer to the Hebrews mentions in Hebrews 2. But for our purposes we will be studying it in the context of its present meaning, and not as messianic.

The title of the Psalm says: "To the chief Musician upon Gittith." Gittith occurs only in two other places in the Scriptures: Psalm 81 and Psalm 84. Gittith is *probably* a reference to a musical instrument that was common among the Hittites, or the inhabitants of Gath. These Hittites were among those that David resided with according to 2 Samuel 6:5. "Then David and all the house of Israel played music before the LORD on all kinds of instruments of fir wood, on harps, on stringed instruments, on tambourines, on sistrums, and on cymbals."

According to 2 Samuel 6, David was bringing the ark up to Jerusalem. It had been captured by the Philistines. There were explicit instructions from the Lord that the Levites could not touch the ark or even look at it because it was holy. But the ox that was carrying the ark began to stumble and Uzzah put his hand out to touch the ark when the ark was shaking, and the Lord struck him dead. David then became afraid and removed the ark to the house of Obed-Edom, the Gittite, for three months. We do not know if this instrument was a stringed instrument or a wind instrument. All three of the Psalms that have this title are of a joyous nature so more than likely it was an instrument that was used for joyous occasions, like the occasion of bringing up the ark. Some also believe that the title to Psalm 9 really was a *footnote* to Psalm 8. The reason being: "To the chief Musician upon Muthlabben." Muthlabben is a Hebrew expression which means "death of a champion," which would be Goliath. Scholars tell us that this is a direct reference to the story of David and Goliath. Another question we might want to ask is: when was this psalm of praise written? It appears that David penned this psalm after his victory over Goliath. This is probably true because a Gittite was an inhabitant of Gath, and Goliath was of Gath. Now I will say that some believe David wrote this Psalm after he took the ark up to the house of Obed-edom. But I believe that it was most likely written after David's victory with Goliath. It also appears that David wrote this psalm at night, as he refers to the moon and stars. Let's look first at the

Praise for the Lord's Excellent Name
Psalm 8:1

> O Lord, our Lord,
> How excellent is thy name in all the earth!
> (Psalm 8:1)

When David says Lord, he is actually saying, O Jehovah, our ruler! This name expresses the idea of Sovereign or Master. In fact, this is the word for God that David used when he said to Goliath in 1 Samuel 17:45, "You come to me with a sword, with a spear, and with a javelin. But I come to you in the name of the LORD of hosts, the God of the armies of Israel, whom you have defied." The name Lord stresses God's dominion over His creation. David knew that God was the ruler and master not of himself only, but of everyone, as he demonstrates by using the term *our* Lord. What kind of a name does the Lord have? David says it is excellent. This means it is exalted, powerful and splendid. It is interesting that in 1 Samuel 17:45 David said to Goliath "You come to me with a sword, with a spear, and with a javelin. But I come to you in the *name* of the LORD of hosts, the God of the armies of Israel, whom you have defied." David knew that God's name was powerful and could conquer any giant, and now he reflects on the excellency, the power of the name of the Lord. And notice the Lord's name is excellent *in all the earth*, which would mean in all parts of the world. Whether mankind wants to acknowledge it or not, the splendor and majesty of our Lord are shown throughout the earth. As Paul says in Romans 1:20, "For since the creation of the world His invisible attributes are clearly seen, being understood by the things that are made, even His eternal power and Godhead, so that thcy arc without excuse." You can travel anywhere and see God's majesty—it is displayed throughout the whole world. David goes on to speak of the Lord in his prayer and says: "who set Your glory above the heavens." David says, "God, Your glory, Your majesty, Your splendor is higher than the heavens." Now what does David mean by this statement? He means that the glory of God is above the heavens, even the heavens which David was gazing upon. To the Jew, there were three heavens. The first one was the atmosphere, where we see the birds fly. The second one was the starry heavens (the heavens declare the glory of God, Psalm 19:1). And the third heaven was the place where God resides. God's glory is above all the heavens and yet none of the heavens can even contain God's glory, as Solomon declares in his prayer in 1 Kings 8:27. "But will God indeed dwell on the earth? Behold, heaven and the heaven of heavens cannot contain You. How much less this temple which I have built!"

David knew it was only Jehovah God and His glorious power which is above the heavens that won him the victory. His heart must have been exuberant as he praises God for the victorious slaying of Goliath. And now in verse two, he turns from praise for the Lord's excellent name, to

Praise for the Lord's Enemies' Defeat
Psalm 8:2

> Out of the mouth of babes and nursing infants
> You have ordained strength,
> Because of Your enemies,
> That You may silence the enemy and the avenger.
> (Psalm 8:2)

"Lord, you have used a boy, a nursing infant like me!" This might sound a little strange to us, but we need to remember that the Hebrew mothers would nurse their children much longer than we do, usually until about the age of three. Hannah did not wean her son until he was old enough to appear before the Lord and abide in the temple. (I Samuel 1:22) David says, "You have used just a mere babe to ordain strength, or perfect or establish praise." The Septuagint version reads *perfected praise*. Jesus refers to this in Matthew 21:16 after He had driven the money changers from the temple. Matthew states that the chief priests saw that, and the children crying in the temple, "Hosanna to the Son of David", and they were displeased. To them Jesus replied "Yes. Have you never read, 'Out of the mouth of babes and nursing infants you have perfected praise'?" David is reflecting and marveling at the goodness of God in the fact that he can use even children and infants to bring praise to His name. David was just a youth and yet was used by God. It is estimated that he was between 16-18 years old. 1 Samuel 17:14 tells us that David was the youngest of his brothers, and it appeared that he was not even old enough to go out to battle with his three older brothers. And in verse 42 of the same chapter, it says Goliath disdained him because he was but a youth. David was not the only youth to be used by God. 2 Kings 22:1,2 tells us that King Josiah was only 8 years old when he became King and he did right in the sight of the Lord. Paul says in 1 Corinthians 1:27 that "God has chosen the foolish things of the world to put to shame the wise, and God has chosen the weak things of the world to put to shame the things which are mighty." Paul tells Timothy, in 1 Timothy 4:2, "let no one despise your youth." Even Jesus prayed in Matthew 11:25 after the Jews' refusal to repent: "I thank You, Father, Lord of heaven and earth, that You have hidden these things from the wise and prudent and have revealed them to babes." Ladies, these are encouraging verses to share with your children if they feel like they are unable to do anything for God. God can use the weak, the simple, and the young, and He usually does, in order to magnify His great and Holy name. But why did God use someone such as David? David says, "because of Your enemies, that You may silence the enemy and the avenger." The *enemy* would be the Philistines. The word *silence* means to rest or cease, to end the purposes of the enemy. David not only calls Goliath the enemy, but the avenger as well. The word *avenger* means in its root word, to breathe forcibly. *Enemy* and *avenger* are certainly appropriate names when referring to Goliath. Goliath is described in 1 Samuel 17 as one who defied the armies of the living God (verses 10 and 45). And so David praises the Lord for the enemies' defeat. He used a child like David, but David knew that the praise went to the Lord. These thoughts cause David to further contemplate God's greatness and man's insignificance. We see this in the next part of David's prayer of praise:

Praise for the Lord's Evaluation of Man
Psalm 8:3-8

> When I consider Your heavens, the work of Your fingers,
> The moon and the stars, which You have ordained,
> 4What is man that You are mindful of him, and the son of man that You visit him?
> 5For You have made him a little lower than the angels,
> And You have crowned him with glory and honor.
> 6You have made him to have dominion over the works of Your hands;
> You have put all things under his feet,
> 7All sheep and oxen-- even the beasts of the field,

> [8]The birds of the air, and the fish of the sea that pass through the paths of the seas.
> (Psalm 8:3-8)

David says: "When I consider, when I view or inspect Your heavens, it is amazing that you even consider me!" Notice David says *Your* heavens, not the heavens. David knew that the Heavens belonged to God, and that He had created them. Now why would David be inspecting the heavens, why wasn't he inspecting the ground his feet were on? Because the heavens are where God is and where He resides. It is a wonderful blessing to be able to look outside, day or night and contemplate the heavens and worship God. David would have had numerous opportunities to inspect the heavens and contemplate the stars, as he was a shepherd boy. His occupation was an outside job. Can you imagine how majestic the heavens must have looked back then without the city lights and the pollution that we contend with? I have had the wonderful joy of being out in the dessert at night and gazing up at the stars. It is truly magnificent! And David describes some particular things he sees in the heavens: the moon and the stars. He describes them as *the work of Your fingers*. David uses a human illustration that we can identify with—fingers. Our fingers are the instruments we use when we make something. We know God spoke and the heavens came into being, and yet fingers illustrate the skill by which they were formed. They were *ordained*, David says, they were *prepared.* The fact that David mentions the moon and stars instead of the sun is perhaps an indication that this Psalm was composed at night, as David is gazing at the night heavens. And as David meditates on these awesome works of God, the moon and the stars, it causes him to stop and think about his insignificance again. And so, he has two questions that he poses to God in verse 4.

> What is man that You are mindful of him,
> And the son of man that You visit him?
> (Psalm 8:4)

The word for *man* here means mortal man, man in his weakness. The Hebrew word contains the meaning of man in his miserable state of sin, and mortality. Man is only mere dust and yet God is mindful of him, David says. The word *mindful* means to remember, to mention. The fact that God meditates on us is an astounding thought indeed. Why should Almighty God do that? The only answer I can give to that question is because of His great love toward us—a love that sent His Son to die for us. He is mindful of us, but how mindful are we of Him? And so David not only asks, "Lord why you are mindful of weak, miserable man," but he then asks a second question: "And the son of man, that You visit him?" *The son of man* has a different meaning than the first man. *Son of man* means son of Adam, the son of a sinful father. The Hebrew word is dust; any descendant of man, any one of the human race. "Lord what is man that you should visit him or look after him?" The Hebrew indicates a visitation for any purpose, for inspection, for mercy, for friendship, for judgment. Job says something similar in Job 7:17-18, "What is man, that You should exalt him, that You should set Your heart on him, That You should visit him every morning, and test him every moment?" When we consider the majesty of God, and the fact that He is the Creator over all, it is a wonder that He thinks upon you and me, and that He looks after us for mercy, for friendship! We, who are mere grass! In verse 5 David continues in his thoughts regarding man's insignificance.

> For You have made him a little lower than the angels,
> And You have crowned him with glory and honor.
> (Psalm 8:5)

The Hebrew rendering of *angels* here is God. You have made man a little lower than God. We know from Genesis 1:26 that God made man in His own image, after His likeness, which is amazing! We were made a little lower than God! (Now the writer to the Hebrews quotes from this Psalm and in its messianic meaning it is a reference to Jesus who was made a little lower than the angels, as He came to earth to redeem mankind.) And if that isn't enough, David goes on to say, "You have crowned him with glory and honor." *Crowned* means to encircle or encompass. The word *glory* means to esteem and it is a different meaning from the term used in verse one, as we know God will not give His glory to another. David seems to be amazed that God would give to finite man such a place or position of honor. And what is that position of honor? He states in verses 6-8 what that position of honor is: dominion over creation.

> You have made him to have dominion over the works of
> Your hands;
> You have put all things under his feet,
> (Psalm 8:6)

God gave man the power to rule over the things *He* made (See Genesis 1:26-28). It is amazing that God would entrust to mere man, mere dust, the power to rule over His creation. David uses the illustration of God's creation as being made with His hands; this is similar to the work of His fingers as seen in verse 3. *You have put all things under his feet* refers to the acts of treading down enemies in battle. The idea is of complete subjection. All things from the beginning were to be under man, to be in subjection to mankind. What are the things that we have power over? Well, in verse 7 and 8 David describes the creatures that man has dominion over.

All sheep and oxen—
Even the beasts of the field,
[8]The birds of the air,
And the fish of the sea
That pass through the paths of the seas.
(Psalm 8:7-8)

David lists all kinds of creatures here: the wild beasts of the field, the birds that fly, the fish in the sea, and even those things that pass through the paths of the seas, which would include everything that moves in the waters. It is very interesting that David uses this terminology here for two reasons. First, in 1 Samuel 17:34-36 we read:

> But David said to Saul, "Your servant used to keep his father's sheep, and when a lion or a bear came and took a lamb out of the flock, [35]I went out after it and struck it, and delivered the lamb from its mouth; and when it arose against me, I caught it by its beard, and struck and killed it. [36]"Your servant has killed both lion and bear; and this uncircumcised Philistine will be like one of them, seeing he has defied the armies of the living God." (1 Samuel 17:34-36)

David had a real life experience of bringing those animals under subjection. Secondly, consider 1 Samuel 17:44-46:

> And the Philistine said to David, "Come to me, and I will give your flesh to the birds of the air and the beasts of the field!" [45]Then David said to the Philistine, "You come to me with a sword, with a spear, and with a javelin. But I come to you in the name of the LORD of hosts, the God of the armies of Israel, whom you have defied. [46]"This day the LORD will deliver you into my hand, and I will strike you and take your head from you. And this day I

> will give the carcasses of the camp of the Philistines to the birds of the air and the wild beasts of the earth, that all the earth may know that there is a God in Israel. (1 Samuel 17:44-46)

David would give the head of Goliath the enemy to the beasts of the field and the birds of the air. David perhaps is reflecting that very night after his victory with Goliath on the fact that man has dominion over all the fish of the sea and the fowl of the air. It's amazing, when you think of it, isn't it, that God has given us that privilege to have dominion over His creation? I want to note something here that we as women need to be reminded of from time to time: James reminds us in chapter three of his epistle, that even though man has the privilege of having dominion over all the animal creation, we can't seem to control that one little member that gets us into trouble—the tongue! He says: "For every kind of beast and bird, of reptile and creature of the sea, is tamed and has been tamed by mankind. But no man can tame the tongue. It is an unruly evil, full of deadly poison" (James 3:8).

David now ends the Psalm of praise the same way he began it:

Praise for the Lord's Excellent Name
Psalm 8:9

> O LORD, our Lord,
> How excellent is Your name in all the earth!
> (Psalm 8:9)

David ends the Psalm with a reminder of the Excellency of God's name. As he reflects again on the day's events with Goliath, he has to sing out "O Lord, our Lord, how excellent is Your name in all the earth!" One man calls this an envelope Psalm, because the opening and the closing statements wrap up the truth which lies between. "God has no more to say. If we still want to argue He will simply bring us back to verse 1. 'Very well, let's go over it again.' The Psalm begins where it ends; ends where it begins, and completes the cycle endlessly and forever. How excellent is thy name in all the earth."[9]

9 Phillips, John--*Exploring the Psalms*-Volume 1-Loizeaux Brothers-Neptune, New Jersey; page 69.

Summary

As we contemplate this prayer of praise from King David, we see 1. Praise for the Lord's excellent name (vv. 1, 9). In your prayers to God do you praise Him for His excellency? Do you recall the fact that His glory is above the heavens? 2. Praise for the Lord's enemies' defeat (v. 2). Have you defeated any Goliaths in your life recently? Have you praised the Lord for the victory? 3. Praise for the Lord's evaluation of man (vv. 3-8). God used David, a young boy, and a small stone to kill the giant. David reflects upon this at the end of the day and is overcome with God's remembrance of him—mere man. In what ways has God visited you today? Are you humbled by that fact? Have you praised His name? May we all echo with King David, "O Lord, our Lord, how excellent is Your name in all the earth!"

Questions to Consider

A Prayer of a Young Man

Psalm 8

1. Read 1 Samuel 17. It is said that Psalm 8 was written after this great event in David's life. (a) What things happened on that day that would cause David to praise God? (b) What similarities do you see between Psalm 8 and 1 Samuel 17?

2. Compare Psalm 8 and Hebrews 2. What could be some of the reasons the writer to the Hebrews quotes from Psalm 8?

3. Compare and contrast Psalm 8 and Psalm 148.

4. In Psalm 8, David refers to the Lord's name as excellent. (a) What else do we learn about the Lord's name in the following verses? Psalm 18:49; 33:21; 61:5; 63:4; 69:36; 72:17; 74:10; 76:1; 80:18; 111:9. (b) How would you describe the Lord's name?

5. (a) In what ways do you consider the Lord's name to be "excellent?" (b) What are some ways you can teach your children or grandchildren or others to revere the Lord's name?

6. Spend some time this week looking at nature, and meditating on God's marvelous creation and His glory. Write some thoughts of praise.

7. Come with a written praise to God for the fact that "He is mindful of you," especially considering that you are mere man (woman!).

Chapter 6

The Prayer of the First Martyr

Acts 7:54-60

"In dark filthy places, forsaken, forgotten, our brothers and sisters are paying a price. They will not deny Him to purchase their freedom for these are the faithful, the martyrs for Christ."[10] Martyrdom—a word we don't hear much about in the United States of America, but nonetheless we have brothers and sisters around the world who have been martyred for their faith, and others continue to be martyred. It is estimated that more than 50 million Christians died for their faith in the Dark Ages. It is also estimated that a million Christians died for their faith when the Communists seized China. Unnumbered thousands died as martyrs in the revolutions and civil wars in Africa. And still today martyrdom is happening. "While solid numbers are difficult to ascertain, it has been estimated that as many as 160,000 Christians are martyred each year worldwide."[11] Tertullian said it well when he said: "The blood of the martyrs is the seed of the church." It is interesting that the word *martyr* means "a witness unto death." As we think about those who have been martyred, those who have been "a witness unto death" for their faith in Christ, we might ask questions

10 Words and music by Michael Card and Phil Naish. Copyright 1998 Meadowgreen Music.

11 Ron Strom 2005WorldNetDaily.com.

like, "How did they die?", "What went through their minds as they died?", "What were their last words?", and "What did they pray?" We have the wonderful privilege of examining the Word of God to look at the prayer of Stephen, the first martyr of the early church. How was he martyred? What went through his mind, and most of all, what did he pray?

Before we look at Stephen's prayer and at his death, I want us to look at some background regarding Stephen and what was happening to bring him to this point. First of all, Stephen's name means "a crown." Stephen, as his Greek name indicates, was probably of Hellenistic origin. Where or when he was born, we don't know. The first account we have of Stephen is in Acts 6:5.

> Now in those days, when the number of the disciples was multiplying, there arose a murmuring against the Hebrews by the Hellenists, because their widows were neglected in the daily distribution. [2]Then the twelve summoned the multitude of the disciples and said, "It is not desirable that we should leave the word of God and serve tables. [3]Therefore, brethren, seek out from among you seven men of good reputation, full of the Holy Spirit and wisdom, whom we may appoint over this business; [4]but we will give ourselves continually to prayer and to the ministry of the word." [5]And the saying pleased the whole multitude. And they chose Stephen, a man full of faith and the Holy Spirit, and Philip, Prochorus, Nicanor, Timon, Parmenas, and Nicolas, a proselyte from Antioch, [6]whom they set before the apostles; and when they had prayed, they laid hands on them. [7]Then the word of God spread, and the number of the disciples multiplied greatly in Jerusalem, and a great many of the priests were obedient to the faith. [8]And Stephen, full of faith and power, did great wonders and signs among the people. (Acts 6:1-8)

Here we have the account of the distribution of the common fund that was entrusted to the apostles for the support of the poorer brethren. The Hellenists complained that partiality was shown to the natives of Palestine and that their own widows were neglected. The apostles took measures immediately to remove the cause of the complaint. They did not want to be taken from the work of the preaching ministry, so they advised the church to select seven men of honest report, full of the Holy Spirit and wisdom, for this business (v. 3). The brethren proceeded immediately to select these men, among whom Stephen is first mentioned in verse 5. It is very possible that he was the head of this group, as his name is mentioned first. From the first, Stephen occupied a prominent position. He is described as "a man full of faith and the Holy Spirit" (v. 5), "full of faith and power" (v. 8), and of irresistible "wisdom and the Spirit" (v. 10). He attracted attention by the great wonders and miracles that he did among the people (v. 8).

Stephen was not long in the ministry—maybe five minutes—before he was falsely accused. One man describes Stephen like a battery charged and in action. Read the following account:

> Then there arose some from what is called the Synagogue of the Freedmen (Cyrenians, Alexandrians, and those from Cilicia and Asia), disputing with Stephen. [10]And they were not able to resist the wisdom and the Spirit by which he spoke. [11]Then they secretly induced men to say, "We have heard him speak blasphemous words against Moses and God." [12]And they stirred up the people, the elders, and the scribes; and they came upon him, seized him, and brought him to the council. [13]They also set up false witnesses who said, "This man does not cease to speak blasphemous words against this holy place and the law; [14]"for we have heard him say that this Jesus of Nazareth will destroy this place and change the customs

> which Moses delivered to us." [15]And all who sat in the council, looking steadfastly at him, saw his face as the face of an angel. (Acts 6:9-15)

The people could not stand against this wisdom. They spoke blasphemous words against Stephen and got false witnesses to testify against him. These false witnesses caused his arrest and brought him to the council. The charge against him was blasphemy, in speaking "against this holy place, and the Law" (v. 13.) Stephen probably knew at this time that he was going to be a victim, and yet he stood serene and collected. "All who were sitting in the Council saw his face like the face of an angel" (v. 15). Some have imagined this to be like Moses when his face shone with the glory of God. Peter mentions this type of countenance in his epistle in 1 Peter 4:14 when speaking of someone who is going through suffering. He states that the "spirit of glory and of God rests upon you." And having been brought before the counsel, the high priest asks Stephen about the accusations against him.

> Then the high priest said, "Are these things so?" (Acts 7:1)

Now, I would encourage you to open your Bible and read Stephen's masterful sermon in chapter 7. I would also like to make a few remarks before we look into Stephen's final prayer. First of all, this is the longest recorded sermon in Acts. Stephen gives a masterful summary of Israel's history beginning with the call of Abraham, and proving historically that the presence and favor of God had not been confined to the Holy Land or the Temple of Jerusalem. He also states that there was nothing new under the sun, as the Jews of old had the same ungrateful and questioning spirit as did those listening to him. Then suddenly, in verse 51, Stephen breaks away from his narrative about Israel and accuses his audience of being "stiff-necked and uncircumcised in heart and ears," that they "always resist the Holy Spirit." (See 7:51-53) These were strong terms Stephen used there to describe them, as *stiff necked* was used to describe an ox that refused to be yoked. He is telling them they're obstinate. Also, the term *uncircumcised* would cut to the Jews' hearts, since they prided themselves in their physical circumcision. Their response to Stephen's sermon was not falling on their faces to repent, but "they were cut to the heart, and they gnashed at him with their teeth." Let's look now at verses 54-60:

Acts 7:54-60

> When they heard these things they were cut to the heart,
> and they gnashed at him with their teeth. 55But he, being
> full of the Holy Spirit, gazed into heaven and saw the
> glory of God, and Jesus standing at the right hand of
> God, 56and said, "Look! I see the heavens opened and the
> Son of Man standing at the right hand of God!" 57Then
> they cried out with a loud voice, stopped their ears, and
> ran at him with one accord; 58and they cast him out of
> the city and stoned him. And the witnesses laid down
> their clothes at the feet of a young man named Saul.
> 59And they stoned Stephen as he was calling on God
> and saying, "Lord Jesus, receive my spirit." 60Then he
> knelt down and cried out with a loud voice, "Lord, do not
> charge them with this sin." And when he had said this, he
> fell asleep. (Acts 7:54-60)

In this portion of Scripture we will see: *the methods of Stephen's persecutors* (vv. 54, 57-59a); *the meekness of Stephen's response* (vv. 55, 56); and *the martyr's selfless prayer* (vv. 59, 60).

The Methods of Stephen's Persecutors
Acts 7:54

When they heard these things they were cut to the heart, and they gnashed at him with their teeth. (Acts 7:54)

Verse 54 says *when they heard these things they were cut to the heart*. What are the things Luke is referring to? They are those things mentioned in chapter 7—Stephen's profound and convicting sermon, specifically the accusations that they were stiff necked (obstinate), uncircumcised in their hearts and ears, and resistant to the Holy Spirit. What happened when they heard these things? (Well, they did not get warm fuzzies—that is for sure!) Instead, they were *cut to the heart* (which means they were sawn asunder or sawed in two) and they weren't cut to the heart with sorrow, but with rage. Ladies, there is a *big* difference. What's more, it says they gnashed at him with their teeth. This is the first method we see of the persecutors. They were so enraged that they gnashed their teeth. This means they grated their teeth in pain and rage. Originally this meant to eat greedily, with a noise, as wild beasts. Literally, they began to gnash their teeth, or grind their teeth at him—just like a pack of hungry, snarling wolves. Now Stephen knew that this meant death for him. Ladies, this can happen to us as well, as we stand firm for Christ. If you and I are going to tell people the truth about their sin and its consequences, then you can guarantee they will gnash their teeth at you. It has happened to me on more than one occasion and some occasions stand out more vividly than others. My husband and I have had people shake their fingers at us in rage at restaurants and at church; I have had people cuss me out and hang up the phone on me, all because of speaking the truth in love. So what did Stephen do? Well, the fleshly thing to do is to gnash back, but Stephen did not. Now we'll see:

The Meekness of Stephen's Response
Acts 7:55-56

> But he, being full of the Holy Spirit, gazed into heaven and saw the glory of God, and Jesus standing at the right hand of God, [56]and said, "Look! I see the heavens opened and the Son of Man standing at the right hand of God!" (Acts 7:55-56)

As we think of the meekness of Stephen's response, we must first notice that an important key to having a meek response to such wickedness is to be full of the Holy Spirit. It states that Stephen was full of the Holy Spirit. When you and I are full of the Holy Spirit we will then respond righteously to difficult circumstances and difficult people, and we will respond in the Spirit. Stephen, being filled with the Spirit, gazed into heaven. This means he gazed intently. "Why would he look to heaven?" you might ask. Because heaven was where His Lord and Savior was—Stephen's help came from the Lord. The Psalmist states this well in Psalm 121:1, 2: "I will lift up my eyes to the hills—from whence comes my help? My help comes from the LORD, who made heaven and earth." This is where we should all look when going through suffering. And so, as Stephen looks to heaven, he saw the glory of God, and Jesus standing on the right hand of God. Notice Jesus is standing—not sitting—as we see in other places in Scripture. Consider Hebrews 1:3: "Who being the brightness of his glory, and the express image of his person, and upholding all things by the word of His power, when He had by Himself purged our sins, sat down on the right hand of the Majesty on high." Also consider Colossians 3:1, which says,

"If then you were raised with Christ, seek those things which are above, where Christ is sitting at the right hand of God." This sitting down indicates Christ's finished work on the cross. But here we see Him standing. Why? Why is He standing? He is standing to receive Stephen into glory, as we will see in a moment. What a comfort to us all. One man has commented that He was "Rising from the throne to protect and receive his servant." So Stephen, being filled with the Spirit, responds in meekness and looks to heaven. And since he is filled with the Spirit, he continues to respond with a spirit of meekness as he says in verse 56: *Look! I see the heavens opened and the Son of Man standing at the right hand of God!*

You might ask "Why is this exhibiting a spirit of meekness?" Because Stephen could have said, "Okay guys, I see God and He is going to make you pay someday—you'll see, you'll get what is your due!" But not Stephen; being righteous and full of the Holy Spirit, he said righteous things even in the face of death. There is no need for any of God's children to make threats or call fire down from Heaven because they are undergoing suffering. We should repay evil with good.

Stephen's persecutors obviously didn't care for Stephen's vision, as evidenced in verse 57, where we continue with:

The Methods of Stephen's Persecutors
Acts 7:57-59a

> Then they cried out with a loud voice, stopped their ears, and ran at him with one accord; 58and they cast him out of the city and stoned him. And the witnesses laid down their clothes at the feet of a young man named Saul. 59And they stoned Stephen as he was calling on God and saying, "Lord Jesus, receive my spirit." (Acts 7:57-59a)

We see in verses 57-58 five more methods of persecution. Remember, the first one was gnashing their teeth in verse 54. Their second method was that *they cried out with a loud voice. Cried out* means to croak as a raven or scream, shriek. I have recently had the experience of hearing this first hand when I walk in the morning. My friend and I walk at a local park and we have seen and heard the shriek of a raven. It is piercing indeed! Their third method was that they *stopped their ears. Stopped their ears* means literally that they held them together. They put their hands over their ears. They did not want to hear any more blasphemy. "A manifest specimen of their willful obstinacy; they were resolved they would not hear what had a tendency to convince them, which was what the prophets often complained of: they were like the deaf adder, that will not hear the voice of the charmer."[12] This is exactly what Stephen described in 7:51 when he said they were *uncircumcised in their ears*. Isn't it interesting that they held their ears, in light of the fact that God in a way of righteous judgment stopped their ears from hearing? Fourthly, they *ran at him with one accord.* The word *ran* means they plunged. They were rushing impetuously as the pigs did in Luke 8 when demons were cast out of a man and entered into them. It says they ran violently down a steep place and drowned in the lake. Fifthly, *they cast him out of the city.* This would be to keep from defiling the place with blood. Casting one out of the city was also a requirement by the law in cases of blasphemy. See Numbers 15:35, I Kings 21:13 and Luke 4:29. And in the sixth and final method of persecution, they *stoned him.* So, they had gnashed their teeth, they shrieked, they held their ears and began to run toward him like animals, threw him out of

12 Henry-Matthew- *Matthew Henry's Commentary*-MacDonald Publishing Co.-volume 6-page 91.

the city, and if that wasn't enough, they stoned him! Verse 58 tells us, *they cast him out of the city and stoned him. And the witnesses laid down their clothes at the feet of a young man named Saul.* They did not wait for any sentence to be pronounced upon Stephen; they were determined to stone him first, and then prove afterward that it was done justly. You might say, "They had no right to do this!" However, they had accused Stephen of blasphemy, and stoning was the Jewish punishment for blasphemy according to Leviticus 24:14-16:

> "Take outside the camp him who has cursed; then let all who heard him lay their hands on his head, and let all the congregation stone him. [15]"Then you shall speak to the children of Israel, saying: 'Whoever curses his God shall bear his sin. [16]'And whoever blasphemes the name of the LORD shall surely be put to death. All the congregation shall certainly stone him, the stranger as well as him who is born in the land. When he blasphemes the name of the LORD, he shall be put to death. (Leviticus 24:14-16)

Stoning was not a very pleasant way to die. According to the Rabbis, the scaffold to which the criminal was to be led, with his hands bound, was to be twice the size of a man. One of the witnesses was to smite him upon the breast with a stone, so as to throw him down. If that did not kill him, the second witness was to throw another stone at him. Then, if he was still alive, all the people were to stone him until he was dead. Then the body was to be suspended until sunset.

After this horrible method of persecution, it says *the witnesses laid down their clothes at a young man's feet, whose name was Saul* (whom we know as Paul) What is the significance of laying down their clothes at Saul's feet? The laying down of their clothes would mean that they would loose their outer garments, to be taken charge of while they did their murderous work. The laying aside of outer garments was a normal practice. We have an example of this with Jesus in John 13 when He laid aside His garments before washing the disciples' feet. However, unlike our Lord, who did servant's work, they were readying themselves to do murderous work. And in the remaining verses we read Stephen's prayer as he is being martyred for his faith. This is the prayer of a dying man; he prays first for himself and then for his persecutors.

The Martyr's Selfless Prayer
Acts 7:59, 60

> And they stoned Stephen as he was calling on God and saying, "Lord Jesus, receive my spirit." 60Then he knelt down and cried out with a loud voice, "Lord, do not charge them with this sin." And when he had said this, he fell asleep. (Acts 7:59-60)

Luke records for us that they *stoned* Stephen. The tense of this verb indicates that "they kept on stoning"—they kept it up as he was calling upon the Lord Jesus. So we know one stone did not kill him. Stephen first prays for himself and says, "Lord Jesus, receive my spirit." The Greek is in the aorist middle imperative which indicates urgency: "Lord, receive my spirit now!" Stephen said almost the same words the Lord had said as he was dying on the cross as recorded in Luke 23:46:

> And when Jesus had cried out with a loud voice, He said, "Father, 'into Your hands I commit My spirit.'" Having said this, He breathed His last. (Luke 23:46)

What did Stephen mean when he asked God to receive his spirit? He meant: "Lord, receive it to Yourself; take it to your abode in heaven." Stephen knew, as all God's children should know, that to be absent from this body is to be present with the Lord (2 Corinthians 5:8) Jesus left these comforting words to his disciples and to all of us before leaving this life to go back to His Father in John 14:1-3:

> "Let not your heart be troubled; you believe in God, believe also in Me. [2]In My Father's house are many mansions; if it were not so, I would have told you. I go to prepare a place for you. [3]And if I go and prepare a place for you, I will come again and receive you to Myself; that where I am, there you may be also. (John 14:1-3)

Jesus is telling His disciples that He comes for us at the moment of our death. Jesus came and received Stephen unto Himself at the moment his spirit left his body. That is the hope of each of us. Now, not only does Stephen pray for himself, but he also doesn't leave this earth without praying for his persecutors, a remarkably selfless prayer.

> Then he knelt down and cried out with a loud voice, "Lord, do not charge them with this sin." And when he had said this, he fell asleep. (Acts 7:60)

This seems to have been a voluntary kneeling, placing himself in this position for the purpose of prayer, choosing to die in this attitude. Stephen kneels in humility to worship as Christ stands to receive him into glory. Stephen then cries with a loud voice. *Cry* is the same Greek word as in verse 57, a loud shriek like a raven. This would be natural, as he is almost dead and probably bloody to the core. And he utters his last words in the form of a prayer for his persecutors *Lord, do not charge them with this sin*. Literally, this means: Lord, fix not this sin upon them. Stephen dies praying for his persecutors. It's as if he thought he could not die in peace until he had done this. He wanted to be at peace with God and man, as we all should, before we step into eternity. Stephen followed the command of our Lord when He said in Matthew 5:44, "But I say to you, love your enemies, bless those who curse you, do good to those who hate you, and pray for those who spitefully use you and persecute you"

Stop for a moment and consider what these men must have been thinking. These men had just stoned Stephen in a fit of rage and anger because of the truth he had spoken, and yet Stephen's last words were a prayer for God's mercy on them. I imagine how those words haunted them for the rest of their lives. Perhaps even some came to salvation as a result of what they had witnessed. Stephen followed in the steps of his Savior who uttered almost the same words from the cross "Father, forgive them, for they do not know what they do." Luke 23:34. Stephen was just like our Lord, who exhibited forgiveness in the midst of mental and physical pain. He prayed for them that did the wrong. I have a book in my office at home entitled *The Prayers of the Martyrs*, and in it there is a prayer of a father regarding the murder of his son. Almost every time I read it, I think, "How did this man have this attitude?" "O God our son's blood has multiplied the fruit of the Spirit of the soil of our souls, so when his murderers stand before thee on the Day of Judgment, remember the fruit of the Spirit by which they have enriched our lives, and forgive."[13] I know it is only by the grace of our Lord that this father had this attitude, that Stephen had this attitude and that you and I can have this attitude, if we are allowed to follow in those steps. The verse ends with this: *And when he had said this he fell asleep*. This is a word picture of rest and calmness, which stands in dramatic contrast

13 Arnold, Duane W.H.- *Prayers of the Martyrs*- Zondervan Publishing House-page 108-109.

to the rage and violence of the scene. It is interesting that there were 2 sets of expressions found in the catacombs of the early Christians. The first expression was “in peace” or “in sleep” and the second set referred to the life which follows sleep. And so Stephen dies. But he dies as a victor, not a victim.

Summary

The methods of Stephen's persecutors (vv. 54, 57-59a). They gnashed their teeth, they cried out with a loud voice, they stopped their ears, they ran at him with one accord, they cast him out of the city, and they stoned him. *The meekness of Stephen's response* (vv. 55, 56). Stephen responded in meekness as He was filled with the Spirit and looked to heaven. *The martyr's selfless prayer* (vv. 59, 60): "Lord do not charge them with this sin."

If you read on in Acts you know that this is not the end of the story. Not only does Stephen enter into eternal glory, but also, because of his death, persecution breaks out. When there is persecution, as we know from the Scripture, there is a scattering of God's people. Acts 8:4 states just that, "and they went everywhere preaching the word." If you read on in Acts 11, you'll see in verse 21 that it says "a great number believed and turned to the Lord." Ladies, Stephen's death was not in vain. We might say "what a waste of a good and godly man," but the Lord had something else in mind—a bigger picture. I think of Cassie Bernall who was killed in the tragic Columbine shootings, and I have read how many countless people have come to the Lord as a result of her dying faith—a bigger picture. I think of a woman I read about named Betty Stam, who lived only a few brief decades because in 1931 her courage and fearless faith led her to serve in China as a missionary. She was caught in a Communist uprising and kneeling by her husband, bowed her head and was decapitated. Her life verse was "For to me, to live is Christ, and to die is gain" (Philippians 1:21). Later, 700 Moody Bible Institute students stood at her memorial service and dedicated their lives to missionary work whenever and wherever God might call them—a bigger picture. Spurgeon said it well, "suffering saints are living seed."[14]

14 Charles Haddon Spurgeon, 1834-1892.

Who will be the martyrs in this century and who will be their persecutors? Perhaps another question would be: What will be the last words of those who die in this century for their faith? Will they die as Stephen did with a prayer of forgiveness? I'm going to get a little more personal here: Are *you* willing to suffer for His name? *Are* you suffering for His name? Paul says in 2 Timothy 3:12 "Yes, and all who desire to live godly in Christ Jesus will suffer persecution." If you are not going through any persecution for your Lord, then perhaps your life is not manifesting godliness. Now, your persecution may not come in the form of death, like Stephen, but perhaps in the form of ridicule, or loss of friends or family members. But it is better, my friend, to suffer for doing what is right than to suffer for doing what is wrong. Will you make a difference? Will you be counted among the saints who have not compromised their convictions for Christ? Or will you tolerate ungodliness and conform to the world, allowing it to squeeze you into its mold? Amy Carmichael once wrote:

"Hast thou no scar? No hidden scar on foot, or side, or hand? I hear thee sung as mighty in the land, I hear them hail thy bright ascendant star, Hast thou no scar? Hast thou no wound? Yet I was wounded by the archers, spent, Leaned Me against a tree to die; and rent By ravening beasts that compassed Me, I swooned: Hast thou no wound? No wound, no scar? Yet, as the Master shall the servant be, And pierced are the feet that follow Me; But thine are whole: can he have followed far Who has no wound nor scar?"[15]

These are sobering things to ponder, and yet perhaps needful, as we examine our own faith and wonder: would we stand in that day? Would we be martyrs for

15 Carmichael, Amy-*Toward Jerusalem*-Christian Literature Crusade- ISBN-0-87508-080-4-page 85.

our faith? What would be our last words uttered to the Lord if we faced death in that way? Could we with Stephen pray, "Lord, do not charge them with this sin"?

Questions to Consider

The Prayer of the First Martyr

Acts 7:54-60

1. Stephen is first mentioned in Acts 6:1-15. (a) Write down all the character qualities of Stephen that are mentioned. (b) What happened as a result of his faith? See verses 9-15.

2. Read Stephen's masterful sermon in Acts chapter 7. (a) What does he say that provokes unbelievers to hate him? (b) Why are his words so inflammatory? (c) What did these hard words cost Stephen? See Acts 7:54-60. (d) Are you willing to say hard things, when needed, to unbelievers or believers? Why or why not?

3. (a) How would you describe the prayer of the first martyr in Acts 7:59, 60? (b) What can you pray on behalf of those who persecute you? (c) What encouragement can you take from Matthew 5:10-12 and 5:43-48 regarding persecution?

4. (a) What happened as a result of Stephen's death? See Acts 8:1-4 and Acts 11:19-26. (b) How does this relate to what Paul says in Romans 8:28? (c) How does this encourage you during times of persecution, and when you stand up for the truth of God's Word?

5. (a) Looking back over question 1, how would Stephen's *character qualities* incite hatred from unbelievers? (b) What did Jesus say would happen to us in John 15:18-27? (c) If one is not receiving persecution from the world, what might it indicate according to these verses?

6. (a) Do you fear persecution? Why or why not? (b) How are you preparing yourself and your children to suffer righteously amidst persecution?

7. Are you suffering today because of your faith? Come with a prayer request for your persecutors. If you are not currently suffering, then come with a request for yourself, that you will be strong when that day comes.

Chapter 7

The Prayer of a Downcast Soul

Psalms 42 and 43

This past year, as my counseling opportunities have increased, I have become deeply troubled concerning the number of women I see in my office who are depressed. I am not as alarmed about their depression, even though it is reason for concern, as I am with the number of women who are turning to anti-depressants as a solution to their depression. When they arrive in my office for their first appointment, I usually discover that they have been on these drugs for as long as a few months to a few years, and yet their mental health has not improved. In fact, many have reached the point of suicide, which is why they feel desperate for counseling. The number of Americans who are taking antidepressants is staggering! It is estimated that over ten million Americans are on antidepressants, and more than one out of ten women are taking these drugs! Recent reports have indicated that those who are on antidepressants are no better off than those who are not on them. Consider the following: "Clinical Psychiatry News online reports that an independent analysis of the suicide rate in psychotropic drug trials—for drugs approved by the FDA between 1985-2000—found that the NEW DRUGS did NOT REDUCE the risk of suicide—they INCREASED the risk."[16]

Depression can and does occur in many believers in

16 http://www.namiscc.org/Research/2002/AntipsychoticSuicideRisk.htm

Jesus Christ. Sometimes nothing will trigger these emotions, other times it could be triggered by a natural disaster like a hurricane, an earthquake, a tornado, or an out-of-control fire. Or it might be a late night phone call bringing bad news, or perhaps a friend who lets you down, or a troubled marriage which can cause the blues. These situations can trigger feelings of depression or discouragement. What does a person do when feeling depressed? Where does a person turn?

In this prayer we are going to look at a man who was depressed: King Hezekiah. Where did he turn? What did he do? A few years ago, for the first time in my life, I faced a real struggle with depression. I had never before had these emotions tug on me. One minute I was despairing, the next minute I was trusting in God. It was a seesaw of emotional ups and downs. This is the case of King Hezekiah in Psalm 42 and 43. He finds out that he will soon be attacked by a great army. And by the way, this is not just any army, but one that is ruthless. If that isn't enough bad news, he is told that he is sick, and that his sickness will result in his death. This is a difficult time in the life of King Hezekiah. As he contemplates the challenges he faces, he becomes depressed and cries out to God and prays:

Psalm 42

As the deer pants for the water brooks,
So pants my soul for You, O God.
2My soul thirsts for God, for the living God.
When shall I come and appear before God?
3My tears have been my food day and night,
While they continually say to me, "Where is your God?"
4When I remember these things,
I pour out my soul within me.
For I used to go with the multitude;

I went with them to the house of God,
With the voice of joy and praise,
With a multitude that kept a pilgrim feast.
5 Why are you cast down, O my soul?
And why are you disquieted within me?
Hope in God, for I shall yet praise Him
For the help of His countenance.
6 O my God, my soul is cast down within me;
Therefore I will remember You from the land of the Jordan,
And from the heights of Hermon,
From the Hill Mizar.
7 Deep calls unto deep at the noise of Your waterfalls;
All Your waves and billows have gone over me.
8 The LORD will command His lovingkindness in the daytime,
And in the night His song shall be with me—
A prayer to the God of my life.
9 I will say to God my Rock,
"Why have You forgotten me?
Why do I go mourning because of the oppression of the enemy?"
10 As with a breaking of my bones, my enemies reproach me, while they say to me all day long, "Where is your God?"
11 Why are you cast down, O my soul?
And why are you disquieted within me?
Hope in God;
For I shall yet praise Him,
The help of my countenance and my God.
(Psalm 42:1-11)

Psalm 43

Vindicate me, O God,
And plead my cause against an ungodly nation;
Oh, deliver me from the deceitful and unjust man!
2 For You are the God of my strength;

Why do You cast me off?
Why do I go mourning because of the oppression of the enemy?
[3]Oh, send out Your light and Your truth!
Let them lead me;
Let them bring me to Your holy hill
And to Your tabernacle.
[4]Then I will go to the altar of God,
To God my exceeding joy;
And on the harp I will praise You,
O God, my God.
[5]Why are you cast down, O my soul?
And why are you disquieted within me?
Hope in God;
For I shall yet praise Him,
The help of my countenance and my God.
(Psalm 43:1-5)

These two Psalms together open book 11 of the Psalter. We are studying them together because most scholars feel it was the translators that divided them, and that originally they were one Psalm. If you will notice in your Bible, Psalm 43 has no title, which may seem to indicate that the translators divided it. There are a lot of suggestions as to the author of these Psalms. Some suggest that this prayer was written by King David when he was fleeing from Absalom. But the best suggestion for the author seems to me to be that of King Hezekiah. King Hezekiah was the greatest king to sit upon the throne of Judah besides David. He was only 25 years old when he became king, and he did more to bring the nation back to God than any other king. In fact, 2 Kings 18:5, 6 says: "He trusted in the LORD God of Israel, so that after him was none like him among all the kings of Judah, nor who were before him. For he held fast to the LORD; he did not depart from following Him, but kept His commandments, which the LORD had commanded Moses." Even though Hezekiah was a great king and trusted God, he had troubles. These troubles were sent by God. Bad things do happen to God's children, despite what you may hear taught today. Hezekiah had two very significant trials in his life. The first trial was an invasion by the Assyrians, from which he was rescued by a miracle of God. In fact, Jehovah slew 185,000 Assyrians according to 2 Kings 19:35. The second significant trial was his illness, which the prophet Isaiah warned him of in 2 Kings 20. This illness was intended to take his life. But God in His great mercy healed him and gave him fifteen more years. This prayer in Psalm 42 and 43 appears to have been written during these two trials. Both events were threatening the life of this godly king, and both were miraculously intervened by a Sovereign God. We get a glimpse of this man's heart as we look at the struggles and emotional distress he goes through as he faces these two very difficult trials. The outline for this prayer is as follows: *Hezekiah's hunger for God* (Psalm 42:1-4); *Hezekiah's haunted soul* (Psalm 42:5-11); and *Hezekiah's hope in God* (Psalm 43:1-5)

Hezekiah's Hunger for God
Psalm 42:1-4

As the deer pants for the water brooks,
So pants my soul for You, O God.
2My soul thirsts for God, for the living God.
When shall I come and appear before God?
3My tears have been my food day and night,
While they continually say to me, "Where is your God?"
4When I remember these things,
I pour out my soul within me.
For I used to go with the multitude;
I went with them to the house of God,

With the voice of joy and praise,
With a multitude that kept a pilgrim feast.
(Psalm 42:1-4)

We are not told what type of illness Hezekiah had; some think he had the plague. 2 Kings 20:7 simply refers to it as a boil. However, due to his illness, he was cut off from the temple that he had been renovated and destroyed. He could not go to the house of God and worship, and yet that was his desire. *As the deer pants for the water brooks, so pants my soul for You, O God. My soul thirsts for God, for the living God. When shall I come and appear before God?* The word *pant* means to cry. It is easy to understand why someone would cry out for water when you consider that many people live in countries where it is especially hot and there are times of drought. Just as a deer needs water to sustain its physical life, you and I need God to sustain our spiritual lives. Hezekiah was in a time of spiritual drought because he was unable to go to the temple. He describes this condition by using the imagery of a deer panting after the water. It has been said that when deer are extremely thirsty you can come very close to them before they will flee. Are you and I that thirsty for God; are we that focused that nothing distracts us from His presence? Are our hearts that fixed upon God that we cry out for worship even when we are unable to go to the house of worship? Hezekiah did not even allow his illness to keep him from longing to worship God. His depression did not keep him from longing for God's house. Hezekiah is a rebuke to our current day Christian mentality which allows even the smallest ache to give us excuse to miss worship. But not Hezekiah; it upset him that his illness kept him from the house of God. He longed for the *living* God, not the dead gods of the heathen. He was thirsty to be in the house of God; it was an intense craving. Does that describe you? Does your soul pant and long to come to church? Can you hardly wait to get there? What about when you have to miss church for some reason? Are you disappointed, or relieved? Hezekiah puts many of us to shame, as some of us can come up with some pretty silly excuses for not assembling in God's house. Some of the excuses I have heard over the years are: "I am too tired;" "that's our family day;" "we have company from out-of-town;" "I have a terrible headache;" "I can't miss some program on television;" "I went last week." The Holy Spirit warns us very strongly about this attitude in Hebrews 10:25, where we are told to be "not forsaking the assembling of ourselves together, as is the manner of some, but exhorting one another, and so much the more as you see the Day approaching." In addition to describing Hezekiah's thirst for God as a deer that pants for water, verses 3 and 4 provide us with yet another description of his hunger for God.

> 3My tears have been my food day and night,
> While they continually say to me, "Where is your God?"
> 4When I remember these things,
> I pour out my soul within me.
> For I used to go with the multitude;
> I went with them to the house of God,
> With the voice of joy and praise,
> With a multitude that kept a pilgrim feast.
> (Psalm 42:3-4)

Hezekiah had lost his appetite for food, apparently because of the mocking he was receiving from others. Hezekiah had rebelled against the King of Assyria, Sennacherib, which precipitated an invasion by the Assyrian army. According to 2 Kings 18, the Assyrians' top officials were casting doubt on the people, telling them not to listen to Hezekiah. They were saying "don't let Hezekiah make you trust in the Lord, saying the Lord will deliver you!" Also, 2 Chronicles 32:17, 18 says that they were telling the people that Hezekiah did not have the power to deliver the city; neither did the Lord. Verse 19 says they spoke against the God of Jerusalem, as against the gods of the people of the earth saying, *"Where is your God?"* This made the people terrified and afraid. When King Hezekiah got word of this (2 Kings 19), he tore his clothes and went to pray. It is very possible that this Psalm was his prayer. He was so upset about what was happening, that he couldn't eat, but he did weep. Have you ever been so upset for the cause of Christ, that you were unable to eat? This is one of the reasons for Hezekiah's depression. It is somewhat different then some of our modern day reasons. When was the last time you were depressed for the cause of Christ? Hezekiah says, *When I remember these things, I pour out my soul within me*. What *things* is he referring to? Things like the fact that he used to be able to worship freely; the fact that his enemies were mocking. When Hezekiah remembers these things, he *pours out his soul*. To *pour out* means "to bear one's soul in tears and complaints." Hezekiah did not allow his illness or the fact that his enemies were attacking him to cause him to become so down that he lost his spiritual balance. He certainly did not turn to drugs to aid his discouragement. He cried out to God! In fact, Hezekiah does not become bitter, but he does pour out his soul to God! What does he cry and complain about? He cries about the fact that he used to be able to go to the house of God with joy and praise, and that he did this with God's people who kept the day of worship. Hezekiah's thirst for God is described as a deer that pants after water; his hunger for God is more intense than his hunger for food. Having seen Hezekiah's hunger for God, we turn to Hezekiah's haunted soul. He gives six descriptions regarding his soul.

Hezekiah's Haunted Soul
Psalm 42:5-11

5 Why are you cast down, O my soul?
And why are you disquieted within me?
Hope in God, for I shall yet praise Him
For the help of His countenance.
6 O my God, my soul is cast down within me;
Therefore I will remember You from the land of the Jordan,
And from the heights of Hermon,
From the Hill Mizar.
7 Deep calls unto deep at the noise of Your waterfalls;
All Your waves and billows have gone over me.
8 The LORD will command His lovingkindness in the daytime,
And in the night His song shall be with me—
A prayer to the God of my life.
9 I will say to God my Rock,
"Why have You forgotten me?
Why do I go mourning because of the oppression of the enemy?"
10 As with a breaking of my bones, my enemies reproach me, while they say to me all day long, "Where is your God?"
11 Why are you cast down, O my soul?
And why are you disquieted within me?
Hope in God;
For I shall yet praise Him,
The help of my countenance and my God.
(Psalm 42:5-11)

Hezekiah teaches us a great principle to keep in mind when we are depressed. We should talk to ourselves instead of listening to ourselves. Do you ever do that? Do you ever ask yourself, "Self, why are you cast down, why are you depressed? What is up with you?" He repeats this phrase in verse 11, and again in verse 5 of the following Psalm. Many times we have to talk to ourselves over and over again, reminding ourselves during trying times that God is faithful, we should trust in Him, hope in Him, and praise Him. These are the answers to Hezekiah's question, *Why are you cast down?* Hezekiah's first description of his haunted soul is *cast down*, which means he is despairing; he is bowed down. Secondly, he describes his soul as *disquieted*, which means he is troubled; he is sad. It also has the idea of growling as a bear, or moaning internally. Hezekiah tells his haunted soul to *hope in God*. The word *hope* means to wait, and to wait with expectation. Notice Hezekiah's hope is rooted in God. He also says God is the help or health (verse 11) of his countenance. The phrase "the help (or health) of his countenance" has been taken by some to indicate that his illness was some sort of disfiguring of his face. That might be true. However, the word itself means "the salvation of His face." The idea is that Hezekiah believes that God would look favorably on him. His hope and his trust were in God. Hezekiah waited with an expectation that was rooted in God. When you are facing trials, and feel discouraged, do you wait with an expected hope in the Lord? Psalm 118:8 says, "It is better to trust in the Lord than to put confidence in man," and that is what we see Hezekiah doing here.

Hezekiah cries out once again about the condition of his soul in verse 6. What is the remedy for his despairing soul? Drugs? Food? No! To *remember God*, he says. Now what does Hezekiah mean when he says that he remembers God *from the land of the Jordan, and from the heights of Hermon, from the Hill Mizar*? The *land of the Jordan* in the Old Testament was a typology of the river of death. It had its source in the heights of Mount Hermon. *Hermon* was a mountainous region northeast of Palestine, near the Jordan. *Mizar* was a little hill on the east side of the Jordan. Hezekiah had come to the river of Jordan, the river of death. His friend Isaiah had told him to put his house in order, because he was going to die. Perhaps these were the areas that Hezekiah was reminiscing about, yet he longed to be on Mt. Zion (see 43:3). The *holy hill* is a reference to Mt. Zion. The psalms speak often about Mt. Zion being the city of God, the city of worship (see Psalm 87:2). That's where Hezekiah's heart longed to be.

Thirdly, Hezekiah goes on to describe his haunted soul as being *overwhelmed* in verse 7. Hezekiah says it is like *deep calls unto deep at the noise of your waterfalls*; one wave speaks to another. A waterfall represents that which makes a noise or seems to give forth a voice. What is Hezekiah saying here? His troubles seemed to be like waves, one after another, and they seemed to be calling to each other to come down like waterfalls. His problems were calling to each other like a waterfall—one after another after another. He was overwhelmed. Hezekiah recognized that the trials of his life were sent by a Sovereign God, and he demonstrates this twice by mentioning *Your* waterfalls, *Your* waves! Hezekiah felt consumed with sorrows and problems, and yet in verse 8 he affirms his trust in God. Hezekiah knew a time of prosperity would return; there would be better days. God's kindness would be shown to him once again. *The Lord will command* indicates a word of authority. And not only will the Lord command His loving-kindness in the daytime, but even in the night, in the shadow of death, his song shall be with him. Even though he faces the river of Jordan, the river of death, even though he has been told he is going to die, his prayer is unto the God of his life. When it is dark (night), His song will be with him! I remember when my husband was going through one of the darkest days of his life. We received a call from our son that we were going to be first-time grandparents. I went right in to where my husband was and told him this news. He replied with, "There *are* songs in the night!"

Hezekiah goes on to describe in verse 9 two more conditions of his haunted soul. Hezekiah calls God his *Rock*, the rock on which he stands. Hezekiah doesn't need a drug upon which to stand; he needs a rock which is founded upon the Almighty God! Hezekiah knows that all other ground is sinking sand. And yet, Hezekiah feels like God has forsaken him. This is the fourth description of his soul. I know we all can identify with these cries, "Lord, where are you in all this? I can't see you, I can't hear you—have you forgotten me?" In the fifth description of his soul, Hezekiah goes on to say his soul is *mourning*: *Why do I go mourning because of the oppression of the enemy? Mourning* means to be gloomy. "Why am I mourning my God, my rock, because of these Assyrians?"

The sixth and final description of Hezekiah's soul is found in verse 10. The mocking from his enemies was like a sword in his bones; his soul felt like it was cut deep into the flesh. You know exactly what Hezekiah is saying here if you have ever been deeply hurt. It cuts like a knife in your ribs. And sometimes you wish for the physical pain over the emotional pain. Hezekiah says, "Lord what is really difficult is that my enemies have reason to reproach me, and say, 'where is your God?' And God, they are saying this daily—over and over again—not just one time." II Chronicles 32 says that they spoke *yet more*, indicating more than one time, against the Lord, and even wrote letters to rail on the Lord God of Israel and to speak against Him.

Hezekiah continues to cry out in verse 11, *Why are you cast down on my soul? And why are you disquieted within me?* These are two good questions for us all to ask when facing difficulties. What is the problem anyway? Hezekiah answers his question with these answers: hope in God; praise Him; He is the health of my countenance; and He is my God. You might say, "Well, what hope is there anyway?" In verses 1-5 of Psalm 43 we see five reasons why Hezekiah hopes in God, and why you and I should hope in God when we feel depressed.

Hezekiah's Hope in God
Psalm 43:1-5

Vindicate me, O God,
And plead my cause against an ungodly nation;
Oh, deliver me from the deceitful and unjust man!
2 For You are the God of my strength;
Why do You cast me off?
Why do I go mourning because of the oppression of the enemy?
3 Oh, send out Your light and Your truth!
Let them lead me;
Let them bring me to Your holy hill
And to Your tabernacle.
4 Then I will go to the altar of God,
To God my exceeding joy;
And on the harp I will praise You,
O God, my God.
5 Why are you cast down, O my soul?
And why are you disquieted within me?
Hope in God;
For I shall yet praise Him,
The help of my countenance and my God.
(Psalm 43:1-5)

In verse 1, he is referring to the Assyrian King Sennacherib. The country that Hezekiah loved was being threatened by unjust and ungodly men, so he pleads for vindication. The first reason he hopes in God is because he knows God is just! *Vindicate me, O God,* he says! As Paul says in Romans 12:19: "'Vengeance is Mine, I will repay,' says the Lord." Will not the God of the earth do what is right?

Hezekiah puts his hope in God not only because He is just, but secondly, because He is strong, as we see in verse 2. He hopes in God because he knows God is strong. He calls God *the God of my strength.* And yet, he says: *Why do You cast me off?* Hezekiah expresses his feeling of abandonment again, as he did in 42:9. The Hebrew word *cast off* means to be foul, rancid, abominable, and then to be treated as such. He complains of his mourning again, *because of the oppression of the enemy,* as he did in 42:9 as well. Oh why, why Lord? This is a common question that King Hezekiah asks in his prayer to God. Actually, there are ten *why*'s in Hezekiah's prayer. Why God? We do the same thing, don't we? Why, Lord, did this happen? And why am I feeling this way, Lord? And why this Lord, and why that, Lord? What is the solution to all these *why* questions? To remind ourselves of the truth that the just live by faith. Our hope is in God. Trust is the solution, not knowing all the answers.

Hezekiah gives two more reasons in verse 3 for hoping in God. *Oh, send out Your light and Your truth! Let them lead me; let them bring me to Your holy hill and to Your tabernacle.* Darkness, in the Scripture, represents distress and danger; *light* represents relief and deliverance. Hezekiah hopes in God, thirdly, because He knows that God will deliver. And not only will He deliver, but Hezekiah knows God is truth, which is his fourth reason for his hope. The word for *truth* here means faithfulness and stability. Hezekiah goes on to pray, *Let them lead me; let them bring me to Your holy hill and to Your tabernacle.* What is he saying here? Lord, I am hoping in Your deliverance (You are the help of my countenance).

I am hoping in Your truth. I will be restored to worship on Mt. Zion. Hezekiah firmly believed that he would be able to return to the place his soul longed for, the place of worship.

Hezekiah continues on with this hope of restored worship, in verse 4. God is his joy: *Then I will go to the altar of God, to God my exceeding joy; and on the harp I will praise You, O God, my God.* Hezekiah calls God *my exceeding joy.* This is his fifth hope. It is not in a pill, or a person, or a place, but in His God! That is his joy! When he calls God his exceeding joy it literally means, "The gladness of my joy." God was his source of joy, and he knew happiness was found in Him. Hezekiah's circumstances seemed pretty bleak, yet his joy was in the Lord, and the Lord was preeminent above all circumstances.

Hezekiah ends his prayer with those familiar words in verse 5. *Why are you cast down, O my soul? And why are you disquieted within me? Hope in God; for I shall yet praise Him, the help of my countenance and my God.* Hezekiah was cast down because of the Assyrians. He could only see disaster ahead. He was disquieted because of the illness he was facing that threatened to take his life. All looked bleak and hopeless. But that wasn't the end of the story. Hezekiah recalls the healing of his countenance from the deadly disease from which God had delivered him. Hezekiah's hope was in God; He was the help of his countenance!

Summary

Hezekiah's hunger for God (Psalm 42:1-4); *Hezekiah's haunted soul* (Psalm 42:5-11); and *Hezekiah's hope in God* (Psalm 43:1-5). Hezekiah is so hungry for God that his soul pants like a deer for water. His hunger for God is more intense than his hunger for food. Does your soul thirst for God to that degree? Have you ever felt like Hezekiah: cast down, disquieted, overwhelmed, forsaken, mourning, like you had a sword in your bones? Do the trials in your life seem like waves—one after another? My dear sister, there is hope, there are answers. The solution is with God. Have hope, as Hezekiah did, that: God is just; God is strong; God will deliver; God is truth; and God is your joy.

What is causing your discouragement or depression this day, dear one? Do you believe that God is just in your situation? Is He strong enough to deliver your disquieted heart? He will! Do you believe in the truth of His word, His promises? Are you seeking joy in your trial in a pill or in the person of Jesus Christ? That, my dear sister, is where the answer is found to all of the trials of life!

Questions to Consider
The Prayer of a Downcast Soul

Psalms 42 and 43

1. (a) Read Psalms 42 and 43. What would you say is the theme of these Psalms? (b) What emotional difficulties does the psalmist have? Support your answer from what you read.

2. Some scholars believe King Hezekiah wrote Psalms 42 and 43. (I am taking this view.) With that in mind, read 2 Kings 18. (a) Against whom did King Hezekiah rebel? (b) What were the results of that rebellion? (c) Who won the war? See 2 Kings 19:35. (d) How do these facts help you understand the prayer in Psalms 42 and 43?

3. Read 2 Kings 20:1-11 and 2 Chronicles 32. What similarities do you see between these two passages and Psalms 42 and 43?

4. (a) What characteristics of God does Hezekiah mention in Psalms 42 and 43? (There should be at least 10) (b) How do these give you hope when facing troubles? *Example*: (42:9) My rock—when all around me seems to be shifting and unstable, I can count on the solid rock—God—He is stable, He is strong.

5. (a) Why do some believers not thirst for God as King Hezekiah did? (b) Do you personally get excited when you think about coming to church to worship or is it a burden to you? (c) Do you enjoy taking regular time in the Word and prayer, or is that a burden for you?

6. Make a list of all the things that are causing you to be

downcast, disturbed, and disquieted. How can you take the prayer of Psalms 42 and 43 and turn those troubles into trusting in God?

7. Write a prayer request petitioning God for a situation that seems hopeless to you. Then trust in Him with all your heart.

Chapter 8

The Prayer of Ten Lepers

Luke 17:11-19

The story is told of a pastor who was giving his congregation an update on some answers to prayer which were a result of prayer requests that had been given earlier by his congregation. He reported the following: "Nine persons were lost at sea." His congregation was shocked, and saddened. The pastor went on to say "Well, eleven people asked for prayer for those going out to sea, and only two asked me to give thanks for a safe return, so I assumed that the other nine were lost at sea." This story illustrates a very tragic truth. The truth is that we live in an ungrateful society. The apostle Paul says in 2 Timothy that in the last days men would be unthankful: "But know this, that in the last days perilous times will come: For men will be lovers of themselves, lovers of money, boasters, proud, blasphemers, disobedient to parents, *unthankful,* unholy" (2 Timothy 3:1-2; emphasis mine).

We are indeed an ungrateful generation, and unfortunately we are rearing the generation after us to be just like us. In fact, a few years ago I was speaking at a women's conference, and before one of the sessions, the lady in charge of women's ministries got up and announced a new policy for new moms and new brides. She went on to say that it was not going to be required anymore to send "thank you" notes after receiving gifts at a baby shower or a bridal shower. I was surprised, and privately commented later about it to the woman who had invited me to come to speak. I mentioned to her that I thought it sent a wrong message, and gave allowance for these women to develop a potentially ungrateful spirit. We have come to one of the most tragic stories, I think, in all of the New Testament—a lesson in prayer, yes, but more than that, a lesson in ungratefulness. Let's look together at Luke 17:11-19.

Luke 17:11-19

> Now it happened as He went to Jerusalem that He passed through the midst of Samaria and Galilee. 12Then as He entered a certain village, there met Him ten men who were lepers, who stood afar off. 13And they lifted up their voices and said, "Jesus, Master, have mercy on us!" 14So when He saw them, He said to them, "Go, show yourselves to the priests." And so it was that as they went, they were cleansed. 15And one of them, when he saw that he was healed, returned, and with a loud voice glorified God, 16and fell down on his face at His feet, giving Him thanks. And he was a Samaritan. 17So Jesus answered and said, "Were there not ten cleansed? But where are the nine? 18"Were there not any found who returned to give glory to God except this foreigner?" 19And He said to him, "Arise, go your way. Your faith has made you well." (Luke 17:11-19)

In this short account of the prayer of the ten lepers we will observe the following: *the scene* (vv. 11, 12), *the prayer* (v. 13), *the answer* (v. 14), *the tragic ending* (vv. 15-19). By the way, Luke is the only gospel which records this particular story of the healing of the ten lepers.

The Scene
Luke 17:11, 12

> Now it happened as He went to Jerusalem that He passed through the midst of Samaria and Galilee. (Luke 17:11)

Now Samaria was located between Galilee and Jerusalem, and in order for Jesus to go to Jerusalem, it was necessary for Him to pass through Samaria. It is important to note here that Jesus would be taking a risk by passing through Samaria. "Why?", you might ask. Well, in John chapter 4, in the account of Jesus and the woman at the well, it states in verse 9 that the Jews had no dealings with the Samaritans. Jesus was a Jew, and the Jews were not buddies with the Samaritans, that's for sure. Samaritans were the adversaries of the Jews. Jews considered the Samaritans of mixed origin and half-breeds. The Jews were extremely malicious toward the Samaritans; in fact, they looked upon them as having no part in the resurrection. They considered them to be accursed by God. The Jews ate nothing that was a Samaritan's because to do so would have been considered eating pig's flesh. It was said that the Jews were under no kind of obligation to the Samaritans. They did not borrow anything from them, they did not drink out of the same cup or well with them, and they did not sit down to meals with them, or eat out of the same vessel. They had no religious connection, and no commercial dealings with them. The deadly hatred that existed between these two nations was known to all. With these facts in mind, being a Jew and passing through Samaria was risky. And so, in verse 12 we continue with the scene. Jesus enters into a village where He encounters 10 lepers.

> Then as He entered a certain village, there met Him ten men who were lepers, who stood afar off. (Luke 17:12)

The New King James Version says *there met him.* In other words, they were in His way, or in His path, as He was entering the village. They were not allowed to enter the village while they were afflicted with the leprosy. Leviticus 13:46 says that lepers were to dwell alone outside the camp, so that they would not infect others. They were unclean, and it was not lawful for them to come near to those who were healthy. So, they stood afar off. Now before we go on, I think we need to define leprosy in order that we may better understand the misery these men were in and the desperateness of their prayer. What is leprosy? Leprosy is a chronic, infectious disease characterized by sores, scabs, and white shining spots beneath the skin. There are several types of leprosy. Biblical leprosy was most likely a severe type of psoriasis, a form of the disease that is relatively rare in modern times. No disease was more dreadful in Bible times than leprosy. It first exhibited itself on the surface of the skin. The appearance was not always the same, but it commonly resembled the spot made by the puncture of a pin or a small bump on the skin filled with pus. The spots generally made their appearance very suddenly, and would usually appear first on the face, nose, and eyes, and increased in size until they become as large as a pea or a bean. There were three kinds of leprosy, distinguished by the appearance of the spots: the white, the black, and the red leprosy. These spots, though few at first, gradually spread until they covered the whole body. A leprous person would live twenty, or thirty, or even fifty years if he received the disease at his birth. But the years he would live would be years of indescribable misery. When the disease advanced, the upper part of the nose would swell, the nostrils became enlarged, and the nose itself grew soft. Tumors appeared on the jaws; the eyebrows would swell; the ears became thick; the points of the fingers, and also the feet and the toes would swell; the nails became scaly; the joints of the hands and feet separated and dropped off. In the last stage of the disease the patient would become a hideous spectacle, and fall to pieces. This disease was also contagious and hereditary. It was easily communicated from one person to another, and was transmitted to the third and fourth generation. As we think of the awfulness of this disease we can understand the desperation of these ten lepers. They were outcasts of society, they were in pain, they were disfigured, and they were in need of mercy.

So the scene is Samaria where Christ encounters ten lepers afar off. In all likelihood, these 10 lepers had heard of similar cleansings, as Jesus had healed other lepers whose accounts are recorded in Matthew 8:2-3 and 11:5. These men must have known something of Christ's reputation or who He was, as verse 13 seems to indicate. Let's look at their prayer.

The Prayer
Luke 17:13

> And they lifted up their voices and said, "Jesus, Master, have mercy on us!" (Luke 17:13)

As they were companions in suffering, they were also companions in prayer, and they lifted up their voices together and cried out, *Jesus, Master, have mercy on us!* What did they mean *have mercy on us*? Have compassion on us. These lepers were throwing themselves upon the mercy of God. What a lesson we can learn from them: where can we go, but to the Lord, when we are in need of mercy?! Their prayer consisted of six words—that's all. *Jesus, Master, have mercy on us!* Sometimes in our misery and pain, we don't have the energy to pray some of these lengthy and noble prayers that we have been studying. All we can do is cry out for mercy! It is interesting that leprosy was a disease that the Jews felt was inflicted on others for the punishment of some particular sin. They felt it was a sign of God's displeasure. Yet these lepers did not let that keep them from begging for mercy from the One who could cleanse them. Many have compared leprosy to sin, as both are diseases that grow and grow until they destroy a person. We must cry out to our Master, whether it is for physical healing, or spiritual healing. *Lord, have mercy on us!* Did Jesus answer their prayer for mercy? Yes, He did.

The Answer
Luke 17:14

> So when He saw them, He said to them, "Go, show yourselves to the priests." And so it was that as they went, they were cleansed. (Luke 17:14)

You might be asking, "If Jesus could heal them, then why did He send them to the priest?" The reason Jesus sent them to the priest was so that they could be inspected by him, which was the requirement of the law. The priest was the judge of the leprosy. The ceremonial law was still in effect, and so Christ made sure that it was observed. Based on Leviticus chapter 13 and 14, we know that on the basis of a hair in a scab, a pimple, or a spot on the skin that had turned white, the priest would declare a person to be a leper and would quarantine him for seven days. If no change in the spot occurred by then, the quarantine would be extended another week. At that time, if the spot had started to fade, the leper would be pronounced cured and returned to his normal life. However, if the spot remained or had spread, he was declared unclean and banished. The inspection of the disease was the duty of the priest; he would declare whether a person was healed or not, and restore him to the congregation. It was required, also, that the leprous person bring an offering to the priest of two birds, probably sparrows, one of which was to be killed, and the other was to be let loose into an open field.

Luke goes on to say, *and so it was that as they went, they were cleansed.* Now Jesus intended that their cure should be received by faith. They were depending on His goodness and power. The healing done by Christ was immediate, and it was done as they obeyed his commandment. Luke says: *as they went they were cleansed.* It may have been tempting for the lepers to quarrel with the Lord and say "Why should we go to the priest? We know you can heal us! We don't need to let the priest check us out." But they didn't. They immediately obeyed and went in faith. And their faith is what made them well. (Jesus says that in verse 19.) What a contrast between this story and the story of Naaman in 2 Kings 5 who had leprosy. Remember when Elisha told him to go and wash in the Jordan seven times for healing. Naaman became so angry that he turned and went away in a rage. Those that expect Christ's blessings in their life must receive them in His way and by His method. Many times we want to do things our way, but Christ commands that we follow His way. He also expects immediate obedience, not delayed obedience. God highly honors this kind of faith, and makes it the instrument in His hand of working many miracles. So we have seen the prayer for mercy, and we have seen the glorious answer of healing. Now we see the tragic ending.

The Tragic Ending
Luke 17:15-19

> And one of them, when he saw that he was healed, returned, and with a loud voice glorified God, [16]and fell down on his face at His feet, giving Him thanks. And he

> was a Samaritan. [17]So Jesus answered and said, "Were there not ten cleansed? But where are the nine? [18]"Were there not any found who returned to give glory to God except this foreigner?" [19]And He said to him, "Arise, go your way. Your faith has made you well." (Luke 17:15-19)

Luke records that only one gave thanks. One out of ten. But this leper praised God with a loud voice. He could not keep silent! He had to return to give thanks to God. Luke records that he gave glory by falling on his face, and giving thanks. (See verse 16.) Now all ten were healed and yet only *one* came back to say thank you. They all ten joined hand-in-hand praying for mercy and for the healing of their bodies, but only one came back to complete his prayer, which was the giving of thanks. That is the tragedy of this story, and the tragedy of many whom God shows mercy upon by answering prayer. Just think with me for a minute. How many things have you petitioned God for just this week? How many of those prayers has He answered? Have you thanked Him for those answers?

The Samaritan falling on his face was a posture of reverence and worship to the Lord. He gave him thanks immediately. Luke does not record what he said in his prayer of thanksgiving, but nonetheless he was grateful. God's mercy was fresh on his mind, and so he immediately gave thanks. Many times we are so busy with life, and fail to stop and realize how much God is doing every day in our lives. We just don't stop to give thanks. And Luke adds an interesting footnote: *and he was a Samaritan.* The Spirit of God lets us know this leper was a Samaritan for a reason. This phrase colors the whole incident. The one man who felt grateful enough to come back and thank Jesus for the blessing *was a despised Samaritan!* The fact that it was a hated Samaritan who gave thanks would have been striking in the sight of the Jews. Remember, they considered the Samaritans as *especially* wicked, and themselves as *especially* holy. Luke records another story about a Samaritan in Luke 10. Remember the man who was robbed by thieves and was beaten and left for dead? The story tells us that a priest came by and ignored him, a Levite came by and ignored him, but a certain Samaritan came by and did not ignore him, but had compassion on him and took care of his wounds and made sure he got help for him.

It has been suggested that in this account the other nine lepers were Jews. The nine religious Jews would not humble themselves enough to give thanks, but this poor and contrite and despised Samaritan did. It reminds me of what Paul says in 1 Corinthians 1:27-31:

> But God has chosen the foolish things of the world to put to shame the wise, and God has chosen the weak things of the world to put to shame the things which are mighty; and the base things of the world and the things which are despised God has chosen, and the things which are not, to bring to nothing the things that are, that no flesh should glory in His presence. But of Him you are in Christ Jesus, who became for us wisdom from God—and righteousness and sanctification and redemption—that, as it is written, *'He who glories, let him glory in the Lord.'* (1 Corinthians 1:27-31)

The Lord uses a despised, weak leper to bring him glory. What is the Lord's response to this one grateful leper? Well, let's read His response in verses 17-19:

> So Jesus answered and said, "Were there not ten cleansed? But where are the nine? [18]Were there not any found who returned to give glory to God except this foreigner?" [19]And He said to him, "Arise, go your way. Your faith has made you well." (Luke 17:17-19)

Jesus says "Where are the nine? Why did they not return to give thanks?" Of the many that receive mercy from God, there are few, very few, that return to give thanks. One in ten. This is a striking illustration of human nature, and of the ingratitude of man! One had come back to give thanks, and the others were heard of no more. Commentator Albert Barnes puts it so well:

> When people are restored from dangerous sickness, here and there one comes to give thanks to God; but 'where are the nine?' When people are defended from danger; when they are recovered from the perils of the sea; when a steamboat is destroyed, and a large part of the crew and passengers perish, here and there one of those who are saved acknowledges the goodness of God and renders him praise; but where is the mass of them? They give no thanks; they offer no praise. They go about their usual employments, to mingle in the scenes of pleasure and of sin as if nothing had occurred. Few, few of all who have been rescued from 'threatening graves' feel their obligation to God, or ever express it. They forget their Great Benefactor; perhaps the mention of his name is unpleasant, and they scorn the idea that they are under any obligations to him. Such, alas, is man, ungrateful man![17]

Jesus then says, "Were there not any found who returned to give glory to God except this foreigner?" This man, who might have been least "expected" to express gratitude to God is the one who does. The most unlikely men sometimes are the ones who are found to be most consistent and grateful. The other nine remind me of those who want a Jesus who will make them healthy and wealthy, but not a Jesus who will save

17 Barnes, Albert- *Barnes Note* -Baker Book House; ISBN-0-8010-0843-3– page 122,123.

them from their sins, and cleanse the leprosy of their souls. Their lack of gratitude shows their desire for material blessings, but not a desire to acknowledge Him as their Lord who is worthy of their worship and praise. How grieved Christ must have been and how grieved He must be when we ask for something and yet never give Him thanks. So the story ends in verse 19.

> And He said to him, "Arise, go your way. Your faith has made you well." (Luke 17:19)

"Arise," Jesus says, and "go your way." In other words, go to the priest. Why? He still needed to do that so that he could be restored to society and to his friends, and to the public worship of God. What did Jesus mean when He said *your faith has made you well*? The Greek word for *made you well* is the same word used for *salvation.* What He meant was *your faith has saved you.* Jesus used this term in other accounts of healing, including Luke 8:43-48:

> Now a woman, having a flow of blood for twelve years, who had spent all her livelihood on physicians and could not be healed by any, came from behind and touched the border of His garment. And immediately her flow of blood stopped. And Jesus said, "Who touched Me?" When all denied it, Peter and those with him said, "Master, the multitudes throng and press You, and You say, 'Who touched Me?'" But Jesus said, "Somebody touched Me, for I perceived power going out from Me." Now when the woman saw that she was not hidden, she came trembling; and falling down before Him, she declared to Him in the presence of all the people the reason she had touched Him and how she was healed immediately. And He said to her, "Daughter, be of good cheer; your faith has made you well. Go in peace." (Luke 8:43-48)

Notice in this account that Jesus calls her *Daughter,* indicating she was now part of His kingdom. She was a daughter of the King. Her faith not only healed her physically, but also spiritually. Her faith *made her well* just as the leper who returned was made well. The other nine lepers were healed, but the one who returned showed faith in action by returning to Christ in recognition of Who He was. We know God sends rain on the just and the unjust, but not all recognize the source of this mercy. The other nine experienced God's mercy but did not fully benefit from it. Faith responds to God's goodness, and it is to this one leper alone that Jesus says "your faith has saved you." And so there is no other mention of the other nine. They did not return to praise and thank God. They missed the moment to give thanks and to be spiritually healed. They missed the opportunity to acknowledge His Lordship. Beware of receiving God's mercy in your life and yet not acknowledging that it is your Lord who extends such mercy.

Summary

The scene (vv. 11-12): Samaria, where Christ encounters 10 lepers afar off. *The prayer* (v. 13): *Jesus Master have mercy on us! The answer* (v. 14): they were all shown mercy by the healing of their leprosy. *The tragic ending* (v. 15-19): only one came back to give thanks and glorify God.

Ungratefulness is really not a new problem for mankind. It was a problem in Jesus' day and it is a problem in our day. As wise old Solomon said, there is nothing new under the sun. What about you? Do you have a grateful spirit, especially as it relates to answered prayer? Do you come back and give thanks? You might say, "Well, of course the leper had something to be thankful for—he was healed. You don't understand my situation, Susan; life for me is difficult right now. I really don't have anything to be thankful for." Matthew Henry, the famous scholar, was once accosted by thieves and robbed. He wrote these words in his diary, "Let me be thankful first, because I was never robbed before, second, because although they took my purse, they did not take my life, third because although they took my all, it was not much, and fourth because it was I who was robbed, not I who robbed." I would like to close this chapter by giving you some help in cultivating a grateful spirit. I would like to leave you with three thoughts for maintaining a thankful heart. Keep these tucked away in your heart:

1. *A grateful spirit begins in your thought life.* A thankful heart begins with a thankful mind. We should begin in our minds with thoughts of God, His power, wisdom, goodness, grace, love and care. These are just some of the things we can meditate on which should create a thankful spirit.

2. *Think of yourself.* Not how great you are, but how insignificant you are, in light of who God is. We should think about

our privileges in Christ and how blessed we are to be among the ones whom Christ loved and died for. We are accepted in the Beloved. These types of thoughts will cultivate a grateful spirit.

3. *Think of others.* Begin to think of others and be thankful for the opportunities we have to serve others. We serve God by serving others. The reason we are probably not more thankful is because we don't stop and think. This one despised Samaritan stopped and thought. Having a thankful heart is really the fruit of a determined resolve to think about God, ourselves (and how insignificant we are), and others.

Why not determine with God's help to have a mind that is grateful? We should be thankful, and yet we are a people who lack this character trait. Beware of the sin of ingratitude. Recognize God's blessings in your life and let them fill your mind, your heart and your lips with humble, sincere praise.

Questions to Consider
The Prayer of Ten Lepers

Luke 17:11-19

1. Read Luke 17:11-19. (a) Skim Leviticus chapter 13 and write down five facts regarding leprosy. (b) How do these facts help you to better understand the lepers' cries for mercy in Luke 17:13?

2. (a) What was the requirement of the cleansed leper according to Leviticus 14:2? (b) Read Leviticus 14:1-32 and summarize what the priest did regarding the cleansing of lepers. (c) Why do you think Jesus sent the ten lepers to the priests in Luke 17:14?

3. (a) What was the nationality of the leper who gave thanks? See verse 16. (b) According to John 4:1-9, why was this so significant? (c) What does this teach you about Jesus?

4. What do you think Jesus meant in verse 19, "your faith has made you well?"

5. Compare and contrast Luke's account of the healing of the ten lepers with the following accounts of other healed lepers: Matthew 8:1-4; Mark 1:40-45. What similarities and differences do you notice?

6. (a) When God answers your prayers, do you come back and give Him thanks? (b) Why do you think we are negligent in giving thanks to God when He answers our petitions? (c) How can we cultivate a spirit of thankfulness in ourselves, and pass that on to our children and grandchildren or others?

7. List 10 specific blessings God has given you this week and thank Him for each one.

8. Write a prayer of thanksgiving to God.

Chapter 9

A Prayer for Mercy

Psalm 51

At the age of 18, I left the security of my home and went away to another state to Bible school. After a few months of being away at college, I remember being under conviction about a lie I had told my parents when I was in high school. I had told them that someone had run into my car in the high school parking lot one day after school. It was a lie, as the truth was I had backed into someone as I was pulling out of my parking space. I remember feeling very scared as I returned home on my break from college, as I knew I needed to make this right. So I asked if I could speak to them one evening, and off we went to the den of our home. I poured out my heart and begged for their forgiveness. Of course, they forgave me and all was well. Their mercy was extended to me. But the greater sin was the sin against the Lord. And His Mercy was extended to me as well. Puritan writer, Richard Sibbes, once said: "No sin is so great but the satisfaction of Christ and His mercies are greater; it is beyond comparison. Fathers and mothers in tenderest affections are but beams and trains to lead us upwards to the infinite mercy of God in Christ."

In this chapter we will focus on a prayer for mercy. It is a prayer from King David, a sinner who was in desperate need of forgiveness of his sin and cleansing of his heart. Many years ago I memorized this Psalm, and it has been one of my favorite scriptures to use when I need to be cleansed of sin or am feeling remorse over sin.

Before we look at this prayer for mercy, we need to understand the context. The background takes place in 2 Samuel, chapters 10-12. King David should have gone out to battle with his men, but instead he stays back at home. One evening he is walking on the roof of his house and notices a beautiful woman bathing. He inquires about her, sends for her, and commits adultery with her. The woman becomes pregnant. There is another problem however, and that is that she is married, and married to one of King David's soldiers—Uriah. So King David begins to connive to cover his sin. The cunning deceit ends with Uriah being killed on the front lines of battle. So David sends for this woman, Bathsheba, and takes her as his wife. Of course, this does not please the Lord, and He sends His prophet Nathan to confront David, which results in his confession of his sin. This prayer for mercy was said to have been written after Nathan confronted him. He cries out to God and says:

Psalm 51:1-19

Have mercy upon me, O God,
According to Your lovingkindness;
According to the multitude of Your tender mercies,
Blot out my transgressions.
2Wash me thoroughly from my iniquity,
And cleanse me from my sin.
3For I acknowledge my transgressions,
And my sin is always before me.
4Against You, You only, have I sinned,
And done this evil in Your sight—
That You may be found just when You speak,
And blameless when You judge.
5Behold, I was brought forth in iniquity,
And in sin my mother conceived me.

[6]Behold, You desire truth in the inward parts,
And in the hidden part You will make me to know wisdom.
[7]Purge me with hyssop, and I shall be clean;
Wash me, and I shall be whiter than snow.
[8]Make me to hear joy and gladness,
That the bones You have broken may rejoice.
[9]Hide Your face from my sins,
And blot out all my iniquities.
[10]Create in me a clean heart, O God,
And renew a steadfast spirit within me.
[11]Do not cast me away from Your presence,
And do not take Your Holy Spirit from me.
[12]Restore to me the joy of Your salvation,
And uphold me by Your generous Spirit.
[13]Then I will teach transgressors Your ways,
And sinners shall be converted to You.
[14]Deliver me from bloodshed, O God,
The God of my salvation,
And my tongue shall sing aloud of Your righteousness.
[15]O Lord, open my lips,
And my mouth shall show forth Your praise.
[16]For You do not desire sacrifice, or else I would give it;
You do not delight in burnt offering.
[17]The sacrifices of God are a broken spirit, a broken and a contrite heart—
These, O God, You will not despise.
[18]Do good in Your good pleasure to Zion;
Build the walls of Jerusalem.
[19]Then You shall be pleased with the sacrifices of righteousness,
With burnt offering and whole burnt offering;
Then they shall offer bulls on Your altar.
(Psalm 51:1-19)

This Psalm was written by David, directed to the chief musician, which indicates that the Psalm was not merely written to express the feelings of David, but it was to be used in public worship. Psalm 51 is one of the seven Psalms which are called Psalms of penitence. The others are Psalm 6, 32, 38, 102, 130 and 143. The Psalm is easily outlined: *the confession of David's sin* (vv. 1-6); *the cleansing of David's sin* (vv. 7-11); *and the consequences of David's repentance* (vv. 12-19). We begin with David's confession of his sin in verse one.

The Confession of David's Sin
Psalm 51:1-6

David begins his plea for mercy by saying:

> Have mercy upon me, O God,
> According to Your lovingkindness;
> According to the multitude of Your tender mercies,
> Blot out my transgressions.
> (Psalm 51:1)

It is interesting to note that David's first cry to God is for mercy, even before he confesses his sin. It is very different from some of our prayers for forgiveness. "Lord, I blew it again today, and Lord, if it weren't for my husband leaving his dirty clothes out, I probably wouldn't have lost my temper. So glad you understand—see ya!" Not David; he knew he needed mercy for his guilty heart. What is David pleading for here when he asks God for mercy? *Mercy* means to be favorable, and it always implies pity to the miserable, grace to the guilty. David knew *he* was guilty before God. He did not shift the blame to anyone else. In fact, did you notice throughout the whole Psalm, that David uses the pronoun *my* or *me*? Have mercy upon *me*, *my* transgressions, wash *me*, *my* iniquity, cleanse *me*, *my* sin, *my* transgression, *my* sins, *I* sinned, purge *me*, wash *me, my* sins, *my* iniquities, create in *me*, renew a right spirit within *me*, cast *me* not away, take not the Holy Spirit from *me*, deliver *me*! There is not one mention of blaming Bathsheba, blaming his parents, or even shifting the blame to the devil. David takes full responsibility for his sin. Many of us refuse to take responsibility for our sin: "you don't understand my situation," "if they had done to you what they did to me," "you aren't married to my husband." But sin is a choice; always has been, always will be.

Notice that David knew that the only basis for cleansing was God's loving-kindness and His tender mercies. This was his only hope. There was another time in David's life when he sinned greatly against the Lord by numbering the Israelites, in II Samuel 24. After being confronted by the prophet Gad with his sin, David was given three choices. He could either receive seven years of famine, three months of his enemies pursuing or three day's of pestilence. Note David's response to Gad. "I am in great distress. Please let us fall into the hand of the LORD, for His mercies are great; but do not let me fall into the hand of man." (2 Samuel 24:14) David understood that the mercy of the Lord was greater then man's mercy. Jeremiah says in Lamentation 3:22, 23, "Through the LORD's mercies we are not consumed, because His compassions fail not. They are new every morning; great is Your faithfulness." Now lest you think, oh well! I will just sin, and God's mercy will get me through. You are thinking wrong! Paul says in Romans 6:1, 2, "What shall we say then? Shall we continue in sin that grace may abound? Certainly not! How shall we who died to sin live any longer in it?" The attitude of the child of God should not be *how much can I sin and get away with?* but, instead, *how little can I offend a holy God?* What is David asking for here when he asks for his transgressions to be blotted out? *Blot out* means to be wiped out or to be destroyed. What were the transgressions, or sins, which David desired to have destroyed? The obvious ones of course were adultery and murder. But David also committed the sins of discontentment, ingratitude, covetousness, pride, selfishness, worldliness, just to mention a few. One sin usually always leads to another, if not dealt with and forsaken. Such was the case of David. David goes on to pray:

> Wash me thoroughly from my iniquity,
> And cleanse me from my sin.
> (Psalm 51:2)

The word *wash* means to bleach or to purify. David wants not just to be washed, but to be washed thoroughly which means "multiply to wash me." It is a reference to repeated or constant washings in order to remove a stain. The word used in this context means "to trample with the feet." During biblical times clothes were often washed in this manner. The dirt that David had in his life was so ingrained that a simple rinsing would not do it. Cleanse me from my sin, Lord; remove it entirely, Lord! Cleanse me and make me pure. Help me to be guiltless. Notice that David uses three verbs in verses 1 and 2 when asking for forgiveness: blot out, wash, and cleanse. These verbs express David's desire for complete forgiveness and cleansing. Also, it is interesting to note that David uses three terms for sin as well. The first one is *transgression*—a high-handed revolt against divinely constituted law; rebellion. The second one is *iniquity*, which means perversion and twisting of moral standards. The third one is *sin*, which we know is missing the mark, a stumbling, a falling short, and a missing of the goal that has been set for us. David continues his prayer and says:

> For I acknowledge my transgressions,
> And my sin is always before me.
> (Psalm 51:3)

Acknowledge is a verb that is in the future tense, indicating David knew he would retain a deep sense of his sin as long as he lived. I know there are sins in my past for which I know I have been forgiven, but I do remember them with great remorse. "My sin is always before me," David says. It is now constantly before my mind. Remember David had dealt with this unconfessed sin for almost a year now. His confession came right before his child died, according to 2 Samuel 12:13-18. If you have ever dealt with unconfessed sin, then you know what David is saying here. It is always before you: when you lie down, when you wake up, in the middle of the night, in the middle of the day. It continually haunts you. Everywhere David turned, he probably saw Uriah's face and rehearsed the sin with Bathsheba. Along with this, perhaps the thought of people finding out his sin haunted him for 12 long months. And to think, David had continued to sit as king as if he had done no wrong. David knew that this sinful act was done against a holy God, as evidenced in verse 4.

> Against You, You only, have I sinned,
> And done this evil in Your sight—
> That You may be found just when You speak,
> And blameless when You judge.
> (Psalm 51:4)

Now we know that David sinned greatly against Bathsheba, Uriah and even the nation of Israel as their leader. But the one David had sinned against the most was God. He had violated God's law. In 2 Samuel 12:13 after Nathan confronted him; David said "I have sinned against the Lord." Remember in Genesis 39, when Potiphar's wife was trying to get Joseph to commit adultery with her? What was his response? He said, "How then can I do this great wickedness, and sin against God?" (verse 9) Joseph knew that this would be a sin against a Holy God. This is where some of us fall short, as we do not see our sins as sins against a Holy God. We wink at sin, we excuse it, and we justify it. We should abhor sin and fight hard not to violate God's law. We should flee from all sin. David acknowledges that this evil was done in God's sight: *done this evil in Your sight.* Nothing was hidden from God's view. He saw the adulterous act between David and Bathsheba. He saw the plotted murder of Uriah, the Hittite. God saw it all, and David knew it. Many of us wouldn't think of sinning if the pastor was present or our best friend were there, but do we ever stop to consider that when we sin there is One who indeed sees all and is ever present with us? As the writer to the Hebrews says in 4:13, "all things are naked and open to the eyes of Him to whom we must give account." What does David mean when he goes on to pray: *that You may be found just when You speak, and blameless when You judge?* Speaking and judging are parallel terms which signify the pronouncement of a sentence. David is saying, God, your character is vindicated in all that You have said. David knew that his sin deserved all that God said it did, which was death according to the Old Testament law. Speaking of David's sin, he now acknowledges a fact we must remind ourselves of often, that is, we are born sinners. I know we like to think those cute babies are innocent, but they are not. Verse 5 says:

> Behold, I was brought forth in iniquity,
> And in sin my mother conceived me.
> (Psalm 51:5)

David is saying here that he knew he was born a sinner. Psalm 58:3 states "The wicked are estranged from the womb; they go astray as soon as they are born, speaking lies." What does David mean when he says in sin my mother conceived me? David is not blaming his mother for the way he is. He is rehearsing the fact he was born a sinner. The reason that David mentions his mother here instead of his father, is perhaps because of the fact that she had a greater part in the birthing process. David knew that sin was a heart problem, an inward problem. That's why he goes on to pray in verse 6:

> Behold, You desire truth in the inward parts,
> And in the hidden part You will make me to know wisdom.
> (Psalm 51:6)

Lord, you desire, or take delight in, the inward parts. The *inward parts* here would be a reference to the seat of the mind, the feeling, the intellect. David knew that God was pleased with purity in his innermost being. Do you ever pray for the purity of your heart? Jesus says in the Sermon on the Mount that only the pure in heart will see God (Matthew 5:8). God isn't impressed with outward manifestations of religion, but He is interested in truth, in purity in the inward parts. David says *in the hidden part You will make me know wisdom.* In the depth of my soul you will make me know knowledge. We now turn from David's' *confession* of his sin, to the *cleansing* of his sin.

The Cleansing of David's Sin
Psalm 51:7-11

David longs for cleansing and prays:

> Purge me with hyssop, and I shall be clean;
> Wash me, and I shall be whiter than snow.
> (Psalm 51:7)

The word *purge* means to purify from uncleanness. *Hyssop* was a common herb, which sprouted on walls, and was used to cleanse someone who had been in contact with a dead body, or had been defiled by someone who had leprosy. (See Leviticus 14:4 and Numbers 19:18) David felt contaminated by sin; his impurity was great, and he knew that he needed something to cleanse him which had a strong purifying power. He goes on to say *wash me, and I shall be whiter than snow*. David wanted to be entirely clean, as white as snow. As Isaiah the prophet said in Isaiah 1:18, "'Come now, and let us reason together,' says the LORD, 'Though your sins are like scarlet, they shall be as white as snow; though they are red like crimson, and they shall be as wool." David did not even want a speck of dirt to defile him. David not only wanted to be washed internally, but he desired the joy that had vanished because of his sin to be returned.

> Make me to hear joy and gladness,
> That the bones You have broken may rejoice.
> (Psalm 51:8)

David no longer heard joy and gladness; he had become deaf to the voice of God. Unrepentant sin makes us deaf to the voice of our Lord. As Psalm 66:18 says: "If I regard iniquity in my heart, the Lord will not hear." Repentance and forgiveness would have to take place in order for the joy and gladness to return to David's life. What does David mean when he says, "that the bones You have broken may rejoice?" I have never broken any bones, but I understand that breaking a bone can cause great pain. You might be diverted temporarily from the pain by medication or distraction, but you always come back to the reality of the pain. David's bones were not literally broken, that we know of, but the pain from his sin weighed on him as if they were. He couldn't stop thinking about it. His bones felt crushed by the weight and guilt of sin. David desires that his bones would rejoice, or be free from suffering. He wanted the burden lifted. If you have ever suffered under a heavy load of sin, then you know exactly what David is talking about. Unconfessed sin and undealt-with sin can cause numerous illness and diseases. Before we call a doctor, we might need to call on the Lord to see if there is a reason for our illness. James 5 indicates the man mentioned was sick because of sin. Also in I Corinthians 11, Paul indicates that many in the church at Corinth were sick and had even died because of sin. David was very ashamed of his sin, as we see in verse 9.

> Hide Your face from my sins,
> And blot out all my iniquities.
> (Psalm 51:9)

David is saying, Lord, do not look on my sins; refuse to see them. It is terrible to have people find out about our sin, but we forget that God knows about every one of our sins. David not only wants God to not see his sins, but to blot out all his iniquities. Let them be erased, Lord, please cancel them! It is interesting to note that David makes the same three requests in verses 7-9 as he did in verses 1 and 2, only now they are in reverse order. David's cry for mercy continues with a plea for the inward man to be pure.

> Create in me a clean heart, O God,
> And renew a steadfast spirit within me.
> (Psalm 51:10)

Create is the Hebrew word *bara* which is used in Genesis 1:1. In the beginning God created (bara) the heaven and the earth. It means to create something out of nothing. When David asks for God to create a new heart, he is asking the Lord to not only change his heart, but to create a new one. He asks the Lord to create in him such a clean heart that he will never sin again. The heart would indicate the center where all thoughts and plans originate. What is David saying when he asks for God to *renew a right spirit within me? Within me* literally means in the midst of me in my innermost parts. And the word *right* means that which is able to stand up; that which is upright or proper. David wants a heart that will be able to stand up against temptation and do what is right. In verse 11 we see a portion of David's prayer that we as New Testament believers do not need ever to pray—praise God for that! David fears a permanent separation from God.

> Do not cast me away from Your presence,
> And do not take Your Holy Spirit from me.
> (Psalm 51:11)

An interesting side note is that this is the first time in the Old Testament that *Holy Spirit* is used. And it is only used one other time in the Old Testament, in Isaiah 63:10. More than likely David did not understand the third person of the Trinity as we do, as in Old Testament times the Holy Spirit came and went and did not indwell believers. So what is David saying when he prays this? If you recall in 1 Samuel 16:13, when Samuel anointed David as King, it says "the Spirit of the Lord came upon David from that day onward." David had the experience of the Holy Spirit upon him, and he did not want that taken away. David knew that the Spirit had departed from Saul, and he did not want that to happen to him. Now this is not a prayer that we have to pray, as Jesus said in John 14:17 that the Spirit will dwell with us and will be with us and, in verse 16, that He will abide with us forever. Paul also states in Ephesians 1:13 that after we believed we were sealed with the Holy Spirit of promise and that sealing is until the day of redemption. Well, what are the results of David's *confession* and *cleansing* from his sin? We see in verses 12-19 the *consequences* of David's repentance. What blessings they are!

The Consequences of David's Repentance
Psalm 51:12-19

> Restore to me the joy of Your salvation,
> And uphold me by Your generous Spirit.
> (Psalm 51:12)

David prays, "Cause the joy of thy salvation to return." *Joy* comes from two Hebrew words, one meaning bright and the other meaning lily or whiteness. David's joy would be returned to him, and it would be as bright and beautiful as the lily. Notice David did not say restore unto me my salvation, but the joy of my salvation. Sin does not cause us to lose our salvation, but it certainly causes us to lose the joy of it. David goes on to pray: *And uphold me by Your generous Spirit.* Lord, keep me from falling, and keep me willing. Make my spirit willing to be obedient. Do you ever pray that? God, I want to obey—help me to be willing. It is like the father of the child possessed with a demon in Mark 9:24 who prayed, "Lord I believe, but help my unbelief." David's joy would not only be restored as a result of his repentance, but he will also be able to help others.

> Then I will teach transgressors Your ways,
> And sinners shall be converted to You.
> (Psalm 51:13)

The word *converted* means to turn around. David wants to help sinners to turn around. David wanted to be able to help others as a result of his own dreadful experience. As painful as our past sins can be, many times God will allow us the privilege of helping someone who is perhaps contemplating that same sin or already involved in it. Before I embraced Christ as my Lord, I had several sinful patterns that needed to be broken. The Lord helped me immensely, and now I am able to help others in putting off sin. Not only will David's joy be restored, not only will he be able to help others, but he will also sing again!

> Deliver me from bloodshed, O God,
> The God of my salvation,
> And my tongue shall sing aloud of Your righteousness.
> (Psalm 51:14)

God deliver me from bloodshed, from the guilt of murder! Nothing could change what David had done. Uriah was dead, and no prayer would bring him back to life. But nonetheless, David's soul needed peace. In this verse it is interesting that David confesses his awful sin, and in the same breath, calls God the God of his salvation. As Charles Spurgeon said, "Growing upward and downward at the same time are perfectly consistent." *And my tongue shall sing aloud of Your righteousness*, David says. Lord, after you forgive and cleanse me I can sing again of your righteousness, but not until then. Not only will David be joyful again, and turn sinners from their sin, and sing again, but he will also once again praise God with his mouth.

> O Lord, open my lips,
> And my mouth shall show forth Your praise.
> (Psalm 51:15)

It is hard to praise the Lord with a sinful heart. David's lips had been sealed for a year. To have opened them at that time with praise would have been hypocrisy. But now, with his sins forgiven, he desires to declare praises unto the Lord once again. It is very hard, as you know, to praise the Lord and at the same time have unconfessed sin in your life. Praise from our lips should be the natural expression, not only of David, but of all who have had sins forgiven. David goes on to express what the Lord desires from each of us, and it is not animal sacrifices.

> For You do not desire sacrifice, or else I would give it;
> You do not delight in burnt offering.
> 17The sacrifices of God are a broken spirit,
> A broken and a contrite heart—
> These, O God, You will not despise.
> (Psalm 51:16-17)

David was willing to offer sacrifices and burnt offerings, but God was more interested in David's heart than a bloody lamb. What is a sacrifice to God? A broken and contrite spirit. God is interested in a broken and contrite spirit. *Broken* means to break in pieces and *contrite* means to crouch. God delights in those whose hearts are broken over sin, and yet he detests the proud in heart. In fact, they are an abomination to Him according to Proverb 6:17. The results of David's repentance will also help the whole nation of Israel as can be seen in verses 18 and 19.

> Do good in Your good pleasure to Zion;
> Build the walls of Jerusalem.
> 19Then You shall be pleased with the sacrifices of righteousness,
> With burnt offering and whole burnt offering;
> Then they shall offer bulls on Your altar.
> (Psalm 51:18-19)

David now turns his thoughts from his sin to Zion, the place of worship, the city of God. Did his sin affect God's people? Yes. David was the King of Israel, and because of his sins, he had weakened the nation. He had pulled down the walls. He asks God to repair and build the walls of Jerusalem which had been weakened by his sin. David is asking God to turn His favor upon the holy city so that others may profit by his insight. He knows that then and only then will God *be pleased with the sacrifices of righteousness, with burnt offering and whole burnt offering; then they shall offer bulls on Your altar*. Because of David's repentance, God would again pour out His favor to Zion and His blessing on Jerusalem. A whole burnt offering was a sacrifice which was utterly consumed by flames. Usually only the head, fat, and certain other portions were offered, but sometimes, when the person's heart was full and he wanted to show his complete and undivided surrender to God, the entire animal was consumed. This must have been how David felt, as he wanted nothing held back. After David's repentance, all the offerings prescribed in the law would then be able to be offered. Bullocks were the largest and the most costly sacrifices. But the cost of the sacrifice from God's people would mean nothing until David's heart was right. Then and only then would God be pleased with the sacrifices required of the nation. When the walls of Jerusalem would be built up again, then the cause of true religion would flourish.

Summary

The confession of David's Sin (vv. 1-6): David knows his sin was committed against a Holy God: *against thee, thee only, have I sinned.* And so he cries out to God for mercy, and he cries for washing and cleansing. In your prayers of confession, do you justify your sin, or blame others, or do you acknowledge you have sinned against a Holy God? *The cleansing of David's sin*: (vv. 7-11): This cleansing would involve a washing that would leave David as white as snow: *wash me and I shall be whiter than snow.* In your prayers for cleansing do you desire a thorough washing that leaves not one speck of dirt? *The consequences of David's repentance*: (vv. 12-19): David's joy would return; he would sing again; be used by God to turn sinners from their sin; praise God again; and once again God's favor would be restored to Israel. Is there any sin you have not confessed and forsaken this day? What are the consequences in your life, in the lives of others? For those of you who have confessed and forsaken sin in your life, what have been the consequences of your repentance? Joy? Singing and praising God again? Helping others to turn from their evil ways? May God help us to be women who are thorough in our confession and repentance of our sin!

Questions to Consider

A Prayer for Mercy

Psalm 51

1. Read 2 Samuel 11-13. (a) What were the sins that David committed? (b) What were the results of his sins? (c) What does this teach you about sin in your own life?

2. Psalm 51 was written after the events of 2 Samuel 11-13. (a) According to Psalm 51, who does David say he sinned against? (b) Why doesn't he mention sinning against Bathsheba or Uriah? (c) What parts of this Psalm are not applicable to New Testament believers and why?

3. (a) Where did Hyssop grow according to 1 Kings 4:33? (b) What did Moses say to do with hyssop in Exodus 12:21, 22? (c) What were the uses for it according to Leviticus 14:1-6 and Numbers 19: 6, 18? (d) How does this help you to understand David's plea in Psalm 51:7?

4. David says in verses 16 and 17 of Psalm 51 that God is not merely interested in outward sacrifices, but He is interested in a broken and contrite heart. (a) What do the following verses say about those who have a broken and contrite heart? Psalm 34:18; 102:17; 147:3; Isaiah 57:15; 61:1; 66:1, 2. (b) How do these verses motivate you to be mindful of your heart condition?

5. How does David's cry for mercy and forgiveness compare to our modern prayers of forgiveness?

6. Write your own psalm of penitence. (This does not have to be lengthy.)

7. Is there any unconfessed sin in your life? Confess it (and forsake it) now before God, and others, if necessary. Then come with a praise to share concerning God's mercy and forgiveness in your life.

Chapter 10

Lord, Teach Us to Pray

Luke 11:1-4

Someone once said, "Discipleship is not so much taught as caught." I have pondered that sentence often, and I have passed the thought on to others. In fact, when we considered the prayer of the 10 lepers, one of the questions for consideration at the end of the chapter prompted us to consider how we teach our children to be grateful. And one of the things that comes to mind when considering that question is that we have to *live* a grateful attitude before them. Our children learn more by our example than by the things we teach them with our words. In fact, when you think back on your childhood and what your parents taught you, do you remember more from their words or from their example? We can instruct all we want, but the greatest teacher is our living example, not only before our children, but before others also. When we think of that statement, "discipleship is not so much taught as caught," we can see how that is also true in the life of the Lord and His twelve disciples. He did teach them much with His words, but He also taught them great volumes by His example. One of the most important things they learned by His instruction as well as by His example was how to pray. The twelve saw and heard Christ pray on many occasions and, as we will see in a moment, they also heard His instruction on prayer.

Luke 11:1-4

Now it came to pass, as He was praying in a certain place, when He ceased, that one of His disciples said to Him, "Lord, teach us to pray, as John also taught his disciples."
[2]So He said to them, "When you pray, say:

> Our Father in heaven,
> Hallowed be Your name.
> Your kingdom come.
> Your will be done on earth as it is in heaven.
> [3]Give us day by day our daily bread.
> [4]And forgive us our sins,
> For we also forgive everyone who is indebted to us.
> And do not lead us into temptation,
> But deliver us from the evil one." (Luke 11:1-4)

Our outline for this prayer is fairly simple. First, we will see *the Lord's example of prayer* (v. 1). And second, we will see *the Lord's instruction of prayer* (vv. 2-4).

The Lord's Example of Prayer
Luke 11:1

Luke tells us, *Now it came to pass, as He was praying in a certain place*. There are many instances where Luke records for us that our Lord prayed. He prayed at His baptism in Luke 3:21; He prayed in the wilderness, Luke 5:16; He prayed before selecting the 12 disciples and He continued all night in prayer in Luke 6:12; He was alone praying in Luke 9:18; He prayed at the transfiguration in Luke 9:28-29; He prayed here in Luke 11:1-4; He prayed for Simon in Luke 22:32; He prayed on the cross in Luke 23:46. All these references (and by the way, these are just in Luke) point us to the fact that Jesus was in the habit of praying, and that His disciples witnessed many of those times. Now where was Jesus when He was praying here? Luke doesn't tell us, as he simply states that it was *a certain place*. It is possible that this is in the Garden of Gethsemane. Luke goes on to say that *when He ceased, that one of his disciples said to Him....* Did you notice that the disciples did not interrupt His praying? I wish that were the case when we pray, don't you? I find it interesting in my own life to see the different ways the enemy tries to interrupt my praying or distract me from praying. Many times the phone will ring, or a child will interrupt us, or all of sudden we get sleepy. I remember one Saturday night prayer meeting at our house when our instant hot water faucet in the kitchen starting spewing and spitting! (We had already learned to turn the phones off when praying, but this was a new distraction!) I am sure you too have your own list of interruptions that occur when you are trying to pray. How gracious of the disciples to be sensitive to the Lord and this sacred time. Speaking of the disciples, Luke then records that one of them asks a question. He doesn't say which one, but I wonder if it was Peter, since it appears from many of the gospel accounts that he liked to asked questions! One of His disciples said to Him, *"Lord, teach us to pray, as John also taught His disciples."* Evidently the disciples were impressed with Christ's prayer life, and wanted Him to teach them to pray. And so one asks: *"Lord, teach us to pray."* The Greek tense is an aorist imperative, which indicates a slight note of urgency in the request. Have you ever asked the Lord to teach you to pray? I hear people often say, "I don't know how to pray." Perhaps we might do well to ask God to teach us how to pray. May our request be, "Lord, teach us to pray; give us a rule or model by which to go in praying, and put words into our mouths…Lord, teach me what it is to pray; Lord, excite and quicken me to the duty; Lord, direct me what to pray for; Lord, give me praying graces, that I may serve God acceptably in prayer; Lord, teach me to pray in proper words; give me a mouth and wisdom in prayer, that I may speak as I ought; teach me what I shall say."[18] I hope each of us has an attitude of willingness to learn much from the prayers we study. We can learn not only from the prayers themselves, but from the people who pray them, just like the disciples are learning how to pray from the Lord. I would encourage you to pray often with others, and glean from the way others pray.

What does it mean to *teach us to pray, as John also taught his disciples*? What is the reference here to John teaching His disciples to pray? It was the custom in those days for the rabbis to teach formulas for prayer to their disciples. Evidently John the Baptist did that for his followers. We have no record of such a prayer in the Bible, but the disciples must have been aware of it, because they ask Jesus for the same training that John's disciples received.

Having seen the Lord's example of prayer in verse one, we turn to His instruction of prayer in verses 2-4.

The Lord's Instruction of Prayer
Luke 11:2-4

Jesus says, *when you pray, say…* Notice Christ assumes that the 12 are praying. He does not say *if* you pray, but *when* you pray. By the way, all disciples of Jesus Christ should be praying. Even those who are like the disciples, who need

18 Henry, Matthew-*Matthew Henry-Commentary on the whole Bible*-MacDonald Publishing Co.-page 692-Volume V.

instruction in prayer, should be talking to God. Jesus begins His instruction regarding prayer by first telling them whom they should pray to. They should pray to the Father. Ladies, who we pray to is of utmost importance. What does the term *Our Father* mean? This goes back to the Aramaic expression *Abba*. He is our Papa, Daddy! Paul says in Romans 8:15, "For you did not receive the spirit of bondage again to fear, but you received the Spirit of adoption by whom we cry out, 'Abba, Father.'" This term includes respect for the Father's rule, but it also suggests intimacy. We need to remember when we are praying that we are addressing our prayers to the One who is caring and gracious and desires to have fellowship with his children. He is also the One who protects us and helps us in our fears, just as an earthly father would. He showers us with resources and grants us wisdom and direction. He never leaves us nor does He forsake us. This is the One we pray to. Oh, what a blessing! Jesus goes on to say that the Father we are praying to is *in heaven*. This is also a very important element in our prayers. God is not a god that cannot hear us. He is alive and He is in heaven. Notice what the apostle Paul states in his sermon in Acts 17:22-25, "Then Paul stood in the midst of the Areopagus and said, 'Men of Athens, I perceive that in all things you are very religious; for as I was passing through and considering the objects of your worship, I even found an altar with this inscription: TO THE UNKNOWN GOD. Therefore, the One whom you worship without knowing, Him I proclaim to you: God, who made the world and everything in it, since He is Lord of heaven and earth, does not dwell in temples made with hands. Nor is He worshiped with men's hands, as though He needed anything, since He gives to all life, breath, and all things.'" Paul recognized that our Father is in heaven! He is not dead, nor unknown! This is our Father who is in Heaven.

After we acknowledge who we are praying to and where He is, then Jesus says we must reverence or hallow His name. *"Hallowed be Your name."* What does it mean to hallow His name? To *hallow* His name means to make it holy. This means we love and revere His name. We will approach Him as a Father, but we will also approach Him with a reverent, humble spirit, and by doing that, we hallow His name. I hope you are careful about not being flippant in your prayers. I hear some people refer to God as their "buddy" or "pal," or "the man upstairs." This is not hallowing His name. The Jews would often end their worship services with this prayer "Exalted and hallowed by His great name, in the world which He created according to His will. May He let His kingdom rule in your lifetime and in your days and in the lifetime of the whole house of Israel, speedily and soon." Perhaps we should adopt this godly habit in our own prayers. After Christ instructs them about whom they pray to, and hallowing His name, He then instructs them with what they should pray about. He begins with *Your kingdom come*. What does this mean? This means we are praying for Christ to reign on earth as He does already in heaven. *Your kingdom* means "Your rule." This means we are submitting to the will of God, His rule, and therefore God's kingdom or rule to come. This is affirming that you are willing to relinquish the rule of your own life so that the Holy Spirit can use you to promote the Kingdom of God in whatever way He chooses. Not only are we to pray for His Kingdom to come, but also for His will to be done. *Your will be done on earth as it is in heaven.* This literally reads "Whatever you wish to have happen, let it happen immediately." Your choice be done. This is where most of us get tripped up. "Lord, Thy will be done." One man recounts a time when he prayed this prayer and ended up in a serious automobile accident after his freshmen year of college. He said after it was over, he thought "God, if you're going to fight this way, I give up! I can't handle this." He knew God was calling him into the ministry, but he was focusing and heading in another direction. God used this experience to get his attention to serve Him. That man was John MacArthur. Remember Christ's prayer in the Garden in Luke 22:42? "Father, if it is Your will, take this cup away from Me; nevertheless not My will, but Yours, be done." Jesus not only instructs the disciples to pray this way, but He modeled it for them as well in the Garden of Gethsemane. He yielded His will to the Father's will.

The next element of this prayer, found in verse 3, is one most of us probably cannot identify with. *Give us day by day our daily bread.* Most of us have never had to pray this prayer. We probably need to pray for self-control to not eat so much bread! But, this would be a prayer request that the disciples would understand. Many people in those days were dependent on their day's wages to buy food, as there was not the abundance that most of us now enjoy. Many of the disciples would need to pray for daily food just to sustain their lives. This does not mean the principle is not the same for those of us who have enough food. We must acknowledge that all we have is from God, whether it is food, material blessings, spiritual blessings or anything else. James 1:17 says "Every good gift and every perfect gift is from above, and comes down from the Father of lights, with whom there is no variation or shadow of turning." In that context, James is talking about our trials being a gift from Him.[19] Everything we have is from Him. One of the precious gifts we have from Him is forgiveness of sins. This is yet another element of instruction in this prayer, found in verse 4.

19 See *With the Master in the School of Tested Faith: A Ladies' Bible Study of the Epistle of James*, by the author of this volume; pages 73,74.

Verse four reads, *"And forgive us our sins."* What does it mean to *forgive us our sins?* This means to send away, or dismiss. This verb is in the past tense, "we have forgiven," since Christ assumes that he who prays for the remission of his own debts has already forgiven those indebted to him. Christ goes on to say: *for we also forgive everyone who is indebted to us.* This is somewhat different from the expression in Matthew, though the sense is the same. The idea is this: unless we forgive others, God will not forgive us; and unless we come to Him genuinely forgiving all others, we cannot expect forgiveness. It does not mean that by forgiving others we "deserve" forgiveness ourselves, but without the attitude of forgiveness, God cannot consistently forgive us. Now this statement may have caused the disciples to ask, as you may be asking in your mind, "forgive everyone?" You've got to be kidding me!? I must forgive my husband who is harsh with me? You mean I have to forgive that person who slandered me and ruined my reputation? Do I have to forgive that one who abused me when I was a child? I want to stop here and say a few words about forgiveness, because I think it is an element sorely lacking in our Christianity. This is an area that grieves me, but more than that, it grieves the heart of God, and it should not be, my sisters. Many of us have allowed areas of resentment to fester and now they have become full blown areas of unforgiveness. It might have started out as an interruption in your day, or someone who didn't meet your expectations or standards, so you resented their imperfections. Perhaps your resentment comes from broken promises, personality or character flaws such as the way people talk, the way they act, they way they forget and forget, their eating habits, their untidiness, the fact that they are always late, change their minds, and cannot even decide what to order off the menu. And so we fester and fester resentment until we hate the person in our heart. How can we be so petty? How can we not forgive and look over the imperfections of others when we have been forgiven so much by a Father who remembers our frailties and knows we are dust? "Well", you might say, "how do I get rid of all this garbage I am carrying around?" One of the best remedies I know, ladies, it to look back at the cross. It is where we find the only One who had a right to be unforgiving and yet He wasn't. What did Jesus experience? Hebrews 12:3, 4 says: "For consider Him who endured such hostility from sinners against Himself, lest you become weary and discouraged in your souls. You have not yet resisted to bloodshed, striving against sin." Have you and I had to forgive others of the following: a kiss of betrayal by a friend, another friend who is ashamed to even say they know you? Have you had to forgive three of your closest friends for falling asleep on you in your darkest hour? Have you had to forgive false witnesses testifying against you, someone spitting in your face, having your face hit (while being blindfolded), having your clothes stripped off you, a crown of thorns on your head, being beaten so many times that you were too weak to carry your cross? Have you had to forgive others for driving nails in your hands, being hung on a cross, and then, while you were in the deepest pain and agony, all alone, no friends, and even your own Father forsaking you? Have you had to forgive endless mocking, ridiculing and insults? How did Jesus respond? "Father, forgive them, for they know not what they do." Peter says in 1 Peter 2:21-23, "For to this you were called, because Christ also suffered for us, leaving us an example, that you should follow His steps: Who committed no sin, nor was deceit found in His mouth, who, when He was reviled, did not revile in return; when He suffered, He did not threaten, but committed

Himself to Him who judges righteously." You might say, "I can't do that!" You're right, you can't! But Paul tells us how we can through the Spirit's work. Paul tells us in Ephesians 3:20 that God is "able to do exceedingly abundantly above all that we ask or think, according to the power that works in us." We are reinforced with mighty power in the inner man by the Holy Spirit Himself indwelling our innermost being. We have that power if we are a child of God, and therefore we can forgive because He gives us the power and grace to do so. Stephen was able to do this as he was being stoned. (See Acts 7:6) What did he say? "Lord, do not charge them with this sin." I think it is very sobering in the Matthew 6 account of this prayer where Christ adds in verse 15, "But if you do not forgive men their trespasses, neither will your Father forgive your trespasses." Another sobering passage is James 2:13, where he states: "For judgment is without mercy to the one who has shown no mercy. Mercy triumphs over judgment." And yet another in Matthew 5:22-25, "But I say to you that whoever is angry with his brother without a cause shall be in danger of the judgment. And whoever says to his brother, 'Raca!' shall be in danger of the council. But whoever says, 'You fool!' shall be in danger of hell fire. Therefore if you bring your gift to the altar, and there remember that your brother has something against you, leave your gift there before the altar, and go your way. First be reconciled to your brother, and then come and offer your gift. Agree with your adversary quickly, while you are on the way with him, lest your adversary deliver you to the judge, the judge hand you over to the officer, and you are thrown into prison." Jesus is saying that we are not to come to church if we have resentment in our hearts. Jesus says to take care of the offense first, and do it quickly. We should never put off reconciliation. Another principle I would like to bring out before we go on is in Leviticus 19:17, "You shall not hate your brother in your heart. You shall surely rebuke your neighbor, and not bear sin because of him." If we would follow this principle in Leviticus that God gave us, we would not be a people who are filled with festered resentment. We would do well to practice the principle here in Leviticus as well as those in Matthew 18:15-20 and Galatians 6:1, 2. We are to lovingly help each other in areas of offence. I find in my own life, if I let these things go, then I will become resentful and unforgiving. I would plead with you if you are harboring resentment and an unforgiving spirit that you would take care of it today! Jesus ends His instruction with a prayer request that I think we should pray each day. *And do not lead us into temptation,but deliver us from the evil one.* What does it mean to pray that we would not be led into temptation? Here we have a permissive imperative in the Greek. The idea is: "Do not allow us to be led into temptation." Lord, help us! And there is a way out of temptation, as God has promised to help us when we are tempted to do evil. Paul says in 1 Corinthians 10:13 "No temptation has overtaken you except such as is common to man; but God is faithful, who will not allow you to be tempted beyond what you are able, but with the temptation will also make the way of escape, that you may be able to bear it." I am afraid some of us just don't want to take the escape route that the Lord has provided. In fact, in the next verse Paul says "flee!" Run! We like to dabble with temptations, but running and fleeing is the escape hatch which is provided for us. In the Garden of Gethsemane Jesus said to Peter, James, and John: "Pray that you may not enter into temptation" (Luke 22:40). Christ is saying that they should pray that they would be delivered from situations that would cause them to sin. Instead of being led into temptation we should pray that the Lord would deliver us from the evil one. The word *but* here is *alla* in the Greek. The other word for but is de, but this word is the stronger of the two, indicating the seriousness of being delivered from evil. The word *deliver* means *to rescue*; and the *evil one* is the enemy Satan. Did you know Christ prayed this for us in the High Priestly prayer in John 17:15? He prayed, "Keep them from the evil one." Some of you are familiar with the prayer of Jabez and, unfortunately, the hay day that the proponents of the prosperity gospel have had with his prayer. But did you ever notice another part of Jabez's prayer that we have seemed to ignore? 1 Chronicles 4:10 reads, "And Jabez called on the God of Israel saying, "'Oh, that You would bless me indeed, and enlarge my territory, that Your hand would be with me, and that You would *keep me from evil*, that I may not cause pain!' So God granted him what he requested." Just think how much temptation we would be delivered from if we would only ask. We have not because we ask not! Luke's account ends this prayer here. It is not followed with *for thine is the kingdom and the power and the glory forever, Amen.* However, Jesus follows this instruction about praying with two parables in verses 5-13.

> And He said to them, "Which of you shall have a friend, and go to him at midnight and say to him, 'Friend, lend me three loaves; [6]'for a friend of mine has come to me on his journey, and I have nothing to set before him'; [7]"and he will answer from within and say, 'Do not trouble me; the door is now shut, and my children are with me in bed; I cannot rise and give to you'? [8]"I say to you, though he will not rise and give to him because he is his friend, yet because of his persistence he will rise and give him as many as he needs. [9]"So I say to you, ask, and it will be given to you; seek, and you will find; knock, and it will

> be opened to you. [10]"For everyone who asks receives, and he who seeks finds, and to him who knocks it will be opened. [11]"If a son asks for bread from any father among you, will he give him a stone? Or if he asks for a fish, will he give him a serpent instead of a fish? [12]"Or if he asks for an egg, will he offer him a scorpion? [13]"If you then, being evil, know how to give good gifts to your children, how much more will your heavenly Father give the Holy Spirit to those who ask Him!" (Luke 11:5-13)

Why did He do this? Perhaps the disciples needed further instruction about two more aspects of prayer not yet mentioned. The first lesson that was needed was persistence, boldness and aggression in prayer. It is also interesting that this one pertains to food, which was mentioned already when Jesus prayed *give us day by day our daily bread.* Perhaps there would be times when they would need to ask and ask again. Jesus wanted them to not grow weary in praying. "Men always ought to pray and not lose heart" (Luke 18:1). The second lesson needed is that God gives His children what is good for them. He doesn't give them things that will harm them, like a snake or a scorpion. The best gift He will give the disciples is the Holy Spirit, if they ask. And I would be negligent if I did not say to you that if you have never bowed the knee to the Lordship of Jesus Christ and repented of your sins, do so today. What a gift we can have—not only the gift of the Holy Spirit as mentioned here, but the gift of eternal life and knowing Christ!

Summary

In this chapter we have seen, first, *the Lord's example of prayer* in verse 1. And secondly, we have seen *the Lord's instruction in prayer* in verses 2-4. If others learned about prayer by your example only, what would they learn? Are these elements that Jesus taught evident in your prayers? *Our Father in heaven, hallowed be Your name.* When you begin your prayers, is it with a reverent spirit that hallows the name of our Heavenly Father? Or do you make some flippant opening remarks? *Your kingdom come. Your will be done on earth as it is in heaven.* Do others see you asking for the will of God in your current situations, or would they hear you asking God to change His will to suit yours? *Give us day by day our daily bread.* When you look at your day and pray about it, are you aware that God alone is the one you must be dependent on, or do you try and go through the day depending on your own strength and resources? *Forgive us our sins, for we also forgive everyone who is indebted to us.* Do you come to God with bitterness in your heart toward another, or is your conscience clear? Do you keep short accounts with others? *Do not lead us into temptation, but deliver us from the evil one.* Would you say when temptation comes that others see you crying out to God for deliverance, or do they hear you say "Oh, you know, my flesh just gave in—you know I come from a dysfunctional family." Let us soberly evaluate our prayers and attitudes to see if they line up with what Jesus taught us. With that in mind, I would like you to bow your head and pray the Lord's Prayer. This is the account as it is recorded in the Gospel of Matthew, which is probably the one most familiar to you. Pray with me from your heart, will you?

Our Father in heaven,
Hallowed be Your name.
Your kingdom come.
Your will be done
On earth as it is in heaven.
Give us this day our daily bread.
And forgive us our debts,
As we forgive our debtors.
And do not lead us into temptation,
But deliver us from the evil one.
For Yours is the kingdom and the power
and the glory forever. Amen.
(Matthew 6:9-13)

Questions to Consider

Lord, Teach Us to Pray

Luke 11:1-4

1. Read Luke 11:1-4. (a) What elements of prayer do you find in this passage? (b) Do your own prayers include these elements? (c) Do you think we should include these elements in our prayers? Why or why not? (d) What do you notice about your prayers that are different from this one?

2. (a) Why is this prayer a good model for our praying? (b) How would you outline this prayer?

3. Compare and contrast the Luke passage to Matthew's account of this prayer in Matthew 6:9-13. (a) What are the similarities between these two prayers, as well as the incidents surrounding them? (Read a little before and after the prayer.) (b)What are the differences?

4. Following this lesson in prayer, our Lord gives two parables about praying (see vv. 5-13). Why would these parables follow Christ's teaching on prayer?

5. (a) According to this prayer, whom should we forgive? (b) Why should we forgive according to Psalm 66:18 and Mark 11:25, 26? (c) How many times are we to forgive according to Matthew 18:21, 22? (d) If we refuse to forgive, what will be the result according to Matthew 18:22-35 and II Corinthians 2:7? (e) Is there anyone that you are harboring resentment against this day? (f) What will you do about it after contemplating these passages?

6. Jesus says we are to pray, "do not lead us into temptation." (a) What do you think this means? (b) How does this compare to what James says in 1:13, 14? (c) How do you reconcile these two verses?

7. What element(s) from this prayer do you lack in your prayer life? Put your need in the form of a prayer request.

Chapter 11

A Look at Fasting and Prayer—Part 1

Selected Scriptures

When Abraham Lincoln served as the President of the United States, he did something that perhaps would be foreign to our day and age. He proclaimed the day of April 30th as a day of fasting and prayer. The president told the nation that this day would be set aside as a day of national humiliation—a time when men should confess their sins and seek genuine repentance, seeking the truth in the Holy Scriptures. President Lincoln said we have "become intoxicated with unbroken success; we have become too self-sufficient to feel the necessity, too proud to pray to the God who made us. Let us humble ourselves before the offended Power, and confess our national sins and pray for mercy and forgiveness." These words sound a little strange to our modern-day thinking, don't they? Fast and pray? To think of the United States and even other nations setting aside a day to seek God seems absurd to our culture! Miss a meal? You're kidding! Perhaps you, too, are saying to yourself, "I thought that fasting and praying stuff was for the Old Testament saints!" The reason some think this way is because fasting and praying is really a lost element in the life of the 21st century Christian. Because many of us have not considered what the Word says about this most important but forgotten subject, we are going to take the next two chapters to do so. In this chapter, we are going to look at the majority of the passages in the Word of God which pertain to fasting.

Then in the next chapter we are going to see why we as New Testament Christians should be fasting. We also will look at the right ways and the wrong ways to fast, especially considering Isaiah 58 which devotes an entire chapter to this subject.

The questions I would like for us to consider in this chapter include: *Who should fast? Why should we fast? How long should we fast? Where should we fast? What attitudes should accompany our fasting?* And *what are some results of fasting?* (You might want to answer question number one from the homework before reading this chapter.) Before we get into our study, I want to give you a little information about fasting. First of all, let's define fasting. The word "fasting" means "to eat no bread" and "to afflict oneself" or to "afflict one's soul." This would be either by necessity or by deliberate choice, and would include going without food or drink. This is generally done for religious purposes. However, it could also be done for other reasons, such as distress, grief, or repentance.

The Jewish fasts were observed with varying degrees of strictness. When the fast lasted only a single day, it was the practice to abstain from food of every kind from evening to evening; whereas in the case of private fasts of a more prolonged character, it was only certain foods from which one would abstain. It was not unusual to put on sackcloth. Sackcloth was a rough coarse garment which was worn as a symbol of mourning or repentance. Usually there was also a rending or ripping of the garments and a scattering of ashes over the head, as we will discover in this chapter. Fasting would indicate a confession of misery and an act of deepest humiliation before the Lord.

The Mosaic Law prescribed only one public occasion of strict fasting, namely, once a year on the great Day of Atonement. The Hebrews, in the earlier period of their history, were in the habit of fasting whenever they were in hard and trying circumstances (1 Samuel 1:7); misfortune and bereavement (1 Samuel 20:34; 31:13; 2 Samuel 1:12); in the prospect of threatened judgments of God (2 Samuel 12:16; 1 Kings 21:27); on occasions of falling into grievous sin (Ezra 10:6); or to avert heavy calamity (Esther 4:1,3,16). Extraordinary fasts were appointed by the governing authorities on occasions of great national calamity in order that the people might humble themselves before the Lord on account of their sins, to avert His wrath and get Him to look upon them again with favor.

According to Jewish custom, fasting was frequently joined with prayer so that the mind would not be distracted with earthly matters, and might be more devoted to divine things. As the Pharisees were accustomed to fast on Monday and Thursday, the Christians appointed Wednesday and especially Friday as days of half-fasting in commemoration of the passion and crucifixion of Jesus. They did this with reference to the Lord's words, "But the days will come when the bridegroom will be taken away from them, and then they will fast" (Matthew 9:15).

In the second century there arose also the custom of fasts before Easter, which, however, differed in length in different countries, being sometimes reduced to forty hours, sometimes extended to forty days or at least to several weeks. On special occasions the bishops appointed extraordinary fasts and applied the money saved to charitable purposes, which often became a blessing to the poor.

By the sixth century, fasting was made obligatory by the Second Council of Orleans (A.D. 541), which decreed that anyone neglecting to observe the stated time of abstinence should be treated as an offender. In the eighth century it was regarded as praiseworthy, and failure to observe subjected the offender to excommunication. In the Roman Catholic and Greek Orthodox churches fasting remains obligatory; whereas in most

Protestant churches, it is merely recommended. I am hoping that after our study that you will see the necessity of it in your own life and begin to implement times of fasting and prayer.

The following Scriptures include most of the passages in the Bible which pertain to fasting. We will attempt to answer the questions mentioned earlier from the following passages.

> So he was there with the LORD forty days and forty nights; he neither ate bread nor drank water. And He wrote on the tablets the words of the covenant, the Ten Commandments. (Exodus 34:28)

> Then all the children of Israel, that is, all the people, went up and came to the house of God and wept. They sat there before the LORD and fasted that day until evening; and they offered burnt offerings and peace offerings before the LORD. (Judges 20:26)

> So Hannah arose after they had finished eating and
> drinking in Shiloh. Now Eli the priest was sitting on the
> seat by the doorpost of the tabernacle of the LORD. 10And
> she was in bitterness of soul, and prayed to the LORD
> and wept in anguish. 11Then she made a vow and said, "O
> LORD of hosts, if You will indeed look on the affliction
> of Your maidservant and remember me, and not forget
> Your maidservant, but will give Your maidservant a male
> child, then I will give him to the LORD all the days of
> his life, and no razor shall come upon his head." 12And
> it happened, as she continued praying before the LORD,
> that Eli watched her mouth. 13Now Hannah spoke in her
> heart; only her lips moved, but her voice was not heard.
> Therefore Eli thought she was drunk. 14So Eli said to her,
> "How long will you be drunk? Put your wine away from
> you!" 15And Hannah answered and said, "No, my lord,
> I am a woman of sorrowful spirit. I have drunk neither
> wine nor intoxicating drink, but have poured out my soul

before the LORD. [16]Do not consider your maidservant a
wicked woman, for out of the abundance of my complaint
and grief I have spoken until now." [17]Then Eli answered
and said, "Go in peace, and the God of Israel grant your
petition which you have asked of Him." [18]And she said,
"Let your maidservant find favor in your sight." So the
woman went her way and ate, and her face was no longer
sad. (1 Samuel 1:9-18)

So they gathered together at Mizpah, drew water, and poured it out before the LORD. And they fasted that day, and said there, "We have sinned against the LORD." And Samuel judged the children of Israel at Mizpah. (1 Samuel 7:6)

Then they took their bones and buried them under the
tamarisk tree at Jabesh, and fasted seven days. [2 Samuel
1 1:1]Now it came to pass after the death of Saul, when
David had returned from the slaughter of the Amalekites,
and David had stayed two days in Ziklag, [2]on the third
day, behold, it happened that a man came from Saul's
camp with his clothes torn and dust on his head. So it
was, when he came to David, that he fell to the ground
and prostrated himself. [3]And David said to him, "Where
have you come from?" So he said to him, "I have
escaped from the camp of Israel." [4]Then David said to
him, "How did the matter go? Please tell me." And he
answered, "The people have fled from the battle, many
of the people are fallen and dead, and Saul and Jonathan
his son are dead also." [5]So David said to the young man
who told him, "How do you know that Saul and Jonathan
his son are dead?" [6]Then the young man who told him
said, "As I happened by chance to be on Mount Gilboa,
there was Saul, leaning on his spear; and indeed the
chariots and horsemen followed hard after him. [7]Now
when he looked behind him, he saw me and called to me.
And I answered, 'Here I am.' [8]"And he said to me, 'Who

are you?' So I answered him, 'I am an Amalekite.' [9]"He said to me again, 'Please stand over me and kill me, for anguish has come upon me, but my life still remains in me.' [10]"So I stood over him and killed him, because I was sure that he could not live after he had fallen. And I took the crown that was on his head and the bracelet that was on his arm, and have brought them here to my lord." [11]Therefore David took hold of his own clothes and tore them, and so did all the men who were with him. [12]And they mourned and wept and fasted until evening for Saul and for Jonathan his son, for the people of the LORD and for the house of Israel, because they had fallen by the sword. (1 Samuel 31:13 through 2 Samuel 1:12)

David therefore pleaded with God for the child, and David fasted and went in and lay all night on the ground. [17]So the elders of his house arose and went to him, to raise him up from the ground. But he would not, nor did he eat food with them. [18]Then on the seventh day it came to pass that the child died. And the servants of David were afraid to tell him that the child was dead. For they said, "Indeed, while the child was alive, we spoke to him, and he would not heed our voice. How can we tell him that the child is dead? He may do some harm!" [19]When David saw that his servants were whispering, David perceived that the child was dead. Therefore David said to his servants, "Is the child dead?" And they said, "He is dead." [20]So David arose from the ground, washed and anointed himself, and changed his clothes; and he went into the house of the LORD and worshiped. Then he went to his own house; and when he requested, they set food before him, and he ate. [21]Then his servants said to him, "What is this that you have done? You fasted and wept for the child while he was alive, but when the child died, you arose and ate food." [22]And he said, "While the child was alive, I fasted and wept; for I said, 'Who can tell whether the LORD will be gracious to me, that the child may live?' [23]"But now he is dead; why should I fast? Can I bring him back again? I shall go to him, but he shall not return to me." (2 Samuel 12:16-23)

She wrote in the letters, saying, Proclaim a fast, and seat Naboth with high honor among the people; [10]and seat two men, scoundrels, before him to bear witness against him, saying, "You have blasphemed God and the king." Then take him out, and stone him, that he may die. [11]So the men of his city, the elders and nobles who were inhabitants of his city, did as Jezebel had sent to them, as it was written in the letters which she had sent to them. [12]They proclaimed a fast, and seated Naboth with high honor among the people. [13]And two men, scoundrels, came in and sat before him; and the scoundrels witnessed against him, against Naboth, in the presence of the people, saying, "Naboth has blasphemed God and the king!" Then they took him outside the city and stoned him with stones, so that he died. [14]Then they sent to Jezebel, saying, "Naboth has been stoned and is dead." [15]And it came to pass, when Jezebel heard that Naboth had been stoned and was dead, that Jezebel said to Ahab, "Arise, take possession of the vineyard of Naboth the Jezreelite, which he refused to give you for money; for Naboth is not alive, but dead." [16]So it was, when Ahab heard that Naboth was dead, that Ahab got up and went down to take possession of the vineyard of Naboth the Jezreelite. [17]Then the word of the LORD came to Elijah the Tishbite, saying, [18]"Arise, go down to meet Ahab king of Israel, who lives in Samaria. There he is, in the vineyard of Naboth, where he has gone down to take possession of it. [19]You shall speak to him, saying, 'Thus says the LORD: "Have you murdered and also taken possession?" 'And you shall speak to him, saying, 'Thus says the LORD: "In the place where dogs licked the blood of Naboth, dogs shall lick your blood, even yours." ' " [20]Then Ahab said to Elijah, "Have you found me, O my enemy?" And he answered, "I have found you, because you have sold yourself to do evil in the sight of the LORD: [21]'Behold, I will bring calamity on you. I will take away your posterity, and will cut off from Ahab every male in Israel, both bond and free. [22]I will make your house like the house of Jeroboam the son of Nebat, and like the house of Baasha the son of Ahijah, because of the provocation with which you have provoked Me to anger, and made Israel sin.' [23]"And concerning Jezebel the LORD also spoke, saying, 'The dogs shall eat Jezebel by the wall of Jezreel.' [24]"The dogs shall eat whoever belongs to Ahab and dies in the city, and the birds of the air shall eat whoever dies in the field." [25]But there was no one like Ahab who sold himself to do wickedness in the sight of the LORD, because Jezebel his wife stirred him up. [26]And he behaved very abominably in following idols, according to all that the Amorites had done, whom the LORD had cast out before the children of Israel. [27]So it was, when Ahab heard those words, that he tore his clothes and put sackcloth on his body, and fasted and lay in sackcloth, and went about mourning. (1 Kings 21:9-27)

all the valiant men arose and took the body of Saul and the bodies of his sons; and they brought them to Jabesh, and buried their bones under the tamarisk tree at Jabesh, and fasted seven days. (1 Chronicles 10:12)

And Jehoshaphat feared, and set himself to seek the LORD, and proclaimed a fast throughout all Judah. (2 Chronicles 20:3)

Then I proclaimed a fast there at the river of Ahava, that we might humble ourselves before our God, to seek from Him the right way for us and our little ones and all our possessions. [22]For I was ashamed to request of the king an escort of soldiers and horsemen to help us against the enemy on the road, because we had spoken to the king, saying, "The hand of our God is upon all those for good who seek Him, but His power and His wrath are against all those who forsake Him." [23]So we fasted and entreated our God for this, and He answered our prayer. (Ezra 8:21-23)

So it was, when I heard these words, that I sat down and wept, and mourned for many days; I was fasting and praying before the God of heaven. (Nehemiah 1:4)

Now on the twenty-fourth day of this month the children of Israel were assembled with fasting, in sackcloth, and with dust on their heads. (Nehemiah 9:1)

And in every province where the king's command and decree arrived, there was great mourning among the Jews, with fasting, weeping, and wailing; and many lay in sackcloth and ashes. [4]So Esther's maids and eunuchs came and told her, and the queen was deeply distressed. Then she sent garments to clothe Mordecai and take his sackcloth away from him, but he would not accept them. [5]Then Esther called Hathach, one of the king's eunuchs whom he had appointed to attend her, and she gave him a command concerning Mordecai, to learn what and why this was. [6]So Hathach went out to Mordecai in the city square that was in front of the king's gate. [7]And Mordecai told him all that had happened to him, and the sum of money that Haman had promised to pay into the king's treasuries to destroy the Jews. [8]He also gave him a copy of the written decree for their destruction, which was given at Shushan, that he might show it to Esther and explain it to her, and that he might command her to go in to the king to make supplication to him and plead before him for her people. [9]So Hathach returned and told Esther the words of Mordecai. [10]Then Esther spoke to Hathach, and gave him a command for Mordecai: [11]All the king's servants and the people of the king's provinces know that any man or woman who goes into the inner court to the king, who has not been called, he has but one law: put all to death, except the one to whom the king holds out the golden scepter, that he may live. Yet I myself have not been called to go in to the king these thirty days." 12So they told Mordecai Esther's words. 13Then Mordecai told them to answer Esther: "Do not think in your heart that you will escape in the king's palace any more than all the other Jews. 14For if you remain completely silent at this time, relief and deliverance will arise for the Jews from another place, but you and your father's house will perish. Yet who knows whether you have come to the kingdom for such a time as this?" 15Then Esther told them to reply to Mordecai: 16"Go, gather all the Jews who are present in Shushan, and fast for me; neither eat nor drink for three days, night or day. My maids and I will fast likewise. And so I will go to the king, which is against the law; and if I perish, I perish!" (Esther 4:3-16)

…to confirm these days of Purim at their appointed time, as Mordecai the Jew and Queen Esther had prescribed for them, and as they had decreed for themselves and their descendants concerning matters of their fasting and lamenting. (Esther 9:31)

But as for me, when they were sick,
My clothing was sackcloth;
I humbled myself with fasting;
And my prayer would return to my own heart.
(Psalm 35:13)

When I wept and chastened my soul with fasting,
That became my reproach.
(Psalm 69:10)

My knees are weak through fasting,

And my flesh is feeble from lack of fatness.
(Psalm 109:24)

Now the king went to his palace and spent the night fasting; and no musicians were brought before him. Also his sleep went from him. (Daniel 6:18)

Then I set my face toward the Lord God to make request by prayer and supplications, with fasting, sackcloth, and ashes. (Daniel 9:3)

Consecrate a fast,
Call a sacred assembly;
Gather the elders
And all the inhabitants of the land
Into the house of the LORD your God,
And cry out to the LORD.
(Joel 1:14)

"Now, therefore," says the LORD,
"Turn to Me with all your heart,
With fasting, with weeping, and with mourning."
13 So rend your heart, and not your garments;
Return to the LORD your God,
For He is gracious and merciful,
Slow to anger, and of great kindness;
And He relents from doing harm.
14 Who knows if He will turn and relent,
And leave a blessing behind Him--
A grain offering and a drink offering
For the LORD your God?
15 Blow the trumpet in Zion,
Consecrate a fast,
Call a sacred assembly;
16 Gather the people,
Sanctify the congregation,
Assemble the elders,

Gather the children and nursing babes;
Let the bridegroom go out from his chamber,
And the bride from her dressing room.
(Joel 2:12-16)

So the people of Nineveh believed God, proclaimed a fast, and put on sackcloth, from the greatest to the least of them. (Jonah 3:5)

Then Jesus was led up by the Spirit into the wilderness to be tempted by the devil. [2]And when He had fasted forty days and forty nights, afterward He was hungry. (Matthew 4:1-2)

"Moreover, when you fast, do not be like the hypocrites, with a sad countenance. For they disfigure their faces that they may appear to men to be fasting. Assuredly, I say to you, they have their reward. [17]But you, when you fast, anoint your head and wash your face, [18]so that you do not appear to men to be fasting, but to your Father who is in the secret place; and your Father who sees in secret will reward you openly. (Matthew 6:16-18)

However, this kind does not go out except by prayer and fasting." (Matthew 17:21)

Now there was one, Anna, a prophetess, the daughter of Phanuel, of the tribe of Asher. She was of a great age, and had lived with a husband seven years from her virginity; [37]and this woman was a widow of about eighty-four years, who did not depart from the temple, but served God with fastings and prayers night and day. [38]And coming in that instant she gave thanks to the Lord, and spoke of Him to all those who looked for redemption in Jerusalem. (Luke 2:36-38)

There was a certain man in Caesarea called Cornelius,

a centurion of what was called the Italian Regiment, [2]a devout man and one who feared God with all his household, who gave alms generously to the people, and prayed to God always. [3]About the ninth hour of the day he saw clearly in a vision an angel of God coming in and saying to him, "Cornelius!" [4]And when he observed him, he was afraid, and said, "What is it, lord?" So he said to him, "Your prayers and your alms have come up for a memorial before God. [5]Now send men to Joppa, and send for Simon whose surname is Peter. [6]He is lodging with Simon, a tanner, whose house is by the sea. He will tell you what you must do." [7]And when the angel who spoke to him had departed, Cornelius called two of his household servants and a devout soldier from among those who waited on him continually. [8]So when he had explained all these things to them, he sent them to Joppa.

[9]The next day, as they went on their journey and drew near the city, Peter went up on the housetop to pray, about the sixth hour. [10]Then he became very hungry and wanted to eat; but while they made ready, he fell into a trance [11]and saw heaven opened and an object like a great sheet bound at the four corners, descending to him and let down to the earth. [12]In it were all kinds of four-footed animals of the earth, wild beasts, creeping things, and birds of the air. [13]And a voice came to him, "Rise, Peter; kill and eat." [14]But Peter said, "Not so, Lord! For I have never eaten anything common or unclean." [15]And a voice spoke to him again the second time, "What God has cleansed you must not call common." [16]This was done three times. And the object was taken up into heaven again.

[17]Now while Peter wondered within himself what this vision which he had seen meant, behold, the men who had been sent from Cornelius had made inquiry for Simon's house, and stood before the gate. [18]And they called and asked whether Simon, whose surname was

Peter, was lodging there. 19While Peter thought about the vision, the Spirit said to him, “Behold, three men are seeking you. 20Arise therefore, go down and go with them, doubting nothing; for I have sent them.” 21Then Peter went down to the men who had been sent to him from Cornelius, and said, “Yes, I am he whom you seek. For what reason have you come?” 22And they said, “Cornelius the centurion, a just man, one who fears God and has a good reputation among all the nation of the Jews, was divinely instructed by a holy angel to summon you to his house, and to hear words from you.” 23Then he invited them in and lodged them. On the next day Peter went away with them, and some brethren from Joppa accompanied him.

24And the following day they entered Caesarea. Now Cornelius was waiting for them, and had called together his relatives and close friends. 25As Peter was coming in, Cornelius met him and fell down at his feet and worshiped him. 26But Peter lifted him up, saying, “Stand up; I myself am also a man.” 27And as he talked with him, he went in and found many who had come together. 28Then he said to them, “You know how unlawful it is for a Jewish man to keep company with or go to one of another nation. But God has shown me that I should not call any man common or unclean. 29Therefore I came without objection as soon as I was sent for. I ask, then, for what reason have you sent for me?” 30So Cornelius said, “Four days ago I was fasting until this hour; and at the ninth hour I prayed in my house, and behold, a man stood before me in bright clothing, and said, ‘Cornelius, your prayer has been heard, and your alms are remembered in the sight of God. 32Send therefore to Joppa and call Simon here, whose surname is Peter. He is lodging in the house of Simon, a tanner, by the sea. When he comes, he will speak to you.’ 33”So I sent to you immediately, and you have done well to come. Now therefore, we are all present before God, to hear all the things commanded

you by God."
[34]Then Peter opened his mouth and said: "In
truth I perceive that God shows no partiality. [35]But in
every nation whoever fears Him and works righteousness
is accepted by Him. [36]The word which God sent to
the children of Israel, preaching peace through Jesus
Christ--He is Lord of all-- [37]that word you know, which
was proclaimed throughout all Judea, and began from
Galilee after the baptism which John preached: [38]how
God anointed Jesus of Nazareth with the Holy Spirit and
with power, who went about doing good and healing all
who were oppressed by the devil, for God was with Him.
[39]And we are witnesses of all things which He did both in
the land of the Jews and in Jerusalem, whom they killed
by hanging on a tree. [40]Him God raised up on the third
day, and showed Him openly, [41]not to all the people, but
to witnesses chosen before by God, even to us who ate
and drank with Him after He arose from the dead. [42]And
He commanded us to preach to the people, and to testify
that it is He who was ordained by God to be Judge of the
living and the dead. [43]To Him all the prophets witness
that, through His name, whoever believes in Him will
receive remission of sins."
[44]While Peter was still speaking these words, the
Holy Spirit fell upon all those who heard the word. [45]And
those of the circumcision who believed were astonished,
as many as came with Peter, because the gift of the Holy
Spirit had been poured out on the Gentiles also. [46]For
they heard them speak with tongues and magnify God.
Then Peter answered, [47]Can anyone forbid water, that
these should not be baptized who have received the Holy
Spirit just as we have?" [48]And he commanded them to be
baptized in the name of the Lord. Then they asked him to
stay a few days. (Acts 10:1-48)

Now in the church that was at Antioch there were certain prophets and teachers: Barnabas, Simeon who was called Niger, Lucius of Cyrene, Manaen who had been brought up with Herod the tetrarch, and Saul. [2]As they ministered to the Lord and fasted, the Holy Spirit said, "Now separate to Me Barnabas and Saul for the work to which I have called them." [3]Then, having fasted and prayed, and laid hands on them, they sent them away. (Acts 13:1-3)

So when they had appointed elders in every church, and prayed with fasting, they commended them to the Lord in whom they had believed. (Acts 14:23)

And as day was about to dawn, Paul implored them all to take food, saying, "Today is the fourteenth day you have waited and continued without food, and eaten nothing. (Acts 27:33)

Do not deprive one another except with consent for a time, that you may give yourselves to fasting and prayer; and come together again so that Satan does not tempt you because of your lack of self-control. (1 Corinthians 7:5)

Who Should Fast?

Having read through the Scriptures pertaining to fasting, let's consider who should fast. In Exodus 34:28 we see it was Moses. Judges 20:26 mentions all the children of Israel. In 1 Samuel 1:9-18 we see it was Hannah. 1 Samuel 7:6 states that it was all Israel. 1 Samuel 31:13 and 1 Chronicles 10:12 tell us it was the inhabitants of Jabesh-Gilead. We observe from 2 Samuel 1:12 that it was David and his men. 2 Samuel 12:13-23 also mentions David. 1 Kings 21 gives an interesting slant to our study, as an example of evil motives. The fasting was done by the people according to verse 9. However, this is not the end of the story, as we see in verse 27 that Ahab fasts after he hears his verdict. 2 Chronicles 20:3 mentions Jehoshaphat and all the people—see verse 13. In Ezra 8:21-23 it is Ezra and his people. We notice from Nehemiah 1:4 that it is Nehemiah. However, in the same book, Nehemiah 9:1 states it is the children of Israel who are fasting. In Esther 4:3-16 and 9:31 we take note that the Jews, Esther and her maidens were all fasting. In Psalms 35:13; 69:10; and 109:24, it is King David. Daniel 6:18 tells us that the king was fasting. However, in Daniel 9:3 we see it is Daniel. In Joel 1:14 we observe that the elders and all the inhabitants of the land are fasting. Joel 2:12-17 gives us an interesting list of people who are fasting: people, elders, children, those who nurse at the breast, bride and groom, priests and ministers. Jonah 3 mentions the people of Nineveh, with beasts included! (Try that on for size for your dog or cat!) As we come to the New Testament, we see in Matthew 4:2 our Lord fasting. We shift from Christ fasting to hypocrites fasting in Matthew 6:16-18. (Notice *when* you fast, indicating they did; not *if* you fast.) Matthew 17:14-21 is an admonition to the disciples to fast. In Luke 2:36-38 we see a widow named Anna who was fasting. Acts 10 mentions Cornelius as the one who was fasting in verses 2 and 30. In Acts 13:1-3 it is Barnabus, Symeon, Lucious, Manean, and Saul (prophets and teachers). Acts 14:23 tells us that Paul and Barnabus were the individuals who were fasting—see verse 14. Acts 27:33 reveals that it is the men on the boat who are with Paul. And finally, in 1 Corinthians 7:5 Paul mentions husbands and wives fasting for a brief time.

Why Should We Fast?

The next question we need to consider is why we should fast. Why would God call certain individuals to a fast? In Exodus 34:28 we see it was for the purpose of writing the Ten Commandments. Also notice that Moses was with the Lord, which might explain why he did not eat. He was so satisfied with the presence of the Almighty that food was not important to him. In Judges 20:26 we see it was for the purpose of consulting the Lord before going to battle. In 1 Samuel 1:9-18 it was for the begging of a son, and in 1 Samuel 7:6 we learn that fasting took place because of sinning against the Lord. In both 1 Samuel 31:13 and 1 Chronicles 10:12 it is to lament the death of Saul and in 2 Samuel 1:12 it is for the lamenting of the death of Saul and Jonathan. In 2 Samuel 12:13-23 it was in hopes that God would perhaps be gracious to David. In 1 Kings 21, we learn that that fasting was not for a righteous reason, but it was because Ahab did not get his way, i.e. a vineyard he wanted. In verse 2 we see him sulking and in verse 4 his wife takes up an offense and does a number of wicked things. However, when we look at verse 27, Ahab fasts when he hears the evil that will come upon him. In 2 Chronicles 20:3 it is because of a great army which is coming against Jehoshaphat. Ezra 8:21-23 mentions fasting took place in hopes for a safe journey. There would be dangers traveling through the desert, and most travelers usually sought a military escort. But because Ezra had spoken so much to the king about the sufficiency of God's care, he decided to fast and pray and commit their travels to the King of Israel. (I wonder if any have done that before a vacation?! Might not be a bad idea!) In Nehemiah 1:4 we see fasting because the people were in great affliction and reproach; the wall of Jerusalem was broken down and the gates were burning with fire and Nehemiah was distressed for others. In Nehemiah 9:1-3 fasting took place because of sin. Esther 4:3-16 and 9:31 record for us that fasting took place because the Jews were going to be destroyed. In Psalm 35:13;

69:10; and 109:24 it is because of enemies. Daniel 6:18 records that fasting took place for Daniel's safety. However, in Daniel 9:3 it is because of sin—note the entire prayer. Joel 1:14 mentions fasting because destruction is coming—see verse 15. In Joel 2:12-17 fasting took place in order that God would spare His people. Jonah 3 records that the people of Nineveh fasted due to the fact that they believed Jonah's message that God would destroy Nineveh. Matthew 4:2 records that Jesus fasted before He began His earthly ministry. I think we can learn from our Lord that prayer is important (fasting wouldn't hurt) before beginning any type of ministry. In Matthew 6:16-18 we are told not to fast as the hypocrites by being sad or disfiguring our faces (not washing or shaving their faces), but we are to fast to our Father in secret. If you fast so others will notice or think you are more spiritual, then notice that you already have your reward, which is the praise of men. Matthew 17:14-21 records fasting took place for the healing of one's body. Luke 2:36-38 mentions fasting as a service to God. In Acts 10 we are not told what the prayer was (verses 30 and 31), but it is assumed that it was for the way to salvation. Acts 13:1-3 points out that fasting took place before sending out Barnabas and Saul for the work of the Lord (missionary journeys). Acts 14:23 tells us that they fasted when ordaining elders. (Can you imagine the quality of our churches and elders if we would do this today?) In Acts 27:33 fasting took place because of fear of losing their lives—see verses 14-20. And last, we see that there is no reason mentioned in 1 Corinthians 7:5 for fasting.

How Long Should We Fast?

Next, we must consider the length of our fasting. Exodus 34:28 mentions 40 days and 40 nights. Judges 20:26 says they fasted that day until evening. 1 Samuel 1:9-18 doesn't say how long. 1 Samuel 7:6 records fasting took place on that day. 1 Samuel 31:13 mentions seven days. (This perhaps was a fast during the day, broken at night) In 2 Samuel 1:12 they fasted until evening. In 2 Samuel 12:13-23 and 1 Chronicles 10:12 fasting took place for seven days. In 1 Kings 21 it doesn't say how long, and in 2 Chronicles 20:3, Ezra 8:21-23, and Nehemiah 1:4 it just points out that it took place certain days, and in Nehemiah 9:1 it appears it was the whole day (see verse 3). In Esther 4:3-16 and 9:31 it is three days. Psalms 35:13; 69:10; and 109:24 don't say how long. Daniel 6:18 shows fasting at night and yet Daniel 9:3 doesn't mention how long. Joel 1:14, Joel 2:12, and Jonah 3 do not give us the length of time. In Matthew 4:2-40 it states it was days and nights. (Notice He was not hungry until after the fast). Matthew 6:16-18 and Matthew 17:14-21 don't tell us how long, but in Luke 2:36-38 it is night and day (see 1 Timothy 5:5). Acts 10 just mentions praying to God always—verse 2, and in verse 30 it doesn't specify how long. In Acts 13:1-3 and Acts 14:23 we don't know how long it was, as it doesn't record that for us. However, in Acts 27:33 it is for 14 days! Finally, 1 Corinthians 7:5 doesn't indicate a specific length of time.

Where Should We Fast?

Another question for our consideration involves where we fast. Exodus 34:28 reveals it was Mt. Sinai (v. 29). Judges 20:26 mentions the house of God. 1 Samuel 1:9-18 seem to indicate the temple, but in 1 Samuel 7:6 it is a city called Mizpah. In 1 Samuel 31:13 and 1 Chronicles 10:12 it is another city called Jabesh. In 2 Samuel 1:12 we see the mentioning of yet another city—Ziklag. 2 Samuel 12:13-23 records for us that it is the earth. 1 Kings 21 mentions in the vineyard. In 2

Chronicles 20:3 fasting takes place in the house of the Lord (see verse 5). In Ezra 8:21-23 we see it was at the river of Ahava. Nehemiah 1:4 mentions the palace (see verse 1). And in Nehemiah 9:1 it appears it is the house of God (see 8:16). In Esther 4:3-16 and 9:31 we see the place is the palace. Psalms 35:13; 69:10; and 109:24 don't say. In Daniel 6:18 it is the palace. Daniel 9:3 doesn't tell us the place. In Joel 1:14 it is the house of the Lord. Joel 2:12-15 mentions between the porch and the altar (see verse 17). In Jonah 3 it is throughout Nineveh (see verse 7). In Matthew 4:2 it is in the wilderness (see verse 1). Matthew 6:16-18 just says in secret. Matthew 17:14-21 doesn't say. In Luke 2:36-38 it is in the temple. Acts 10 points out it is in his house. In Acts 13:1-3 it is in the church, and in Acts 14:23 it appears that it was in the church. Acts 27:33 tells us fasting took place in a boat. And 1 Corinthians 7:5 doesn't say.

What Attitudes Should Accompany Our Fasting?

Next, let us consider the attitudes that should accompany our fasting. Exodus 34:28 does not give us the attitude. However, in Judges 20:26 we see weeping and the offering of burnt and peace offerings. By the way, a burnt offering was one in which the entire offering was burned up which indicated an entire sacrifice of one's self to God. A peace offering entailed the forgiveness of one's sin and a right relationship with God which resulted in peace. In 1 Samuel 1:9-18 we see that Hannah wept bitterly, made a vow, and poured out her soul, complaining and grieving. In 1 Samuel 7:6 it records for us a pouring out of water which symbolizes a pouring out of one's soul before the Lord. 1 Samuel 31:13 and 1 Chronicles 10:12 don't give any attitude. In 2 Samuel 1:12 we see mourning and weeping. In 2 Samuel 12:13-23 we notice the attitude is humility (see verse 13: "I have sinned"); an attitude of being steadfast is apparent in verse 17. The attitude of evil motives, greed and selfishness is found in 1 Kings 21. However, in verses 27-29 he repents. Then we see tearing of clothes, wearing of sackcloth, going around softly (his head hanging down; barefoot, as if he had no spirit in him); humility. He is also lying in sackcloth, which is interesting because he seems to have gone beyond the usual practice. We do not read elsewhere of mourners passing the night in sackcloth. In 2 Chronicles 20:3 we see an attitude of humility in verses 6-13; being unafraid in verse 17; and praising God in verse 19. In Ezra 8:21-23 the attitude of seeking God in a right way is mentioned in verse 21 and an attitude of believing in verse 22. Nehemiah records weeping in 1:4, and confession of sins in verse 6. Nehemiah 9:1-3 states it was a mournful attitude accompanied by the confessing of sins, reading the word, and worshipping the Lord. Esther 4:3-16 and 9:31 indicates weeping and wailing and laying in sackcloth and ashes, as well as lamentations. Psalm 35:13 records sackcloth, humility of soul. In Psalm 69:10 we see weeping and sackcloth was his garment (see verse 11). Psalm 109:22 tells us the attitude is a wounded heart. In Daniel 6:18 we see a somber attitude of no music and no sleep. Daniel 9:3 points out that it was with sackcloth, ashes and much confession of sin (see the whole prayer). In Joel 1:14 the attitude is sadness. Joel 2:12-15 indicates the same—weeping and mourning, tearing of the heart. Jonah 3 mentions faith in God, putting on sackcloth, crying mightily unto God, turning from their evil way and from the violence that is in their hands. (Interesting note here: violence was Nineveh's monster sin.) Matthew 4:1 says Christ was led by the Spirit. (This could assume, however, that He was led to be tested, but perhaps the Spirit also moved Him to fast.) In Matthew 6:16-18 there was an anointing of the head and washing of the face. We might say, "Get dressed and put your makeup on." In Matthew 17:14-21 the attitude is faith. Luke 2:36-38 records it was as a service to God, but also with thanksgiving. In Acts 10 the attitude was fear of God, and in Acts 13:1-3, it was with a servant's heart of ministering to the Lord. Acts 14:23 doesn't indicate what the attitude was, but that they commended them to the Lord. Acts 27:17 tells us the attitude was fear, no hope of being saved—verse 20. In 1 Corinthians 7:5 we see husbands and wives having an attitude of intentionally giving themselves completely to prayer and fasting.

What Are Some Results of Fasting?

We have come to the last question we want to answer and that is what are some of the results of fasting? And, ladies, this is probably the most exciting of all the questions! In Exodus 34:28 the result was the writing of the Ten Commandments; Moses' face also shone (see verse 29). In Judges 20:26 and 28 we see that the Lord delivered them. In 1 Samuel 1:20 the result was a son! In 1 Samuel 7:9 the Lord heard him, and in verse 14 the Lord answered and delivered them. In 1 Samuel 31:13 and 1 Chronicles 10:12 there are no results mentioned. In 2 Samuel 1:12 the result was a special tribute to Jonathan (see verses 17-27). I do believe sometimes the Lord gives special insights spiritually when one fasts and prays as seen here. In 2 Samuel 12:13-23 the outcome was the child's death, but notice, ladies, David worshipped anyway! So this would be a time when fasting did not result in deliverance, but it did result in trust in a Sovereign God. 1 Kings 21 records for us that the results were devastating, in verses 20-29. However, he repents in verses 27-29 and so the results of this fast were that the evil was spared in his day; his son was not so fortunate. In 2 Chronicles 20:3 the result was that they won the battle and took so much of the spoil that it took 3 days to get it (see verses 24, 25). Ezra 8:21-23 states that they were granted safety during the whole way (see verses 31, 32)! Nehemiah 1:4 records for us the results were that Nehemiah went to Jerusalem and the walls were rebuilt (see 2:9-7:73). In Nehemiah 9:1 (and reading on to the end of the book), we discover amazing results! There was a purifying of the house of God as well as the beginning of a great revival! In Esther 4:3, 16; and 9:31 the result was that the king could not sleep (see chapter 6) and the rest is history! Esther pleads for her people, Haman is hung on his own gallows, the Jews destroy their enemies, and the feast of Purim is instituted! The results in all three of the Psalm accounts are praise (Psalm 35:28; 69:30-36; and 109:30)! In Daniel 6:18 the result was that Daniel's life was spared (see verses 19-23). Daniel 9:3 is totally amazing! Read the following in verses 20-27 of the same chapter:

> Now while I was speaking, praying, and confessing my sin and the sin of my people Israel, and presenting my supplication before the LORD my God for the holy mountain of my God, yes, while I was speaking in prayer, the man Gabriel, whom I had seen in the vision at the beginning, being caused to fly swiftly, reached me about the time of the evening offering. And he informed me, and talked with me, and said, "O Daniel, I have now come forth to give you skill to understand. "At the beginning of your supplications the command went out, and I have come to tell you, for you are greatly beloved; therefore consider the matter, and understand the vision: "Seventy weeks are determined for your people and for your holy city, to finish the transgression, to make an end of sins, to make reconciliation for iniquity, to bring in everlasting righteousness, to seal up vision and prophecy, and to

> anoint the Most Holy. "Know therefore and understand, that from the going forth of the command to restore and build Jerusalem until Messiah the Prince, there shall be seven weeks and sixty-two weeks; the street shall be built again, and the wall, even in troublesome times. "And after the sixty-two weeks Messiah shall be cut off, but not for Himself; and the people of the prince who is to come shall destroy the city and the sanctuary. The end of it shall be with a flood, and till the end of the war desolations are determined. Then he shall confirm a covenant with many for one week; but in the middle of the week he shall bring an end to sacrifice and offering. And on the wing of abominations shall be one who makes desolate, even until the consummation, which is determined, is poured out on the desolate. " (Daniel 9:20-27)

In Joel we see that deliverance is promised as well as the restoration of Israel. In Jonah 3 we see God changed His mind concerning the evil that He said He would do, and He did it not. In Matthew 4:2 the result was that Jesus was able to resist the temptation of Satan (see verses 3-11), and Christ was able to prove He loved God more than bread. Matthew 6:16-18 records for us the result was God shall reward you openly. Matthew 17:14-21 records that anything is possible. In Luke 2:36-38 we see the result was that Anna was blessed in that she got to see the Messiah. In Acts 10 the result was the salvation of Cornelius. Acts 13:1-12, 42-52 tells us that fasting changed the whole course of history! Who says fasting and praying are a waste of time? In Acts 14:23 the result was that the New Testament churches began! In Acts 27:33 we see the result was that all escaped safely to the land (see verse 44). 1 Corinthians 7:5 doesn't give a result, but I imagine when couples fast and pray they can guarantee a better marriage! Now, ladies, notice in every instance, with the exception of David, the results of fasting were incredible. And, if you believe in a sovereign God, David's results were incredible, too! David Brainerd records in his diary that in every instance where he fasted and prayed, the Lord blessed and answered and often before the day ended. I have found the same to be true in my own life. God does not reward our fasting because we are special, or because we give up anything. I believe God rewards our fasting when it is done with a right attitude (as we will see in the next chapter), because it shows our utter dependence on Him. It also indicates that nothing can satisfy our souls other than the living God. When we are satisfied with Him, He is most certainly glorified. So, why don't we fast? We are too comfortable and not desperate enough. We are self-sufficient; we have no need of God. We don't hunger for Him as we should, nor love Him intensely.

I know this chapter has been somewhat different, but I felt it was important that we take each account in the Word of God and examine it thoroughly. We have looked at many Biblical examples of fasting and praying, and I trust you have been touched. Samuel Chadwick, a mighty preacher used of God, would spend whole days fasting and praying. He said, "Such a prayer life costs. It takes time. Hurried prayers and muttered lines can never produce souls mighty in prayer." Andrew Bonar, another great man of God from the past, would rise earlier than usual to fast and pray. He also would set apart one whole day each month for fasting and praying. He said, "The effect upon the body and soul is somewhat like affliction. It brings down the tone of the spirit, subdues the flesh, draws off the soul from self-complacency, and makes the flesh unsatisfying. It discovers much to me that is humbling; it helps to remove my lightness of mind." Jonathan Edwards fasted and prayed for 3 days and nights before preaching his famous sermon, "Sinners in the Hands of an Angry God." People said that when he got up to preach that particular sermon, he looked as if he had been gazing straight into the face of God. Before he even began to speak, conviction fell on the audience. People took hold of the pews, afraid they might slip into the pit of hell. Many thought the Day of Judgment had fallen. It was, and still is, a very powerful sermon.

For what do you hunger? For what are you asking God? Are you willing to fast and pray about it? John Piper says in his book on fasting, "What is at stake here is not just the good of our souls, but also the glory of God. God is most glorified in us when we are most satisfied in Him. The fight of faith is a fight to feast on all that God is for us in Christ. What we hunger for most, we worship." [20]

20 Piper, John. *A Hunger for God: Desiring God Through Fasting and Prayer*—Multnomah- page 10.

Questions to Consider

A Look at Fasting and Prayer—Part 1

Selected Scriptures

1. The following passages are most of the Biblical references to fasting. From them please answer the following questions: *(You also might need to read a little before and after each passage to answer these questions.)* (a) Who is fasting? (b) For what are they fasting? (c) Where are they fasting? (d) How long did they fast? (e) What attitudes accompanied their fasting? (f) What were the results of their fasting? Exodus 34:28; Judges 20:26; 1 Samuel 1:9-18; 1 Samuel 7:6; 31:11-13; 2 Samuel 1:12; 12:16-23; 1 Kings 21:9-27; 2 Chronicles 20:3; Ezra 8:21-23; Nehemiah 1:4, 9:1; Esther 4:3-16; 9:31; Psalms 35:13; 69:10; 109:24; Daniel 6:18; 9:3; Joel 1:14, 2:12-16; Jonah 3:5; Matthew 4:1,2; Matthew 6:16-18; Matthew 17:21; Luke 2:36-38; Acts 10; Acts 13:1-3; 14:23; 27: 33, 1 Corinthians 7:5. *(You may want to chart this, as it will be helpful in your study.)*

2. Look over the passages you've studied, and answer the following questions. (a) Put yourself in the positions of each of these individuals and ask yourself if you would have fasted and prayed in these situations. Why or why not? (b) What have you learned from their examples?

3. Look at Exodus 34:28 and Matthew 4:2. (a) What is similar about these verses? (b) Do you think there is any significance to this? (c) What is significant about these two passages as you compare it with Matthew 4:4?

4. (a) Why was fasting good for David according to Psalm 35:13? (b) Why do you think this would be true?

5. (a) How does David's attitude compare with the attitude of the hypocrites in Matthew 6:16? (b) What do you think Jesus meant when He said, "They have their reward?"

6. (a) Have you ever fasted and prayed? Why or why not? (b) Do you think we as believers should fast and pray? Why or why not? (c) Share a time when God intervened due to fasting and praying in your life.

7. Is there an area in your life where God seems silent? Why not fast and pray? Put your prayer in the form of a request.

**Recommended reading: *A Hunger For God: Desiring God Through Fasting and Prayer*, by John Piper.

Chapter 12

A Look at Fasting and Prayer—Part 2: The Proper Methods of Fasting and Prayer

Isaiah 58

In our last chapter we began our journey through the Old and New Testaments looking at the important but often neglected topic of fasting and prayer. We endeavored to answer the following questions from the Word of God: Who should fast? Why should we fast? How long should we fast? Where should we fast? What attitudes should accompany our fasting? And what are the results fasting? I would like to shift our thoughts in this chapter to answer the question of why we as New Testament Christians should be fasting, and then take a look at the right and wrong ways to fast.

When you think back over your life, has there ever been a time that you have been really hungry? I mean so starved that you felt that if you did not get some food you would physically die? Have you ever been that hungry for God? I mean so starved that you felt that if you did not spend time with him you would spiritually die? John Piper says in his book, *A Hunger for God*, that "If we don't feel strong desires for the manifestations of the glory of God, it is *not* because we have drunk deeply and are satisfied. It is because we have nibbled so long at the table of the world. Our soul is stuffed with small things, and there is no room for the great."[21] Is there room in your busy life for

---

21 Piper, John. *A Hunger for God: Desiring God Through Fasting and Prayer*—Multnomah-page 23.

the Great? Do you set aside times throughout your week to pray? To fast? You might be saying right now in your heart, "that fasting stuff is for the Old Testament saints, or for the really religious nuts." Oh? Turn with me to Matthew 9:14-17 for an interesting word from our Lord about this topic of fasting.

> Then the disciples of John came to Him, saying, "Why do we and the Pharisees fast often, but Your disciples do not fast?" And Jesus said to them, "Can the friends of the bridegroom mourn as long as the bridegroom is with them? But the days will come when the bridegroom will be taken away from them, and then they will fast. "No one puts a piece of unshrunk cloth on an old garment; for the patch pulls away from the garment, and the tear is made worse. "Nor do they put new wine into old wineskins, or else the wineskins break, the wine is spilled, and the wineskins are ruined. But they put new wine into new wineskins, and both are preserved." (Matthew 9:14-17).

In this passage we see that the disciples of John come to Jesus to ask him a question. They wanted to know why they were fasting, and the Pharisees were fasting, but Jesus' disciples were not fasting. It is very possible that the disciples of John had been fasting because John was in prison. Many times fasting was a sign of mourning, and they were sorrowful because of John's imprisonment. So perhaps they wanted to know why Jesus and His disciples were not fasting, too. They also mention to the Lord that the Pharisees fasted. According to Luke 18:11-12, the Pharisees fasted twice a week. So the disciples of John say to Jesus, "Hey, we are fasting, the Pharisees are fasting, but why aren't *you* guys fasting?" Jesus answers them by saying, *Can the friends of the bridegroom mourn as long as the bridegroom is with them? But the days will come when the bridegroom will be taken away from them, and then they will fast.* Now to understand what Jesus is saying here we need to understand that in biblical times, when a marriage would take place, there were men who took special care of the groom before the wedding. That's who the friends of the bridegroom are that Jesus mentions here. These men were the companions of the bridegroom, and they would bring the groom to the house of his father-in-law when he went to bring the bride to his own home. There was a lot of festivity and rejoicing during this time, just like there is in our day. So Jesus says, when the groom gets married, when he is taken away from them, when the rejoicing ends, then the men will fast. At that time there will be sorrow because the groom will be missed. That is the point Christ is trying to make. Why should my disciples fast now when I am here with them in a physical body? We are rejoicing now because we are together. But the day will come when I am taken from them, and that will be the time when they will be sorrowful, that will be the time when they have a need to fast. What Jesus is saying here is that we should be fasting and praying because we are hungry for Him and we miss Him. John Piper says, "The absence of fasting is the measure of our contentment with absence of Christ."[22]

We must agree, when we look at the early church, that fasting was the norm for them. There are numerous accounts recorded in Acts of the early church fasting, as we saw in the last chapter. Paul also mentions in 2 Corinthians 6:5 and 11:27 that he fasted, and even mentions that he fasted often. It was a part of his life.

Not only should we fast because we are hungry for God and desire that closeness with Him, but also because there are those times in our lives when God doesn't seem to

22 Piper, John. *A Hunger for God: Desiring God Through Fasting and Prayer*—Multnomah- page 93.

answer our prayers until we are desperate enough to set aside time for fasting and praying. In Matthew 17 we have the account of a child who has a dumb and deaf spirit and the disciples endeavor to cast it out. They come to Jesus to ask him why they could not perform this miracle and Jesus answers them by saying that this kind comes out only by prayer and fasting (see verses 14-21). This would indicate that there are times in our lives when some things can only be touched by God through fasting. If fasting and praying are not a part of your life, I would encourage you to begin this practice. Now lest we become arrogant and think that there is some magic in fasting to get the things we want, I want to shift our focus to the right and wrong ways to fast. Some of us may be like the Pharisee in Luke 18:11-14, who boasted of all his religious works and prayed with himself saying, "God, I thank You that I am not like other men—extortioners , unjust, adulterers, or even as this tax collector. I fast twice a week; I give tithes of all that I possess." We must shun any type of pride when God calls us to fast, and we must fast with the attitudes that would please Him. With that in mind, I would like to take a look at Isaiah 58, which gives us helps on proper ways to fast.

The outline for this lesson will be as follows: *four helps for fasting* (vv. 1, 2); *four hindrances to fasting* (vv. 3, 4); *nine more helps for fasting* (vv. 5-7, 13); *thirteen results of fasting* (vv. 8-14).

Four Helps for Fasting

Let's look first at the four helps for fasting in verses 1 and 2.

> "Cry aloud, spare not;
> Lift up your voice like a trumpet;
> Tell My people their transgression,
> And the house of Jacob their sins.

> [2]Yet they seek Me daily,
> And delight to know My ways,
> As a nation that did righteousness,
> And did not forsake the ordinance of their God.
> They ask of Me the ordinances of justice;
> They take delight in approaching God.
> (Isaiah 58: 1, 2)

Isaiah begins by saying, *Cry aloud!* This indicates that it would be with an open throat and a loud voice. Next he says, *spare not*; in other words, do not restrain your voice, Isaiah. In fact, Isaiah let your voice be so loud that it would sound like a trumpet. These people evidently needed something loud enough to awaken them to the enormity of their sin. They were guilty. Guilty of what? I mean it must be pretty bad to demand this degree of loudness! When you look at verse 2, you say, "Well, why do they need a rebuke? They were involved in good stuff." In fact, most of us could say, "Hey I do those things!"

First, they seek Him daily. They were in the temple every day. We might say, "I spend time in the Word daily." And not only that but, second, they delight to know His ways. This probably means that they profess to delight in knowing God's ways. This would include His word and His commands. In fact they delighted to know the ways of God to the point that they were known as a people who did what was right, and did not forsake the ordinances of their God. Third, they were even asking God about justice. They prayed to God to intervene for them with righteous judgments. Fourth, they took delight in approaching God. Just because we find pleasure in praise and prayer does not mean we are truly righteous. John Piper warns in his book about emotionally charged singing to the Lord. He says all that is good, but he sees a real danger. "The danger is that we will subtly slip from loving

God in these moments into loving loving God."[23] We really don't savor God Himself, but the atmosphere which is created. That can lead to serious hypocrisy. This is what was happening here. And yet those four things are not bad, as they are helpful in fasting. These things must be in place. But as we see in verses 3 and 4 there are also four hindrances to fasting according to what God says. So we turn from four helps for fasting to four hindrances to fasting in verses 3 and 4.

Four Hindrances to Fasting

> "'Why have we fasted,' they say, 'and You have not seen?
> Why have we afflicted our souls, and You take no notice?'
> In fact, in the day of your fast you find pleasure,
> And exploit all your laborers.
> 4Indeed you fast for strife and debate,
> And to strike with the fist of wickedness.
> You will not fast as you do this day,
> To make your voice heard on high.
> (Isaiah 58:3, 4)

"Why have we fasted and yet you do not see it?" the people cry. "Lord, why aren't you intervening for us?" "I thought you were supposed to hear when we fast and pray?" "Aren't you going to help us?" "We have even afflicted our soul and you don't take knowledge of it!" "Lord, don't you see our acts of self-denial?" So the prophet Isaiah tells them why God is not intervening while they fast and pray. He says *in the day of your fast you find pleasure and exploit all your laborers*. So the first hindrance to fasting is fasting for pleasure. In

23 Piper, John. *A Hunger for God: Desiring God Through Fasting and Prayer*—Multnomah-page 132.

other words, their fasting was for an outward show of religion, and they were enjoying that. They were involved in satisfying their lusts, their pleasures, and at the same time, fasting. If you and I are fasting, and yet only doing it for pleasure and the praise of men, that is hypocrisy and God will not hear our prayers. The second hindrance to their fasting was that they were exploiting their laborers. The idea seems to be that they were being oppressive in demanding all that was due to them. Oh yes, they were fasting, but at the same time they had unforgiving spirits and were oppressive. They were using the day of fasting to collect their debts. They were like the Pharisees and hypocrites that Jesus rebuked in Mt. 23:23 when He pronounced a woe upon them because they did all the religious stuff: they paid tithes of mint and anise and cumin, but omitted the weightier matters of the law, justice, mercy and faith. He called them blind guides who strain at a gnat and swallow a camel. Fasting may be a part of your Christian life, but if you have an unforgiving heart toward anyone, or if you are oppressive toward others, you might as well be praying to the ceiling.

The third and fourth hindrances to fasting are found in verse 4. *Indeed you fast for strife and debate*, God says. They pretended to be fasting to search for sin, but all the while they were bitter and quarreling with each other. So the third hindrance to fasting is a contentious spirit toward others. The fourth hindrance to their fasting was that they did so *to smite with the fist of wickedness*. This means they were abusing poor innocent people with their wicked hands. Fasting brought out the worst in them. If we are fasting, and yet are self-indulgent, harsh, irritable and contentious, then this is not acceptable to God. John Piper says, "How you treat people on Monday is the test of the authenticity of your fasting on Sunday. Woe to the fasting that leaves sin in our lives untouched. The hunger for fasting is a hunger for God, and the test of that hunger is whether it includes a hunger for holiness."[24] Isaiah goes on to say *you will not fast as you do this day, to make your voice heard on high.* You think all this will be heard by God in heaven? I think not! Isaiah goes on to give nine more helps for fasting the proper way in verses 5-7.

Nine More Helps for Fasting

> "Is it a fast that I have chosen,
> A day for a man to afflict his soul?
> Is it to bow down his head like a bulrush,
> And to spread out sackcloth and ashes?
> Would you call this a fast,
> And an acceptable day to the LORD?
> [6]Is this not the fast that I have chosen:
> To loose the bonds of wickedness,
> To undo the heavy burdens,
> To let the oppressed go free,
> And that you break every yoke?
> [7]Is it not to share your bread with the hungry,
> And that you bring to your house the poor who are cast out;
> When you see the naked, that you cover him,
> And not hide yourself from your own flesh?"
> (Isaiah 58:5-7)

God says, "Do you think that because you are going hungry and bowing your head and spreading sackcloth and ashes, that this is acceptable to me?" We might say, "But Lord, I went without food for a whole day and I even lay prostrate on the living room floor and poured my heart out

24 Piper, John. *A Hunger for God: Desiring God Through Fasting and Prayer*—Multnomah- page 135-136.

to you! Isn't this acceptable to you?" No, it isn't. In verses 6 and 7 the Lord states what is the proper way to fast. Fasting is good, but if it doesn't yield godly results, then why bother?

First of all, they must *loose the bonds of wickedness*. This did not mean they were to let everyone out of prison. But it did mean that if anyone was bound contrary to the law of God and the laws of the land, then they were to be released. Secondly, they were *to undo the heavy burdens*. This means that they must release slaves who were under such oppression that they were about ready to sink. Thirdly, they were *to let the oppressed go free*. Those that were oppressed with slavery were to be set free. Fourth, they were to *break every yoke*. This means they were to break the yoke of slavery. You might say, "Well what in the world does this have to do with me? I don't know any slaves that I've oppressed or any who I can set free." True, but we can be oppressive to those who live under the same roof with us. We can lay burdens on our children that they are not meant to bear. We can oppress them and provoke them to the point of discouraging them. We as women can be oppressive to our husbands by nagging them continually and trying to rule them. Some of us can be like the lawyers that Jesus rebuked in Luke 11:46, "And He said, 'Woe to you also, lawyers! For you load men with burdens hard to bear, and you yourselves do not touch the burdens with one of your fingers.'" We cannot be fasting and praying and expect the blessing of God if we are oppressing anyone less fortunate than us.

Isaiah continues in verse seven with five more things that must be present in our lives if God is to recognize our fasting and praying. Fifth, Isaiah says *to share your bread with the hungry*. We are to give to the poor. Perhaps we should think about taking the food we would have eaten the day we fast and give it to someone who is really in need. The meal you would eat, why not take to someone less fortunate? Did you know that about 40,000 children die every day from hunger and from easily preventable childhood diseases? And 400 million people are severely malnourished, and 200 million of those are children. Next time you fast, and you are hungry, think what that would feel like day after day after day! Sixth, Isaiah tells them to *bring to your house the poor who are cast out.* We might say we are to be hospitable, especially to the stranger. Romans 12:13 says we are to be given to hospitality. Peter says in 1 Peter 4:9 that we are to be hospitable without grumbling. How can we be callous to people in need—even the homeless? Seventh, Isaiah says *when you see the naked, that you cover him.* In other words, if you know someone who doesn't have clothes, then get them some. Eighth, they were to *not hide yourselves from your own flesh.* 1 Timothy 5:8 states, "But if anyone does not provide for his own, and especially for those of his household, he has denied the faith and is worse than an unbeliever." We are to provide for our own. Now lest you think this is just Old Testament stuff, I want you to consider Matthew 25:31-46. Look at these very sobering words from our Lord.

> "When the Son of Man comes in His glory, and all the holy angels with Him, then He will sit on the throne of His glory. "All the nations will be gathered before Him, and He will separate them one from another, as a shepherd divides his sheep from the goats. "And He will set the sheep on His right hand, but the goats on the left. "Then the King will say to those on His right hand, 'Come, you blessed of My Father, inherit the kingdom prepared for you from the foundation of the world: 'for I was hungry and you gave Me food; I was thirsty and you gave Me drink; I was a stranger and you took Me in; 'I was naked and you clothed Me; I was sick and you visited Me; I was in prison and you came to Me.' "Then

> the righteous will answer Him, saying, 'Lord, when did we see You hungry and feed You, or thirsty and give You drink? 'When did we see You a stranger and take You in, or naked and clothe You? 'Or when did we see You sick, or in prison, and come to You?' "And the King will answer and say to them, 'Assuredly, I say to you, inasmuch as you did it to one of the least of these My brethren, you did it to Me.' "Then He will also say to those on the left hand, 'Depart from Me, you cursed, into the everlasting fire prepared for the devil and his angels: 'for I was hungry and you gave Me no food; I was thirsty and you gave Me no drink; 'I was a stranger and you did not take Me in, naked and you did not clothe Me, sick and in prison and you did not visit Me.' "Then they also will answer Him, saying, 'Lord, when did we see You hungry or thirsty or a stranger or naked or sick or in prison, and did not minister to You?' "Then He will answer them, saying, 'Assuredly, I say to you, inasmuch as you did not do it to one of the least of these, you did not do it to Me.' "And these will go away into everlasting punishment, but the righteous into eternal life." (Matthew 25:31-46).

If there is any form of hypocrisy in your life, God will not hear your prayers. Psalm 66:18 says that if we regard iniquity in our hearts, God will not hear us. Now there is another hindrance to our fasting, but we must skip down to verse 13 to see it.

> "If you turn away your foot from the Sabbath,
> From doing your pleasure on My holy day,
> And call the Sabbath a delight,
> The holy day of the LORD honorable,
> And shall honor Him, not doing your own ways,
> Nor finding your own pleasure,
> Nor speaking your own words,"
> (Isaiah 58:13)

Ninth, they were to honor the *Sabbath* day. Foot-travel was forbidden on the Sabbath. Many of them were involved in that, as well as doing their own pleasure, and speaking vain words or angry words. And all this was taking place on the Lord's Day! The Sabbath was a burden to them because it kept them from doing their everyday stuff. How can we have a fight with our husband on the way to church; how can we do our own thing on the Lord's Day, and expect to fast and pray on Monday and think God will hear us? We are only fooling ourselves. Ladies, my heart is so grieved as I see the world pulling us into their system on the Lord's Day with endless sporting events and other activities. It is the Lord's Day. I would encourage you to think through the consequences of these issues, if not for yourself, then for your children. These are serious indictments on these people and they are serious indictments on us.

Isaiah now shifts his tone, to encourage them that if they would be obedient in these areas in their lives, the results would be wonderful. If our life is clean and right before God, and if we cry out to Him in fasting and praying, then Isaiah gives some pretty incredible results. In fact, in the last chapter we saw some pretty amazing results of fasting, too. Let's look at some more results in this passage—thirteen to be exact.

Thirteen Results of Fasting

> "Then your light shall break forth like the morning,
> Your healing shall spring forth speedily,
> And your righteousness shall go before you;
> The glory of the LORD shall be your rear guard.
> 9Then you shall call, and the LORD will answer;
> You shall cry, and He will say, 'Here I am.'
> "If you take away the yoke from your midst,
> The pointing of the finger, and speaking wickedness,
> 10If you extend your soul to the hungry

And satisfy the afflicted soul,
Then your light shall dawn in the darkness,
And your darkness shall be as the noonday.
11The LORD will guide you continually,
And satisfy your soul in drought,
And strengthen your bones;
You shall be like a watered garden,
And like a spring of water, whose waters do not fail.
12Those from among you
Shall build the old waste places;
You shall raise up the foundations of many generations;
And you shall be called the Repairer of the Breach, the Restorer of Streets to Dwell In.
13"If you turn away your foot from the Sabbath,
From doing your pleasure on My holy day,
And call the Sabbath a delight,
The holy day of the LORD honorable,
And shall honor Him, not doing your own ways,
Nor finding your own pleasure,
Nor speaking your own words,
14Then you shall delight yourself in the LORD;
And I will cause you to ride on the high hills of the earth,
And feed you with the heritage of Jacob your father.
The mouth of the LORD has spoken."
(Isaiah 58:8-14)

First, their *light shall break forth like the morning*. Light is an emblem of prosperity. The idea being that prosperity would come upon them like the light of the morning. I think we could say that as we fast and pray in a manner that pleases God, then He will send forth light to our darkness. Second, their *healing shall spring forth speedily*. Literally, a long bandage. Here the sense is that, if they would return to God, they would be delivered from the calamities that their crimes had brought on them, and that peace and prosperity would again visit the nation. We have to wonder how much of our nation's healing would take place if we would humble ourselves and fast and pray?! Third, their righteousness shall go before them. In other words, righteousness would lead them. I don't know about you, but I desire that my life would be lived righteously and that it would go before me. Fourth, *the glory of the Lord shall be your rear guard.* God will be in front of them with His righteousness, but behind them with His glory. Fifth, *they shall call, and the LORD will answer.* This is a promise to have our prayers answered. Before the prophet brings up more promises, he lays down the conditions again in verse 10.

> "If you extend your soul to the hungry
> And satisfy the afflicted soul,
> Then your light shall dawn in the darkness,
> And your darkness shall be as the noonday."
> (Isaiah 58:10)

Sixth, *the LORD will guide you continually*. He will go before you and lead you always. How many times in our lives do we ask the Lord to lead us? We can count on Him answering and showing us as we seek Him in the right way. Seventh, the Lord will *satisfy your soul in drought*, and strengthen your bones. He will satisfy our thirsty souls. The Lord is the only one that can truly satisfy our souls. He is the bread of life and He is the living water. He that comes to Him will never thirst again. Eighth, they would be *like a watered garden*. The idea of happiness in the Oriental world consisted much in pleasant gardens, running streams, and ever-flowing fountains, and nothing can more beautifully express the blessedness of the continued favor of the Almighty. This is a picture of happiness. Ninth, the Lord promises blessing to their families. It says *you shall raise up the foundations of many generations*.

Don't we all desire God's blessing upon our families? Then why don't we fast and pray more often? Tenth, there is promise for Jerusalem to be rebuilt: *you shall be called the Repairer of the Breach, the Restorer of Streets to Dwell In*. Now I know that we don't need our cities to be rebuilt, but just imagine what rebuilding could take places in homes, in our churches, in our city, if we would humble ourselves and pray? Eleventh, they would find *delight...in the LORD*. If they would fast in the spirit and manner that God had intended, then and only then, could they delight themselves in God. Worship would be a joy and not a duty. Twelfth, they would *ride on the high hills of the earth*. The idea here is that of rising above earthly difficulties. The idea is like that of Psalm 18:32-33. "It is God who arms me with strength, and makes my way perfect. He makes my feet like the feet of deer, and sets me on my high places." And thirteenth, Isaiah says He would *feed you with the heritage of Jacob your father*. They would possess the land promised to them as in inheritance. For the mouth of the Lord has spoken it! If God has said it, who can stand against it! No one!

Summary

In this lesson we found:

1. *Four helps for fasting* (vv. 1, 2).
    1. Seek God daily.
    2. Delight to know His ways.
    3. Pray for God's justice.
    4. Delight in approaching God.
2. *Four hindrances to fasting* (vv. 3-4).
    1. Fasting to be seen of men or for pleasure.
    2. Fasting while being oppressive to others.
    3. Fasting while having a contentious spirit toward others.
    4. Fasting while abusing the poor.
3. *Nine more helps for fasting* (vv. 5-7, 13).
    1. Relief to the innocent.
    2. Undo the heavy burdens of others.
    3. Let the oppressed go free.
    4. Free the yoke of slavery.
    5. Give to the poor.
    6. Be hospitable.
    7. Clothe the naked.
    8. Provide for your own household.
    9. Keep the Sabbath day.
4. *Thirteen results of fasting* (vv. 8-14).
    1. Light breaks forth into our darkness.
    2. Deliverance from calamity.
    3. Righteousness going before us.
    4. The glory of the Lord behind us.
    5. Answered prayer.
    6. The Lord's guidance.
    7. Satisfaction for our thirsty souls.
    8. Happiness.

9. Blessing on our families.
10. Rebuilding of our nation or city.
11. Delighting of ourselves in God.
12. Rising above the difficulties of life.
13. Inheritance of the land.

We would all do well to heed to these warnings about fasting in a proper way. What have you been nibbling at this day that is perhaps keeping you from hungering for God? Is it the television? Internet-surfing? Shopping? Exercising? Collecting those collectable items? Decorating? Reading? Traveling? Gardening? Why not commit today before God to put aside anything that is dulling your appetite for Him alone? Why not commit to God that you will regularly set aside time for fasting and prayer? For those of you who do fast regularly? What is your attitude in fasting? Do you do it so others will think you are spiritual? Do you somehow think you will gain favor with God? Are you fasting and praying and at the same time yelling at your kids, nagging your husband, become increasingly calloused toward the hurts and needs of others? Not honoring the Lord's Day? Fasting without repentance is hypocrisy. Is there any form of hypocrisy in your life? If there is, then I pray you will repent today and resume a life dedicated to prayer and to fasting for the glory of God!

Questions to Consider

A Look at Fasting and Prayer—Part 2: The Proper Methods of Fasting and Prayer

Isaiah 58

1. Read Matthew 9:14-15 and paraphrase in your own words what Christ says.

2. Read Isaiah 58. (a) What good things was the "house of Jacob" involved in? (b) Despite these good things, why wouldn't God answer their prayers? (c) How does this compare to what Christ says in Matthew 23:14?

3. God says in Jeremiah 14:12 that when the people fast He will not hear them. (a) Skim Jeremiah 14 to see why God would not hear them. (b) How does this compare to the Isaiah 58 passage?

4. (a) What was God's question to the people in Zechariah 7:5? (b) Why did God question their sincerity according to Zechariah 7:8-14?

5. (a)Would you say there is any form of hypocrisy in your life? (b) Would your spouse or others say there is any form of hypocrisy in your life? (c) In light of this lesson, what will you do to put off all hypocrisy? (See Galatians 5:16, Colossians 3:5; and 1 Peter 2:11 for some help)

6. Having considered these passages, why is it important that our lives be holy, especially as we fast and pray?

7. I would like to encourage you to spend time in fasting and praying. What part of fasting and praying is difficult for you? Come with a prayer request to share.

Chapter 13

The Prayer of a Broken-Hearted Man

Psalm 55

I would like for you to do some imaginary thinking with me. First of all, I want you to picture in your mind your very best friend, your bosom buddy, your soul mate. He or she has now betrayed you in the worst way. On top of that, your son has played some part in the betrayal, and is in serious rebellion against your authority. Not only has he rebelled against your authority, but he has also influenced many other people who will also turn against you, and become some of your worst enemies. Last, but not least, your position of mother, employee, or whatever your major role is at this time in your life, is seriously threatened because of the betrayal of your friend and son. Sounds like a pretty awful nightmare, doesn't it? This was not a nightmare for King David, but a reality. The depth of betrayal is real and the pain of it all is horrendous to this man after God's own heart. And so in his deepest pain, he cries out to God and prays:

> Give ear to my prayer, O God,
> And do not hide Yourself from my supplication.
> [2]Attend to me, and hear me;
> I am restless in my complaint, and moan noisily,
> [3]Because of the voice of the enemy,
> Because of the oppression of the wicked;
> For they bring down trouble upon me,
> And in wrath they hate me.

[4]My heart is severely pained within me,
And the terrors of death have fallen upon me.
[5]Fearfulness and trembling have come upon me,
And horror has overwhelmed me.
[6]So I said, "Oh, that I had wings like a dove!
I would fly away and be at rest.
[7]Indeed, I would wander far off,
And remain in the wilderness. Selah
[8]I would hasten my escape
From the windy storm and tempest."
[9]Destroy, O Lord, and divide their tongues,
For I have seen violence and strife in the city.
[10]Day and night they go around it on its walls;
Iniquity and trouble are also in the midst of it.
[11]Destruction is in its midst;
Oppression and deceit do not depart from its streets.
[12]For it is not an enemy who reproaches me;
Then I could bear it.
Nor is it one who hates me who has exalted himself against me;
Then I could hide from him.
[13]But it was you, a man my equal,
My companion and my acquaintance.
[14]We took sweet counsel together,
And walked to the house of God in the throng.
[15]Let death seize them;
Let them go down alive into hell,
For wickedness is in their dwellings and among them.
[16]As for me, I will call upon God,
And the LORD shall save me.
[17]Evening and morning and at noon
I will pray, and cry aloud,
And He shall hear my voice.
[18]He has redeemed my soul in peace from the battle that was against me,
For there were many against me.
[19]God will hear, and afflict them,

> Even He who abides from of old. Selah
> Because they do not change,
> Therefore they do not fear God.
> [20]He has put forth his hands against those who were at peace with him;
> He has broken his covenant.
> [21]The words of his mouth were smoother than butter,
> But war was in his heart;
> His words were softer than oil,
> Yet they were drawn swords.
> [22]Cast your burden on the LORD,
> And He shall sustain you;
> He shall never permit the righteous to be moved.
> [23]But You, O God, shall bring them down to the pit of destruction;
> Bloodthirsty and deceitful men shall not live out half their days;
> But I will trust in You.
> (Psalm 55:1-23)

I have divided this prayer into three sections: *David's suffering* (vv. 1-8); *David's situation* (vv. 9-15); and *David's solution* (vv. 16-23).

Psalm 55 is a psalm of David, and it is a lament Psalm. It is *supposed* that David wrote it during the time of the rebellion of his son, Absalom, and the betrayal of his friend, Ahithophel. Not only does David have to deal with the pain of the betrayal and rebellion, but his enemies are also seeking his life. David realizes he will probably have to flee Jerusalem, the place of his home and his reigning kingdom. All this is weighing very heavy on this king's heart, and he desperately needs the help of his God. Let's begin by looking at the first portion of David's prayer and consider the suffering of this great man of God.

David's Suffering
Psalm 55:1-8

> Give ear to my prayer, O God,
> And do not hide Yourself from my supplication.
> (Psalm 55:1)

David says, *Give ear to my prayer, O God, and do not hide Yourself from my supplication.* The general meaning of what David is saying is, "do not shut your eyes God," "do not hide Your ear." When a man would see his neighbor in distress, and deliberately pass him by, he was said to hide himself from him. It is like the parable in Luke 10 of the Good Samaritan when the priest and Levite passed by the man who was almost dead. They deliberately passed by walking to the other side of the road to avoid the beaten man. David is crying out to God to not treat him like that. Instead of passing him by, David cries out for God to attend to him!

> Attend to me, and hear me;
> I am restless in my complaint, and moan noisily.
> (Psalm 55:2)

The word *restless* means to wander about; to ramble. It is a word which describes one who looks for help in every way, and it is especially applied to animals that have broken loose, and have gotten lost and don't know where to go. David says I wander from one sad thought to another. David was in deep distress and was looking in every direction for help and his desire was that God would help him. David also describes his distress here as a noisy *moan*, which means by prayer or groaning. David did not hesitate to express his grief in prayer by moaning or sobbing. David was the King of Israel and yet he was not afraid to be real in his prayers to God. Are you real in your prayers to God? Now in verse 3, David gives the reason for his groaning, for his mourning.

> Because of the voice of the enemy,
> Because of the oppression of the wicked;
> For they bring down trouble upon me,
> And in wrath they hate me.
> (Psalm 55:3)

The *voice* here would indicate slanderous reproaches and assaults which were made on his character. *Oppression* has the idea of crushing by a heavy weight. The *wicked* would refer to Absalom and Ahithophel and those who were rebelling with them. David felt a heavy weight due to his enemies. What were his enemies doing to David? First of all, they were bringing trouble upon him which is an indication that they were charging David with sin. Secondly, he says *in wrath they hate me*, which would be a reference to Absalom who was driving David from his home and his throne. David goes on to describe his suffering in verse 4.

> My heart is severely pained within me,
> And the terrors of death have fallen upon me.
> (Psalm 55:4)

David describes his heart as *pained*, which means to dance in a circle, to be whirled around, and then to twist in pain. This is a word that is especially applied to a woman giving birth. (Many of you will be able to identify with this!) This phrase expresses a violent mental stress. One can only imagine the pain David was in. Most of us have never experienced the rebellion of a son, betrayal of a friend, multiple enemies and the possibility of losing your job all at the same time! All of this, no doubt, caused much stress and anguish in David's heart. David says *the terrors of death have fallen upon me.* Some think this means David feared that he would die, but more likely it means that the pain he was experiencing was like that of dying. David felt like he couldn't live. The word *fallen* suggests that this rebellion and conspiracy had come upon David suddenly. David goes on to describe his feelings during his suffering in verse 5, in three ways: *fearfulness*, *trembling* and *horror*.

> Fearfulness and trembling have come upon me,
> And horror has overwhelmed me.
> (Psalm 55:5)

David's fear was so great that it produced trembling and horror. It overwhelmed David. This means David's pain and grief covered him or enveloped him entirely. Now keep in mind this was the same David who killed Goliath, and the same David who fought with a bear and a lion. David was no wimp. But even the strongest of men can encounter painful trials that are so severe that they no longer feel strong, but very, very weak. I think many times that is where the Lord wants us, because when we are weak, then we are strong, because His strength is made perfect in our weakness, as Paul says in 2 Corinthians 12:9. This is a time in David's life where it seems that there is not one ray of light, not one ounce of hope. All seemed gloom and doom and horrifying. No wonder he prays in verse 6:

> So I said, "Oh, that I had wings like a dove!
> I would fly away and be at rest.
> (Psalm 55:6)

Literally this reads, "Who will give me wings like a dove?" This is probably a reference to a turtle dove which was a common dove in Palestine. The dove was known to be a gentle bird. It was often pursued, but rarely captured because of its great speed and the fact that they hid in rocks. They must have been known for their ability to go a great distance, as seen in Genesis when Noah sent the dove out to see if the water had receded from the earth. David is saying I want to get as far away as possible. Why does he want to do that? Because he says, *I would fly away and be at rest.* David wishes to get away from all his troubles. Before we criticize him too greatly, there is probably not one of us who hasn't felt this way at some time or another. "Calgon take me away!" However, we all know that running is never the answer as there is only a new set of problems awaiting us there. There is a solution to David's problem and it is not running away, as we will see later on in his prayer. David wishes to fly away not only because he thinks he would be at rest, but also for another reason in verse 7.

> Indeed, I would wander far off,
> And remain in the wilderness. Selah.
> (Psalm 55:7)

David expresses his desire to escape from it all and go to the wilderness; such a place would be uninhabited, where no one lives. Let me say, that might be exciting for a day or two, but after that I am not so sure the isolation would be so luxurious. I love to be alone, but after a day or two, I am ready for someone to talk to and fellowship with. *Selah*, David says. "Pause to consider, is this really what you want to do David? Be alone in the wilderness. What would you do in the wilderness David?" Well, he states in verse 8 what he would do.

> I would hasten my escape
> From the windy storm and tempest.
> (Psalm 55:8)

Doves were known to fly into holes when the storm would come. David says I would hide in a hole, and there would be no delay in my escape from the storm and tempest. *Storm* and *tempest* are words used to describe his trials. With this, David ends his description of his suffering, which he has described in verses 1-8 as a deep pain that has overwhelmed him and produced great fear, horror, trembling, mourning, and a desire to run away! Things have to be pretty awful to feel that way, and indeed they were. David now turns from thoughts of his suffering, to his situation in verses 9-15.

David's Situation
Psalm 55:9-15

> Destroy, O Lord, and divide their tongues,
> For I have seen violence and strife in the city.
> (Psalm 55:9)

The word for *destroy* in verse 9 means to devour or swallow up. *Tongues* is an interesting word as it is a reference to what took place at Babel in Genesis 11:1-9.

> Now the whole earth had one language and one speech. And it came to pass, as they journeyed from the east, that they found a plain in the land of Shinar, and they dwelt there. Then they said to one another, "Come, let us make bricks and bake them thoroughly." They had brick for stone, and they had asphalt for mortar. And they said, "Come, let us build ourselves a city, and a tower whose top is in the heavens; let us make a name for ourselves, lest we be scattered abroad over the face of the whole earth." But the LORD came down to see the city and the tower which the sons of men had built. And the LORD said, "Indeed the people are one and they all have one language, and this is what they begin to do; now nothing

> that they propose to do will be withheld from them. "Come, let Us go down and there confuse their language, that they may not understand one another's speech." So the LORD scattered them abroad from there over the face of all the earth, and they ceased building the city. Therefore its name is called Babel, because there the LORD confused the language of all the earth; and from there the LORD scattered them abroad over the face of all the earth. (Genesis 11:1-9)

Up to this point in Genesis 11, the people were of one language. God had given mankind a command in Genesis 8:17 to be fruitful and multiply and fill the earth. Instead of obeying God we find mankind purposely deciding to disobey God. Genesis 11:4: "And they said, 'Come, let us build ourselves a city, and a tower whose top is in the heavens; let us make a name for ourselves, lest we be scattered abroad over the face of the whole earth.'" Because of their pride and disobedience, the Lord came down and confused their language so that they could not understand one another's speech. Just like the confused language which took place amidst those who were trying to build the tower, to the point that they could not understand one another, David prays that the tongues of his enemies would be confused and their counsel destroyed. It is similar to what David prays in 2 Samuel 15:31, "'O LORD, I pray, turn the counsel of Ahithophel into foolishness!'" There is a reason David asks for his enemies' tongues to be destroyed and confused. He says *for I have seen violence and strife in the city.* More than likely this was taking place in Jerusalem, which would be a cause for sorrow for David, as Jerusalem was David's home and it was a grief to see the downfall of his home and his people. In verses 10 and 11, we see the description of the wickedness that was going on in the city.

> Day and night they go around it on its walls;
> Iniquity and trouble are also in the midst of it.
> (Psalm 55:10)

Day and night would be an indication that the violence and strife was going on continually. Violence and strife were everywhere, even around the walls. This perhaps could be a reference to when Absalom lay with David's concubines on top of the house in the sight of all of Israel. David goes on to say: *iniquity and trouble are also in the midst of it.* This would indicate mischief and perverseness, which is a good description of the scene when Absalom lay with the women. More descriptions of wickedness are seen in verse 11.

> Destruction is in its midst;
> Oppression and deceit do not depart from its streets.
> (Psalm 55:11)

Destruction is connected with rebellion and revolt. *Deceit* and *oppressions* do not depart from the streets. It is everywhere, the walls, the streets. This would be the open square, where interestingly enough, justice was known to have taken place. But instead, injustice was taking place. David now shifts his thoughts in verse 12 to Ahithophel, his dearly trusted friend, or so he thought.

> For it is not an enemy who reproaches me;
> Then I could bear it.
> Nor is it one who hates me who has exalted himself against me;
> Then I could hide from him.
> (Psalm 55:12)

David says it was not an enemy who slandered me.

I would expect that! Shimei, remember, cursed David and threw stones and dust at him. That was expected—he was an enemy. But not Ahithophel; he was David's counselor and his friend. We expect slander from our enemies, but not from our friends. *Nor is it one who hates me who has exalted himself against me; then I could hide from him.* If it was one who hated David openly, then he would have been able to hide in a cave or somewhere safe, like he did when he was running from Saul in 1 Samuel 24, where it states that David hid himself in the wilderness and in caves. I could have handled this, David says, *but* he says in verse 13:

> But it was you, a man my equal,
> My companion and my acquaintance.
> (Psalm 55:13)

The man who betrayed me was a man according to my rank, an equal, a like-soul, a second self, one of the same mind, my soul mate, my companion, one who is familiar to me and a friend, my confidant. David goes on to describe just how intimate this relationship was in verse 14.

> We took sweet counsel together,
> And walked to the house of God in the throng.
> (Psalm 55:14)

Literally, David says, we sweetened counsel together, we consulted together and opened our minds to each other, and we shared our inner-most thoughts with each other. Remember, 2 Samuel 16:23 said that Ahithophel was David's counselor, and it was as if he had inquired at the oracle of God: "Now the advice of Ahithophel, which he gave in those days, was as if one had inquired at the oracle of God. So was all the advice of Ahithophel both with David and with Absalom." Ahithophel was a supposedly godly and trusted man. They also *walked to the house of God in the throng.* This means that they went together to worship with those who were assembled to worship. There is nothing that unites hearts together more than worshipping the Lord with each other. You know, we might be critical of Ahithophel, and rightly so. But what about ourselves? Are we true to our friendships? Are we speaking unkindly to others about our friends? Friends are precious gifts from God, and we should not trample on such precious gifts. David now shifts his thoughts from Ahithophel to his enemies.

> Let death seize them;
> Let them go down alive into hell,
> For wickedness is in their dwellings and among them.
> (Psalm 55:15)

David does not call for God's vengeance upon Ahithophel, but upon all his enemies, as indicated by the word *them.* He doesn't wish ill will on his friend even though he betrayed him. David wants his enemies to *go down alive into hell.* There is an allusion here to the fate of Korah mentioned in Numbers 16:30-33, who quickly went down into the pit. There is a reason David wants them to be destroyed and it is not out of vengeance. It is because of their wickedness; for *wickedness is in their dwellings, and among them.* It is in their houses and it permeates everywhere. Wickedness is indeed with them, but not with David, the man after God's own heart. David's situation is difficult, as we have seen in verses 9-15. Led by his son Absalom, there is widespread wickedness in the city he loves—Jerusalem. His soul-mate and confident has betrayed him. It is a situation that is indeed distressing. But as David closes his prayer, we see him focus in on the solution to his problems.

David's Solution
Psalm 55:16-23

> As for me, I will call upon God,
> And the LORD shall save me.
> (Psalm 55:16)

David knew that the solution to his problem, just like the solution to any problem, came from God. In fact, he was confident that his deliverance came from God. He was forsaken by many, but God had not forsaken him. He knew he could depend on him; he would call upon him, and do so often. How often?

> Evening and morning and at noon
> I will pray, and cry aloud,
> And He shall hear my voice.
> (Psalm 55:17)

Morning and evening were probably an indication of the morning and evening sacrifices offered according to Exodus 29:38-42. The noon time prayer would not have been a command, but would have demonstrated David's devotion to God. Daniel 6:20 tells us that Daniel also prayed three times a day. This indicates that David felt a need to pray and not just in the morning. It was a need he had all day. David could echo with Paul as he commands in I Thessalonians 5:17, "pray without ceasing." To *cry aloud* would mean to murmur, to sigh, to growl, to groan. David is confident that God will hear him, as evidenced by saying *and He shall hear my voice.*[25] And what is the basis for David's confidence? He tells us in verse 18.

25 "He shall hear my voice" is the name of the painting on the front of this book; painter—C. Michael Dudash

> He has redeemed my soul in peace from the battle that
> was against me,
> For there were many against me.
> (Psalm 55:18)

David knew God had *redeemed* him, which means to deliver, rescue, and to be saved. This psalm was either written after the deliverance, or David was so confident that God would deliver him, that he speaks as if were done already. Note that this deliverance was done in peace. When we let God fight our battles for us, and not try and fight them ourselves, it is peaceful. David's deliverance was especially meaningful as he says that there were *many against me.* David expresses again in verse 19 the fact the God will hear him.

> God will hear, and afflict them,
> Even He who abides from of old. Selah
> Because they do not change,
> Therefore they do not fear God.
> (Psalm 55:19)

"He will hear me," David says. But in contrast, He will *afflict them,* which means God (*He who abides from of old*) will bring upon them what they deserve. *Even He who abides from of old* is He who is from everlasting, He who is enthroned from the most distant past; He will do this! *Selah,* David says for the second time in this prayer. This is perhaps a pause to stop and consider the great God who is from everlasting. Think about it! David goes on to pray, *because they do not change, therefore they do not fear God.* Instead of changing, these enemies remain in their wickedness. There is no repentance, therefore they do not fear God. David's thoughts turn to his trusted friend, Ahithophel, in verse 20.

> He has put forth his hands against those who were at peace with him;
> He has broken his covenant.
> (Psalm 55:20)

Ahithophel had put forth his hand; he had taken vengeance against David, who was at peace with him. He went so far as to break his covenant, which is probably a reference to an agreement the two shared. As David's trusted counselor and adviser, Ahithophel would have made a covenant with David. But instead, he broke his covenant by betraying his friend, a betrayal which stemmed from an evil heart as we learn in verse 21.

> The words of his mouth were smoother than butter,
> But war was in his heart;
> His words were softer than oil,
> Yet they were drawn swords.
> (Psalm 55:21)

"Smooth are the butterings of his mouth," David says. Ahithophel was a hypocrite. The words he spoke from his mouth were not what were in his heart, as *war was in his heart*. David adds: *his words were softer than oil, yet they were drawn swords*. What is David saying here? Ahithophel flattered David with his mouth, and then stabbed him in the back. "He lauded and larded the man he hoped to devour. He buttered him with flattery and then battered him with malice…Soft, smooth, oily words are most plentiful where truth and sincerity are most scarce."[26] But David turns again from his thoughts of Ahithophel and the pain he caused to the solution he needs to focus on. And that solution is the Lord.

26 Spurgeon, Charles. *The Treasury of David*—Hendrickson Publishers-pg 451.

> Cast your burden on the LORD
> And He shall sustain you;
> He shall never permit the righteous to be moved.
> (Psalm 55:22)

Cast your burden on the Lord, throw it off, David says. The lot that God has given you, what He has appointed to you, cast it back. Doesn't it make sense to cast to the Lord what He has cast on you? Just give it back. As Peter says, "cast all your care upon Him, for He cares for you" (1 Peter 5:7). There is a reason David casts his cares upon God. First, He *shall sustain you*. He will support you and He will take care of you. Secondly, *He shall never permit the righteous to be moved*. Literally, David says, He will not give moving for ever to the righteous. We cannot take this to mean that all goes well with the righteous, that their circumstances will never change, or that trials will never come. But in all our trials, we are completely in the hands of God who does not change because we are kept by Him and by His awesome power. And so David ends his prayer by contrasting the righteous with the unrighteous.

> But You, O God, shall bring them down to the pit of destruction;
> Bloodthirsty and deceitful men shall not live out half their days;
> But I will trust in You.
> (Psalm 55:23)

Men who are given over to violence *shall not live out half their days*; they die early. It happened in the case of Absalom and it happened in the case of Ahithophel. Both died young in life. Absalom was murdered while caught in a tree. Absalom had violated a direct command of God, which was to honor your father and mother. In fact, this is a command that has a promise attached to it according to Exodus 20:12 and that is, that it will go well with you and that you will live long on the earth. Had Absalom honored David his father, maybe he wouldn't have died young. Ahithophel committed suicide, and thus died early as well. Albert Barnes comments that "thousands of young men are indulging in habits which, unless arrested, must have such a result, and who are destined to an early grave—who will not live out half their days—unless their mode of life is changed, and they become temperate, chaste, and virtuous."[27] In contrast to the bloody and deceitful men who have no fear of God, David ends his prayer with a phrase we all would do well to model: *but I will trust in You.* I will leave all in God's hands. By the way, David lived longer than Absalom and Ahithophel. In fact, He died at a good old age, according to 1 Chronicles 29:28. What a contrast between David and these two men. They do not fear God and are rebellious and evil men who do not live out half their days. David fears God and does what is right and he lives to be an aged man. David's solution is threefold: he will call on the Lord, he will cast his burden on the Lord, and he will trust in the Lord.

27 Barnes, Albert. *Barnes' Notes*—Baker Book House- page 124.

Summary

In this lesson we learned the following: *David's suffering* (vv. 1-8). His deep pain has overwhelmed him, producing fear, horror, trembling, mourning, and a desire to run away! *David's situation* (vv. 9-15). David's situation is difficult: under the leading of his rebellious son, Absalom, there is widespread wickedness in the city he loves—Jerusalem. His soul mate and confidante has also betrayed him. *David's solution* (vv. 16-23). David's solution is threefold: he will call on the Lord, he will cast his burden on the Lord, and he will trust in the Lord.

What a sad and painful story. But sad as it is, painful trials and terrible experiences do sometimes happen to God's people. Do not be surprised at the fiery trial sent to test you, as the Apostle Peter said, (1 Peter 4:12). The question for us is: what will we do when those fiery trials come? Where will we turn? David knew exactly where to go when his pain was at an all time high—he went to the Lord. If the Lord ever assigns you the lot of being forsaken by your closest companion, having your child rebel and turn against you, as well as countless others joining in the rebellion, and your job of mom or employee is in jeopardy due to all of this, where will you turn? What will you do? I hope we all can say with King David, "I will cast my burden on the Lord, I will trust in Him."

Questions to Consider
The Prayer of a Broken-Hearted Man

Psalm 55

1. (a) What are the problems that King David mentions in Psalm 55? (b) What does he petition of the Lord? (c) What solutions does he rest in?

2. It is supposed that David wrote Psalm 55 during the rebellion of Absalom and during Ahithophel's betrayal. Read 2 Samuel 15-18 and write down the heartaches David went through which coincide with his prayer in Psalm 55.

3. From David's prayer in Psalm 55, we learn that David honestly expresses his emotions and requests as he prays. (a) Read Isaiah 38 and Hebrews 5 to see who else expressed great emotion in their prayers. (b) What verbs are used to describe their grief? (c) What were the circumstances in Isaiah 38 and Hebrews 5? (d) What can you learn from these 3 passages about being "real" with God in our prayers? (e) How do you reconcile these passages with what Paul says in Philippians 2:14 that we are to do everything without murmuring and complaining?

4. (a) What do all three of these passages have in common? Matthew 11:28-30, Philippians 4:6, 7, and 1 Peter 5:7. (b) How are they similar to Psalm 55:22? (c) As believers, how do we "cast" our burdens on the Lord?

5. (a) Have you ever been betrayed by a family member or a friend? (b) What was your response, or what should have been your response? (c) How did the Lord sustain you during that time? (Please be discreet in sharing this if done in a group.)

6. What hope and counsel would you give from Psalm 55 to someone who is suffering deep distress due to betrayal?

7. Write a prayer request for any difficulty you or someone else may be encountering due to betrayal.

Chapter 14

Thirsting for God in the Wilderness

Psalm 63

'Twas the week before Christmas, and all through the day, not one single Christian was taking time to pray. The stockings were hung and the tree, it was there, but Jesus had been left out, and no one seemed to care. Then all of a sudden, I awoke to my sin, and discovered I had let Satan, and not Jesus, in. So, I determined to make this year unlike the past, I studied Psalm 63 and found answers at last. (No, this is not Hebrew poetry, but my feeble attempts at English poetry!)

As I get older, I become more and more concerned with what I see and hear at Christmastime. I may be cynical, but it seems to me that as believers we have bought into the world's idea of celebrating of our Lord's birth. Instead of our focus being on the Christ-child, it is on the Christmas rush. Instead of focusing on our Savior, we are focusing on Santa. Instead of Bethlehem, it is bedlam. We usually spend less time feeding our souls, but more time feeding our body. It seems that around this time of year, more than any other, I feel like a stranger in this world, and that I don't belong here. I feel like I am in the wilderness, as David was when he wrote Psalm 63. You might be asking, "What does one do then?" I would like to challenge you as you study Psalm 63 to be different from the world, not only during the Christmas season, but every season of the year. I know of no better Psalm to get our attention away from the world and on to the Lord than to focus Psalm 63.

O God, You are my God;
Early will I seek You;
My soul thirsts for You;
My flesh longs for You
In a dry and thirsty land
Where there is no water.
2So I have looked for You in the sanctuary,
To see Your power and Your glory.
3Because Your lovingkindness is better than life,
My lips shall praise You.
4Thus I will bless You while I live;
I will lift up my hands in Your name.
5My soul shall be satisfied as with marrow and fatness,
And my mouth shall praise You with joyful lips.
6When I remember You on my bed,
I meditate on You in the night watches.
7Because You have been my help,
Therefore in the shadow of Your wings I will rejoice.
8My soul follows close behind You;
Your right hand upholds me.
9But those who seek my life, to destroy it,
Shall go into the lower parts of the earth.
10They shall fall by the sword;
They shall be a portion for jackals.
11But the king shall rejoice in God;
Everyone who swears by Him shall glory;
But the mouth of those who speak lies shall be stopped.
(Psalm 63:1-11)

Now as we study this Psalm, this prayer of David, I plan to keep to the text, but I also want to share with you nine keys from this passage for keeping Christ in your Christmas. And they will form the acrostic C-H-R-I-S-T-M-A-S. (By the way, they are not in order.) And if it is not the Christmas season when you study this chapter, these principles are good for maintaining closeness to God anytime of the year!

Who wrote Psalm 63? We know that David wrote this psalm when he was in the wilderness of Judah. It was probably written when he was fleeing from his son, Absalom, or from King Saul. Located in the northern part of the wilderness between Jerusalem and Jordan, Judah was considered a wild part of the county. (You might want to take the time to look this up on a map.) Judah is mentioned in Matthew 3:1, 2, "In those days John the Baptist came preaching in the wilderness of Judea, and saying, 'Repent, for the kingdom of heaven is at hand!'" So David finds himself in the middle of nowhere. Isolated and without access to a place of worship, this is a rough time in his life. He feels alone, removed from things familiar to him. He was hungry, he was thirsty, and he was exhausted. (Maybe some of you feel like that around the holiday season with all the stress that is added to your already busy life.) But all these things didn't seem to faze David as his all-consuming passion was his God. Even though he was in the wilderness, David didn't quit praying. This prayer is not a prayer of activity, running here and there like most of us do around the holiday season, but it is a prayer of quietness. It is a prayer from a hungry saint, who prefers depth to speed. "There was no desert in his heart, though there was a desert around him."[28] This is a prayer to pray especially when one is prevented from going to public worship, as David was when he prayed Psalm 63. It is even a great song to sing this during the festive season, and a much better song than *Santa Claus is Coming to Town*! David begins his prayer with these words:

Seek Him Early

28 Spurgeon, Charles. *The Treasury of David*—Hendrickson Publishers- page 45.

O God, You are my God;
Early will I seek You;
My soul thirsts for You;
My flesh longs for You
In a dry and thirsty land
Where there is no water.
(Psalm 63:1)

O God, David says, which means, "O Elohim." Next to the word Jehovah, *Elohim* is the most common name given to God. The word occurs more than 2000 times in the Scriptures and is a word that refers to God as Creator. I imagine that David could see a lot of God's creation out in the wilderness, especially the stars at night, which might be the reason he uses this particular word for God. The second word for God that David uses in this prayer is different. The word is *Eli*, which is a word often applied to God which carries the idea of strength. David uses the phrase *my God*, which would indicate that David was in a covenant relationship with God. It's as if he is saying, "my tower of strength, my strong, and my mighty one." So after identifying who God is, David begins by saying to God, *early will I seek You. Early* is a word which means the dawn, the morning, or the early dawn. To *seek* means to seek diligently. David sought God first. David's first words, his first thoughts, his first plans, were all toward God. God was number one on David's agenda for the day. Each day is a gift from Him, so it only makes sense to seek God first as you yield your day to Him. Most of the time our plans are not His plans, but they are the best plans for us! So the first key to keeping Christ in your Christmas or any time of the year is the "S" on our acrostic: *Seek Him early*. If we do not seek the Lord early, then most often the day rushes on and we come to the end of it and wonder, "Did I spend any time with the Lord today?" Other things creep into our day and rob us of time with Him. But early in the morning, there seem to be fewer distractions and the world seems quieter. What or whom do you seek early? What's first on your morning agenda? Calling your best friend? Watching *Good Morning America*? David was not the only one in scripture who sought the Lord early. According to Mark 1:35, Jesus, who is God in the flesh, sought God early: "Now in the morning, having risen a long while before daylight, He went out and departed to a solitary place; and there He prayed." If Jesus had a need to get alone with God early in the morning, how much greater is our need? One man says, "The Psalmist means morning with a dew in it, morning when, instead of being dull as a clod, you are keen as a star, morning when you are at your freshest and best, the sweet morning moments, so clear, so calm, so bright, that come before you are tired, when life has yet no fever in it, no hurry and no delirium, when, while you are meeting at the Throne of Grace, you are all there." Why does David seek God early? Is it so he can check it off of his "to-do" list? No! It is because David longed for God. He wanted to be with Him in a desperate way as evidenced by what he prays next: *My soul thirsts for You; my flesh longs for You in a dry and thirsty land where there is no water. Soul* and *flesh* would include David's entire being. *Soul* refers to the inner man, and *flesh* refers to the outer man. Both David's soul and flesh were equal in their longing for God. The word *long* means that David was fainting for God. This was an actual physical craving for God that David was describing. Why were his soul and body longing for God? Because he was in *a dry and thirsty land where there is no water*. The *dry and thirsty land* would be literal, as Judah was known to be dry and arid. But it is also used figuratively here in this verse suggesting that when one's soul is deprived of God, then one is indeed in a weary land. What a perfect picture of our world during the Christmas rush! People are occupied with things and shopping to get more things! But not David, he is occupied with God, and getting more of Him. Have you ever felt like David? Have you ever felt like you were in a dry and weary land? I remember when we moved from California to Oklahoma many years ago. We searched and searched to find a solid church where the Word of God was taught. I remember one specific morning when I was on my walk I asked God if He had sent us to a desert, as it seemed that we were in a dry and thirsty land with no good churches! We can all praise God for the promise in Matthew 5:6 which says, "Blessed are those who hunger and thirst for righteousness, for they shall be filled." And according to Revelation 7:16 there will come a day when we will thirst no more, as our thirsting for God will be satisfied forever—we will be with Him forever! David goes on to describe this insatiable thirst he has for God in verse two.

Church Must Be a Priority

> So I have looked for You in the sanctuary,
> To see Your power and Your glory.
> (Psalm 63:2)

The sanctuary is a reference to the temple in Jerusalem. David is out in the wilderness and not able to get to the sanctuary in Jerusalem, and yet that is his soul's desire. Most of us are able to attend public worship, and yet some make the choice not to attend worship as regularly as we should. I have especially seen this during the busy rush of Christmas. We are celebrating Christ's birth and yet we bypass worship of Him when the saints collectively gather. Here we find our second key to keeping Christ in our Christmas, as well as in our hearts all year long. This will be the "C" in our acrostic: *Church must be a priority*. The temptation for many is to crowd out church for other well-meaning activities. But that was not David's desire, and it should not be ours. In spite of the fact that David could not go to the sanctuary, he still had a heart to worship and praise the Lord, and he expresses that in verses 3 and 4.

Have a Praise-Worthy Attitude

> Because Your lovingkindness is better than life,
> My lips shall praise You.
> (Psalm 63:3)

The thought of the Lord's loving-kindness caused David to want to praise God. And remember that it was in the wilderness where David was praising God for his loving-kindness. Most of us would have a hard time thinking about God's loving-kindness in the middle of the hot dessert. But not David. He had a praiseworthy attitude no matter where he was. And that is key number 3, and the "H" in our acrostic to keeping Christ first in our lives and during Christmas: *Have a praiseworthy attitude*. There's enough bah-humbug during this time of year. Why not determine to be different, and show the world that there really is a reason to be joyful? Let them see it by your attitude. Even if you feel like you are in the desert you can still find something to be thankful for. David goes on to pray:

> Thus I will bless You while I live;
> I will lift up my hands in Your name.
> (Psalm 63:4)

This would indicate lifting up the hands in prayer toward heaven. Psalm 28:2 says: "Hear the voice of my supplications when I cry to You, when I lift up my hands toward Your holy sanctuary." There is a lot we can do with our hands this time of year. David wanted to use his hands to praise God. We should all pray, "Take my hands and let them move, at the impulse of thy love."[29] Let your hands bake bread for a shut-in. Let your hands give financially to the needy. Let your hands give a hug to someone who is lonely or hurting. Let your hands write a letter of encouragement to someone who is without their loved one for the first Christmas. Lift up your hands in His name and for His name. David returns to the thought of his thirsty soul in verse 5 and says:

Make God Your Appetite—*Not* Your Appetite Your God

> My soul shall be satisfied as with marrow and fatness,
> And my mouth shall praise You with joyful lips.
> (Psalm 63:5)

David had already mentioned in verse 1 that his soul was thirsting for God, and now he speaks of his soul being satisfied. *Marrow* and *fatness* in the Hebrew are two words which signify fat, and would denote rich food. It is said of the Hebrews that they were more fond of fat than we are, (This is hard to believe I know!) as evidenced by the wording here. David probably wasn't surrounded by much food in the wilderness, and yet his appetite did not seem to occupy his thoughts, as his appetite was for God. David found that praising God was satisfying to his soul, just like the richest foods satisfied his body. He found His satisfaction in God, not in food. The fourth key to keeping Christ in your Christmas is the "M" in our acrostic: *Make God your appetite, not your appetite your god.* Statistics tell us that the average person gains around 10 pounds over the holidays. Then around

29 Words by Frances Havergal—1836-1869.

January 1st, we are all making New Year's resolutions to lose weight. Why not grab for the Word, before you grab for that sixth piece of fudge? Well, let's switch from the topic of food, to the topic of bed. David not only longs for God more than food, but even when he's on his bed, David thinks of God:

If You're Up Late, Meditate On Him

> When I remember You on my bed,
> I meditate on You in the night watches.
> (Psalm 63:6)

David's first thoughts in the morning are of God (*early*, as seen in verse one), and his last thoughts at night are of God. There is nothing more calming to the soul, than to fall into bed at night and reflect on the goodness of God during the day. David says *I meditate on You in the night watches.* David was fleeing from either Absalom or Saul, and the reference to night watches would be periods of the night when different people would keep watch around the camp. In those *night watches* David was meditating or pondering on God. David is not in his home where he would have the normal comforts of his own bed, as he is in the wilderness. More than likely, he is not sleeping too well, like most of us don't when we are not at home in our own bed and surroundings. But instead of taking a sleeping pill in order to sleep, David chooses to meditate on God. David reminds me of the godly man mentioned in Psalm 1, who meditates day and night. So, the fifth key to keeping Christ in your Christmas and at any time is the "I" in our acrostic: *If you're up late, meditate on Him*. Many things can keep us up at night around the holidays—things like shopping, writing Christmas cards, decorating, eating too much, which keeps us awake with indigestion. Instead of meditating on how many gifts you still have to buy, or how you are going to pay for them, or how you are ever going to get along with Aunt Sally this year, meditate on Him and commune with Him. David continues:

Ask God for Help

> Because You have been my help,
> Therefore in the shadow of Your wings I will rejoice.
> (Psalm 63:7)

Because of the fact that God has been David's help he has reason to rejoice. The word *help* actually means *helpers*. If you know anything about the life of David, then you know that God had been his helper many times. He helped him defeat Goliath; He helped him win numerous battles; He protected him from Saul, Nabal and Absalom; He spared his life after his adultery; as well as aiding David in many other times of his life. How many times has God been your helper? Do you ask Him for help? My sixth suggestion for keeping Christ in your heart and in your Christmas is the "A" in our acrostic: *Ask God for help*. God can and will be your helper all year long, but especially during the month of December, which is generally a busier time of year for most of us. It is easy to become frustrated, but why not ask Him for help? Lord what do you want me to buy for so and so? How much should I spend? How should we celebrate your birth? Who should we celebrate with? There are so many things that we could ask Him for, but we don't take the time to stop and ask Him for help and guidance. Perhaps we might save ourselves some undue anxiety if we would seek His face. Before we go on to verse 8, notice that because God has been David's helper he cannot remain silent. He can't help but to be joyful, in *the shadow of Your wings*, which is a symbol of God's protection. Contemplating being under the shadow of His wings, David says,

Stay Close to Him

> My soul follows close behind You;
> Your right hand upholds me.
> (Psalm 63:8)

The phrase follows *close* has the idea of being glued to. The idea is found in Ruth 1:14, where it says that Ruth clung to Naomi. Ruth and Orpah, Naomi's daughter-in-laws, had both lost their husbands. And it says that Orpah kissed her mother-in-law goodbye, but Ruth clung to her, so much that she said, "Entreat me not to leave you, or to turn back from following after you; for wherever you go, I will go; and wherever you lodge, I will lodge; your people shall be my people, and your God, my God. Where you die, I will die, and there will I be buried. The LORD do so to me, and more also, if anything but death parts you and me" (Ruth 1:16, 17). Ruth clung desperately to Naomi. That is the idea that David is expressing here, as he clings desperately to God. So, the seventh principle for keeping Christ in your Christmas is also the second "S" in our acrostic: *Stay close to Him*. Follow close behind Him. Stick to Him like glue. As you do He will be the focal-point of your Christmas. With the thought of David glued to God, he then says, *Your right hand upholds me*. The right hand is usually stronger than the left. The picture would be that of God holding David up with all His strength. This is interesting in light of the name *El*, which David uses for God. Both refer to strength. David now shifts his thoughts from God to his enemies in verses 9 and 10.

Take Time to Share Your Faith With the Lost

> But those who seek my life, to destroy it,
> Shall go into the lower parts of the earth.
> (Psalm 63:9)

David's soul (*life*) that is thirsting for God, that is satisfied with him, that is following Him, is the same soul (KJV) that is now being hunted by his enemies. David says those who are doing this will *go into the lower parts of the earth,* which is a reference to the grave. And indeed they did, as the next verse tells us how they died.

> They shall fall by the sword;
> They shall be a portion for jackals.
> (Psalm 63:10)

This is more than likely a reference to Absalom and Saul who were hunting David. We know that Absalom was killed with the sword by Joab, according to II Samuel 18, after his head was caught in a tree. And Saul was wounded in battle according to I Samuel 31. He asked his armor bearer to kill him but he would not do it, and so Saul killed himself with a sword. David says *they shall be a portion for jackals*. There was nothing more humiliating to a Hebrew than to have his body be prey for animals. Now I know that you are saying, "Now, how is she going to fit this one in to a principle for keeping Christ in Christmas?" I know that most of us don't feel hunted by our family members or friends, even though *some* of us might feel that way! For some of us, this time of year is difficult because of family members, and especially lost family members. So, number 8 and the "T" in our acrostic is: *Take time to share your faith with the lost*. I wonder how many opportunities we have missed to share the gospel during Christmas. This is perhaps the only time of year we see some of our relatives. Keep Christ in your Christmas by telling someone about Him. You could begin very simply by just explaining why we celebrate Christmas and Who it is that we celebrate. David was a man after God's own heart, and he paid a price for it. Some of us are not willing to pay a price for our stand for the Lord. But even the threat of David's enemies didn't keep him from being consumed with God. Look what he says as he ends his prayer in the wilderness in verse 11.

Rejoice in the Lord

> But the king shall rejoice in God;
> Everyone who swears by Him shall glory;
> But the mouth of those who speak lies shall be stopped.
> (Psalm 63:11)

It didn't matter to David what the circumstances were. He was determined to joy in the Lord. And not only does David rejoice in God, but *everyone who swears by Him shall glory.* Everyone that bears allegiance to God shall be honored. *Swear* means to pledge allegiance to God by an oath. This would be those who belong to the Lord and that are faithfully serving Him. These shall *glory*, these shall shine, and these shall give radiance. Those that have pledged an oath to God, those who have committed their lives to His Lordship, shall shine. So last on our list is the 9th and final letter, "R" on our acrostic: *Rejoice in the Lord.* We have an opportunity to shine this time of year—especially to the lost around us. Let the world see us rejoicing in the Lord, in the Christ-child, not just in all the festivities, but in Him, the Prince of Peace, the Lord of Lords, our Savior. David ends his prayer with *but the mouth of those who speak lies shall be stopped.* There were probably many lies going around Jerusalem about David during this time. But David comforts himself in the fact that one day the lies would be stopped. In fact, we know from God's Word that all liars will have their place in the lake of fire (Revelation 21:8).

So do you also feel like a stranger in a foreign land this time of year? Do you feel like you're in the wilderness? When you start feeling like you don't belong in this world during the holiday madness, or any time of year, why not turn to Psalm 63 and meditate on how you can keep Christ in your Christmas and in your heart all year long!

Summary

In this lesson we learned:

C—Church must be a priority.

H—Have a praise-worthy attitude.

R—Rejoice in the Lord.

I—If you're up late, meditate on Him.

S—Seek Him early.

T—Take time to share your faith with the lost.

M—Make God your appetite, not your appetite your god.

A—Ask God for help.

S—Stay close to Him.

I challenge you to not allow the tyranny of the urgent to crowd out your pursuit of a meaningful relationship with Christ!

Questions to Consider

Thirsting for God in the Wilderness

Psalm 63

1. (a) What attributes of God does David mention in Psalm 63? (b) What are David's responses to those attributes? (c) What are David's problems? (d) What are his solutions?

2. 1 Samuel 22 and 23 are *perhaps* the setting for Psalm 63. If that is so, what things are happening in David's life that would prompt him to write Psalm 63?

3. (a) According to Psalm 63, David sought the Lord early in the morning (verse 1) as well as late in the night (verse 6). Who else, according to Mark 1:35 and Luke 6:12, had the same need? (b) Do you think He was any busier than we are? Read the context of these verses (before and after) to find out just how busy He was. (c) What principles can you glean from these passages?

4. David says in Psalm 63:8 that God's right hand upholds him. (a) What else do you see from the following verses about God's right hand? Psalm 16:11; 17:7; 20:6; 48:10; 60:5; 78:54; 80:15; 89:13; 98:1; 110:1; 118:15,16. (b) Write a summary statement regarding what you have just learned about the right hand of God.

5. David was out in the wilderness, and yet his heart yearned to be in Jerusalem to worship (see vs. 2). When you are providentially hindered from worshipping the Lord, does your heart ache to be there, or is your worship performed out of duty? (Remember, it is God who sees the heart.) If your heart is not as David's, why not pause now and ask God to change your heart?

6. (a) Can you echo David's cries: "early will I seek You," and "I remember You on my bed and I meditate on You in the night watches?" (b) Is the Lord the first thing on your mind in the morning and the last thing in your thoughts before you go to sleep? (c) If not, what or who usually occupies your mind? (d) What can you do to change that?

7. In light of Psalm 63, what is your need? Please put it in the form of a prayer request.

Chapter 15

A Prayer of Agony

Luke 22:39-46

The following story is told of John Wesley, who was visiting a woman who was ill in bed. She had buried seven of her family members in 6 months, and had just heard that her beloved husband was cast away at sea. John Wesley asked her "Don't you fret at any of these things?" The woman answered with a loving smile on her pale checks. "Oh, no. How can I fret at anything which is the will of God? Let Him take all besides, He has given me Himself. I have learned to love and praise Him every moment." This is quite a statement, isn't it? Here was a woman who had learned a valuable truth, that is, the best way to know God's will is to say "I will" to God. Jim Elliott once said, "God always gives His best to those who leave the choice to Him." In this chapter, we are going to look at the prayer of our Lord when He was facing His most difficult moment: drinking the cup of the wrath of Almighty God. In Luke 22:39-46, we have a prayer from our Lord's lips which leaves us with a tremendous example of one who submitted His will to God's, even though He went through the worst agony known to man. He not only endured the cup of the wrath of Almighty God, but also the sin of the entire world was placed upon Him. And yet even though He knew He was facing such agony, He could pray, "not My will, but Yours be done." In the midst of a trial that most of us could not even imagine facing, our Lord, our perfect example, shows us how to go through suffering by submitting Himself to His Father's will. Let's read together these verses and learn from Christ's prayer of agony.

> Coming out, He went to the Mount of Olives, as He was accustomed, and His disciples also followed Him. 40When He came to the place, He said to them, "Pray that you may not enter into temptation." 41And He was withdrawn from them about a stone's throw, and He knelt down and prayed, 42saying, "Father, if it is Your will, take this cup away from Me; nevertheless not My will, but Yours, be done." 43Then an angel appeared to Him from heaven, strengthening Him. 44And being in agony, He prayed more earnestly. Then His sweat became like great drops of blood falling down to the ground. 45When He rose up from prayer, and had come to His disciples, He found them sleeping from sorrow. 46Then He said to them, "Why do you sleep? Rise and pray, lest you enter into temptation." (Luke 22:39-46)

Our Lord's prayer can be outlined in this way: *the place of His prayer* (vv. 39, 40); *the posture of His prayer* (v. 41); *the petition of His prayer* (v. 42); *the provision during His prayer* (vv. 43, 44); and *the pain after His prayer* (vv. 45, 46).

What has happened in the life of our Lord which has brought Him to this prayer of agony? We know through the prophet Isaiah (Isaiah 7:14) that a virgin would conceive and bear a son, His name would be called Jesus, and He would save His people from their sin. The time that Isaiah spoke of had finally come: the time for Messiah to save His people from their sins. But it would not be an easy death; it would be a bloody filthy death. It would be a death where God's wrath would be poured out upon His Son. It would be a death in which the sin of the entire world would be placed upon Him.

Mary's Son Jesus has grown into adulthood, and in the

gospel of Luke we have recorded for us His earthly ministry. But Christ has now completed that earthly ministry, and beginning in Luke chapter 22, verses 1, 2, we find a plot to kill our Lord. This betrayal would be at the hand of Judas, who is one of the twelve, as recorded in verses 3-6. We see the men prepare for the Passover in verses 7-13, and in verses 14-18 we see our Lord eating His last Passover with His beloved twelve disciples and instituting the Lord's Supper in verses 19, 20. He then announces His betrayal in verses 21-23, and speaks briefly with His disciples regarding their place in the future kingdom in verses 24-30. Warning Peter of his coming denial in verses 31-34, He then warns them all, in verses 35-38, of the conflict that will soon come. All of this brings us to verses 39 and 40, where we see the place where Christ will pray this prayer of agony—the place where He will pour out His heart to God.

The Place of His Prayer
Luke 22:39-40

> Coming out, He went to the Mount of Olives, as He was accustomed, and His disciples also followed Him. (Luke 22:39)

Coming to the Mount of Olives was evidently the custom of our Lord. We see this in Luke 21:37. The disciples must have known this was the place where Christ prayed, as Judas, who had left the group earlier, knew where to find Him, in verse 47. Luke records for us that on this night Christ's disciples followed Him. The word for *disciple* means a learner. The disciples were always following him. They had been following Him since the time He had called them, and they were still following Him. They were not about to leave Him now, at least not yet. In fact, notice what Jesus says about them in verses 28:

"But you are those who have continued with Me in My trials." May I say before you read on that a true disciple of Jesus Christ always follows Him, and follows Him to the end. So the place where He prayed was the Mount of Olives. Verse 40 says:

> When He came to the place, He said to them, "Pray that you may not enter into temptation." (Luke 22:40)

Although Luke does not name the place, both Matthew's and Mark's accounts of this prayer indicate it was Gethsemane. After arriving at Gethsemane, Jesus says to His disciples *pray that you may not enter into temptation*. The word *pray* means supplication. The word *enter* means to go in. The word *temptation* means a putting to the proof. In other words, Christ is saying, "ask that you not be made to enter into a test to see if you are real." The tense in the Greek here conveys the idea of "Keep on praying not to enter, not even once into temptation." It is real temptation here that Jesus is referring to, not just a trial. Jesus knew the power of temptation and the need of prayer. In fact, He knew it so well that He will repeat this warning to them again in verse 46. So what was Jesus saying here? What kind of temptation was He talking about? Jesus knew that all the disciples would forsake Him and flee. He knew that Satan desired to sift Peter as mentioned in verses 31, 32. Jesus knew that during times of persecution and suffering, some don't stand the test of the fire. Some flee, and He had this concern for the eleven. Matthew and Mark both record for us that this is exactly what happens! They all forsake Him and flee. (See Matthew 26:56 and Mark 14:50) Praying would protect them from unfaithfulness and encourage them to persevere, to not waver, and to not run during their crisis. Remember, Peter learned the reality of this as he warned his readers in 1 Peter 5:8, "Be sober, be vigilant; because your adversary the devil walks about like a roaring lion, seeking whom he may devour." This should cause us all to take seriously the admonition from our Lord in Matthew 6:13, where He directs us to pray, "and do not lead us into temptation, but deliver us from the evil one." Do you pray that prayer? We should. We're not any stronger than the disciples. They had been with Jesus, had even seen the miraculous things He had done and yet they still did not pass the temptation. They could not even stay awake with Him during His darkest hour. And so, after Jesus warns the disciples, He withdraws from them to be alone with His Father.

The Posture of His Prayer
Luke 22:41

> And He was withdrawn from them about a stone's throw, and He knelt down and prayed, (Luke 22:41)

For some reason Luke does not record for us that Christ left eight of His disciples by the entrance to Gethsemane, nor does Luke mention that Christ took Peter, James, and John further into the garden with Him. Matthew and Mark however, record that for us. (See Matthew 26 and Mark 14) The word *withdrawn* here means "torn away by an inward urgency." Ladies, have you ever been torn away to pray by an inward urgency? I am sure we can all testify to times that we have been compelled to pray and to pray earnestly. Luke records that Christ withdrew from them about *a stone's throw*. What exactly is a stone's throw? A *throw* is a measure of distance which is about 50-60 paces, or several yards. Some believe that the disciples could hear him praying because it was a short distance, and this is a possibility depending on how loud He prayed. But one thing we see for sure is that Christ had a need to be alone with the Father in this time. There were times when Christ prayed in the presence of others, just as you and I do, but this time was different. He needed to be alone with the Father, evidently because of the deep agony He was in.

And so Jesus, being alone with the Father, *knelt down and prayed.* Kneeling is the posture of His prayer and, may I add, an appropriate posture for this time in our Lord's life? Mark records that He "fell on the ground" and Matthew says He "fell on his face." All could be true at different moments. Falling on the ground would indicate a time of great earnestness. This was not the common posture of prayer for the Jew, as they would usually stand, but here we see our Lord's humility and His utter dependence upon His Father. The Greek word translated pray here is also used in verse 40 when Christ told the disciples to pray; it means supplication to God. In addition, the tense of this word gives the idea that Jesus was praying, and kept on praying. So what was Jesus supplicating for over and over again?

The Petition of His Prayer
Luke 22:42

> saying, "Father, if it is Your will, take this cup away from Me; nevertheless not My will, but Yours, be done." (Luke 22:42)

Notice that Jesus prays "*if* it is Your will." Christ realizes it may not be the Father's will to take away or carry the cup away. The word for *cup* means a lot or fate, as though Jesus is saying, "Lord, take away these bitter sufferings, these approaching trials." In the Old Testament the cup was linked to wrath and suffering, (see question #4 in Questions to Consider), and in the context here, wrath and suffering are hard to separate, as Christ is going to experience both. What would this cup include? What was our Lord getting ready to drink? The cup included not only the wrath of Almighty God, but immense sufferings as well. Betrayal by Judas, denial by Peter, and all of the disciples forsaking Him: the very men He had poured His life into would now turn their backs on Him. Even more, the cup would involve scourging, being stripped of His clothes, a crown of thorns thrust upon His head, laughter, scorn, mocking words like: "crucify Him, crucify Him," "you that destroyed the temple and built it in three days, save yourself and come down from the cross," "He saved others, but He cannot save himself," "Let Christ, the King of Israel descend now from the cross, that we may see and believe." Drinking the cup would include being despised, rejected, spat upon, struck on the head and face. He would be falsely accused, and blasphemed, not to mention the nails driven through His hands and feet, bones out of joint, His tongue cleaving to His jaws, His whole body being poured out like water. But, perhaps the most difficult part of the cup was the separation from His Father, which He had never known before, coupled with the pouring out of His Father's wrath upon Him. Isaiah 53:10 tells us that "It pleased the Lord to bruise Him." This drinking of the cup was for us, ladies. He was wounded for our transgressions. Christ in His prayer gives us a glimpse of His humanity—we cannot ignore that. We cannot deny His humanity as some try and do. We cannot get around the fact that Christ was requesting a change in the plan of God: "Is it necessary Father; is there another way, possibly?" He was God, yet man. If Jesus, being sinless, could pray that, then I don't think it is wrong for us in our agony to ask God for another path, all the while realizing that Christ's prayer did not end there, and neither should ours. Jesus doesn't end His prayer with those thoughts, but submits himself to the Father's will. His primary concern is to accomplish the will of the Father. So He ends His prayer with, *nevertheless, not My will, but Yours, be done.* Jesus knew that, ultimately, the best thing for Him was the will of His Father. He had already said that on numerous occasions. In John 4:34, Jesus said to His disciples, "My food is to do the *will of Him* who sent Me, and to finish His work" (emphasis mine). On another occasion He stated in John 5:30, "I can of Myself do nothing. As I hear, I judge; and My judgment is righteous, *because I do not seek My own will but the will of the Father* who sent Me" (emphasis mine). In John 6:38, He says "For I have come down from heaven, not to do My own will, *but the will of Him* who sent Me" (emphasis mine). The writer to the Hebrews is speaking of Christ when he says this in Hebrews 10:7-9: "Then I said, 'Behold, I have come—in the volume of the book it is written of Me—*to do Your will*, O God.' Previously saying, 'Sacrifice and offering, burnt offerings, and offerings for sin You did not desire, nor had pleasure in them' (which are offered according to the law), then He said, 'Behold, I have come *to do Your will*, O God.' He takes away the first that He may establish the second" (all emphases mine). Jesus came to earth to do the will of His Father, and His work was not complete until the cross was over, and He could say, "it is finished!" Then, and only then, was the work of the will of God done. We, too, should have a mindset determined to do the will of the Father. Would that we all had the attitude of the Psalmist who said, "I delight to do Your will, O my God" (Psalm 40:8). Do you? We must submit cheerfully to the will of God, confident in all of our trials that He is wise, He is merciful, and He is good. We don't know how many times Christ prayed in this way, but as I noted earlier, the Greek tense indicates that He did so over and over again. So much did he agonize and wrestle that an angel came and ministered to Him. And in verse 43 we see the wonderful provision for our Lord during His prayer.

The Provision During His Prayer
Luke 22:43-44

> Then an angel appeared to Him from heaven, strengthening Him. (Luke 22:43)

Luke records for us that an angel came from heaven and strengthened Him. The word for *strengthen* means invigorate. How the angel ministered to Him is not clear, but perhaps it was by relieving His emotions or strengthening Him physically to face the cross. As a man, he needed the assistance of an angel to support his body, worn down by fatigue and suffering. This is not the first time during His earthly ministry that Jesus was ministered to by angels. Remember that in Matthew, chapter 4, Satan came and tested Him in the wilderness. Verse 11 tells us that after the devil left Him angels came and ministered to Him. In that instance, Jesus was ministered to after He was tempted in the wilderness, but here in Luke, He receives comfort in the middle of the conflict. There are many instances in the Bible of angels ministering to God's people. Perhaps two of the more familiar ones to us are in 1 Kings 19, when Elijah was so depressed he wanted to die, and God sent an angel to minister to Him. The other example is in Acts 5, when the apostles were put into prison. It says there that an angel came and opened the doors of the prison and brought them out. Now I don't have time to get into the doctrine of angelology, and I am not saying that the next time you are in agony or trouble that God will send an angel, but isn't it a comfort to know that He will sustain and strengthen us in our trial by some method? If He chooses an angel, then so be it! As the writer to the Hebrews says, speaking of angels, "Are they not all ministering spirits sent forth to minister for those who will inherit salvation?" (Hebrews 1:14). And later on in 13:2 we read that

Paul says some of us have entertained angels unaware. Angels are meant to serve, and here we see one serving our Lord in His deepest trial. What a comfort it is, as we go through difficulties, to know that God will strengthen us too. Luke goes on in verse 44 to describe the depth of our Lord's agony.

> And being in agony, He prayed more earnestly. Then His sweat became like great drops of blood falling down to the ground. (Luke 22:44)

What does this mean that Jesus was in agony? It means that He was in anguish and He was in a struggle. The Greek here is an aorist participle which suggests a "growing intensity" in the struggle. Literally, it is "having become in an agony," having progressed from the first prayer in verse 41 where He began to pray, to an intense struggle of prayer and sorrow. The writer to the Hebrews describes our Lord's agony in Hebrews 5:7 like this: "who, in the days of His flesh, when He had offered up prayers and supplications, with vehement cries and tears to Him who was able to save Him from death, and was heard because of His godly fear." Also in Hebrews 12:3, 4 the writer says, "For consider Him who endured such hostility from sinners against Himself, lest you become weary and discouraged in your souls. You have not yet resisted to bloodshed, striving against sin." Ladies, this was an intense, agonizing time in the life of our Lord. So much so that, in Matthew's account of this prayer, Christ Himself said to the disciples, "My soul is exceedingly sorrowful, even unto death" (Matthew 26:38). And so, being in agony, He now prays more earnestly. The word *earnestly* means that He prayed more intensely. This Greek word is from the same word used in 1 Peter 1:22, where we are told to love each other fervently, from a pure heart. We are to love each other earnestly, more intensely. Christ's prayers were never cold or indifferent. And now, there was a greater intensity in them, which is expressed in His voice and gesture. “Prayer, though never out of season, is in a special manner seasonable when we are in an agony; and the stronger our agonies are the livelier and frequent our prayers should be.”[30]

The prayer is so intense now that Christ sweats, as Luke records. His sweat became like great drops of blood falling down to the ground. What is really happening here? Was this real blood? This phrase *great drops of blood* is only found here in the New Testament. Luke, the beloved physician who is writing this account, is the only one who mentions this phenomenon. As a doctor, he would naturally speak in medical terms. He wants us to know not only what is transpiring spiritually with our Lord, but also what is happening physically to Him. Some have described this as a thick clotted blood, a bloody sweat. It has been generally accepted that the sweat of the brow of Jesus had become bloody in appearance and in character, a symptom called hematidrosis (also called “hematohydrosis”) or “bloody sweat,” a condition may occur when a person is suffering under extreme stress. “Every pore was as it were a bleeding wound, and his blood stained all his raiment. This showed the travail of his soul. He was now abroad in the open air, in a cool season, upon the cold ground, far in the night, which, one would think, would not be enough to strike in a sweat; yet now he breaks out into a sweat, which speaks of the extremity of the agony he was in.”[31] And so He arises from His prayer, a prayer of deep agony, only to face more agony: sleeping disciples. The men He

30 Henry, Matthew-*Matthew Henry Commentary*-MacDonald Publishing Co.-Volume V- Page 815.

31 Henry, Matthew-*Matthew Henry Commentary*-MacDonald Publishing Co.-Volume V-page 815.

loved the most had fallen asleep on Him during His darkest hour. In verses 45 and 46 we see the pain after His prayer.

The Pain After His Prayer
Luke 22:45-46

> When He rose up from prayer, and had come to His disciples, He found them sleeping from sorrow. [46]Then He said to them, "Why do you sleep? Rise and pray, lest you enter into temptation." (Luke 22:45-46)

The Greek word for *prayer* in these verses changes from one meaning supplication to one meaning worship. Jesus must have ended his praying with worship of God. He started with earnest supplication and ended with a yielded heart to the Father's will in worship. He started with, "if it is possible, let it be another way," and He ended His prayer with, "whatever you want Father." The earnest praying had ended, and His will was resolved to the Father's will, and He worshipped. This is very similar to what we see King David doing in 2 Samuel 12:20 after fasting and praying for seven days for his sick child. We read that after the baby died, he arose and worshipped. He prayed for God to raise the child from sickness and when God did not, David worshipped. He yielded his wills to God's and he ended his seven days of praying with worship. In fact, notice what John 18:11 says: "Then Jesus said to Peter, 'Put your sword into the sheath. Shall I not drink the cup which My Father has given Me?'" In this account, Jesus had already been with the Father in the garden (see John 17), and this verse indicates that Jesus must have risen from His prayer with new zeal and determination to delightfully do the will of the Father. This was after He wrestled with God. He had just prayed, "Father, remove this cup," and now He says with firmness, "shall I not drink this cup?" What just happened in the garden? I think we can conclude that He submitted His will to the Father's will; He says yes to the cup, even though it will be bitter.

After He rises, Christ comes to the disciples and finds them sleeping for sorrow. What does it mean that they were sleeping for sorrow? They were sleeping because they were sad. I know many people who suffer with depression and sorrow, and many will sleep as an escape. More than likely, this is what the eleven were doing. Some of you may be thinking, "how could they be asleep? How come they are not with their Lord? How could they even think about leaving Him alone in His agony?" They are frail humans, just like we are. They had just had a full day of ministry, and were probably exhausted. And the words just spoken to them by the Lord in the upper room were pretty depressing. Words like "I am going to suffer;" "one of you will betray me;" "woe to that man by whom I am betrayed;" "Simon, Satan has desired to sift you like wheat;" "Sell your clothes and get a sword." These things weighed heavy on the disciples and, remember, they still had a dull understanding of what all this meant. I am in no way justifying their sleepiness and the fact that they should have died to themselves for the sake of our Lord during His agony. But I am afraid the disciples represent many of us. And finding them asleep, Jesus says to them: "Why do you sleep? Rise and pray, lest you enter into temptation." Jesus says, stand up and pray! Here again, the Greek word is *supplication.* It is the command mentioned again, that was already mentioned in verse 40: "Get up, and pray so that you will not be overcome and oppressed with these trials that are testing your faith." The word *temptation* here means to test their faith. Jesus is saying, "Get up and pray so that you do not deny me in a few hours. Get up and pray!" The disciples were still in danger, and Christ leaves them with a warning—in fact, His last words to the eleven that Luke records before the cross.

Summary

In this lesson we saw: *the place of His prayer* (vv. 39, 40): The Garden of Gethsemane at the Mount of Olives. *the posture of His prayer* (v. 41): Kneeling. *the petition of His prayer* (v. 42): "Lord, if it be possible, remove this cup from me, nevertheless, not my will, but yours." *the provision during His prayer* (vv. 43, 44): An angel came and ministered to Him. *the pain after His prayer* (vv. 45, 46): The disciples were asleep for sorrow. What do we learn from this prayer of agony? Four lessons can be learned from this prayer.

1. *The disciples failed in their test.* They failed to understand the seriousness of the moment. They failed to understand Jesus' warnings. They were insensitive to what was happening, and by not looking to God, they demonstrated a lack of faith. As a result, they failed to stay awake to pray. By their example, we learn the danger of being indifferent during difficulties, of becoming sluggish during trials and letting our guard down. But, how wonderful it is to know they didn't remain sluggish, as the book of Acts shows us an entirely different group of men. We see men who are praying often and praying fervently in the face of persecution of the early church. Are you failing today in your trial by becoming sluggish and apathetic in prayer?

2. *Jesus sets an example for us in what our attitude should be in prayer.* He is very open about His agony and struggle. He is honest with His innermost thoughts. He hides nothing. What difficulty are you going through today? Have you been open and honest with God about it?

3. *Christ teaches us how to respond to difficulties.* He teaches us to turn to God in prayer. He prepares Himself for the anguish of the cross by turning to God. In your current trial, have you prepared yourself by turning to God?

4. *Jesus submits Himself to the Father's will.* To be honest with our innermost thoughts is good, and yet we must also be willing to commit ourselves to do the Father's will. Are you committed to doing the Father's will, no matter the cost? We may ask God to remove the cup, but do we continue on with "not my will, but yours?" What if God had removed this cup of suffering from His Son? Christ would not have gone to the cross, and there would not have been the provision of salvation for mankind! We don't always see the big picture. May I encourage you, the next time God gives you a cup of suffering, to relinquish your will to His and drink it?

Questions to Consider

A Prayer of Agony

Luke 22:39-46

1. Read Luke 22:39-46. (a) Why do you think the Lord told the disciples to "pray that they would not enter into temptation?" (b) Who ministered to our Lord in verse 43? (c) How does this encourage you when going through agonizing times? (See Hebrews 1:14)

2. (a) What is the context of this prayer? (In other words, what comes before it and after it?) (b) How does the context help you to better understand our Lord's prayer in vs. 42?

3. Matthew 26:36-46 and Mark 14:32-42 also describe Christ's prayer in the garden. Read these accounts and note the similarities, as well as the differences, between these accounts and Luke's account.

4. (a) How is the "cup" described in the following verses? Isaiah 51:17, 22; Jeremiah 25:15-17, 27-29; Ezekiel 23:31-34, and Habakkuk 2:16. (b) How do these verses help you to understand what Christ prays in Luke 22:42?

5. In verse 42, Jesus prays for the Father's will. (a) Does this condition apply to our praying? See 1 John 5:14, 15. (b) What are some other conditions for God to answer our prayers? See Jeremiah 29:12, 13; Mt. 7:7-11; Mt. 21:22; John 14:13; John 15:7; James 1:5, 6; James 4:3; James 5:16; 1 John 3:22. (c) Which of these conditions do you think most often hinders God answering your prayers? (d) What will you do about it?

6. (a) Who else relinquished her will to God's? See Luke 1:34-38. (b) What might have happened if Jesus and Mary had refused to do the will of God? (c) What will happen if you refuse to do the will of God? (Answer this question from the Scriptures)

7. When you are going through a trial, do you react like the disciples (verse 45) or like the Lord (verses 42, 44)?

8. (a)What "cup" (or suffering) has God called you to today? (b) Can you honestly pray "not my will, but Yours be done?" (c) What keeps you from praying that?

9. (a) Write a prayer of thanksgiving to Jesus for His willingness to go to the cross. (b) Also, write a request for how you might make necessary changes after pondering question 5.

Chapter 16

A Prayer of Vengeance

Psalm 109

You may be looking at the title of this chapter and thinking, "What in the world is this prayer about?" Perhaps you might be confused in your thinking and wondering, "Didn't Jesus say in the Sermon on the Mount 'love your enemies, bless those who curse you, do good to those that hate you, and pray for those who despitefully use you and persecute you'?" (Matthew 5:44). Maybe you are sensing a contradiction already in your heart. Or maybe you are relieved, thinking, "This is a good prayer I can pray for my friend who has hurt me. I'll get back at her by praying this prayer." Whatever your first thoughts were, I hope any difficulties you may have will be cleared up after we look at this prayer. But before we do that, let's take a look at Deuteronomy 19:15-21, which will aid in clearing up any confusion that you may have.

> "One witness shall not rise against a man concerning any iniquity or any sin that he commits; by the mouth of two or three witnesses the matter shall be established. If a false witness rises against any man to testify against him of wrongdoing, then both men in the controversy shall stand before the LORD, before the priests and the judges who serve in those days. And the judges shall make careful inquiry, and indeed, if the witness is a false witness, who has testified falsely against his brother, then you shall do to him as he thought to have done to

> his brother; so you shall put away the evil from among you. And those who remain shall hear and fear, and hereafter they shall not again commit such evil among you. Your eye shall not pity; but life shall be for life, eye for eye, tooth for tooth, hand for hand, foot for foot." (Deuteronomy 19:15-21).

According to the Mosaic law, those who were unjustly accused had the advantage. (Not so in our day!) Justice was to be done, as previously mentioned in verse 21. Whatever crime had been committed toward an individual was to be done back in return! Once we understand what the punishment was under the Mosaic Law for a false witness, then we can understand David's cry for personal vengeance in Psalm 109. David merely wants justice which is in agreement with his right according to the Mosaic Law. He is crying out for the Judge of all the earth to render to David's enemies, as well as God's enemies, only what is due them. Psalm 109 is one of what we call the Imprecatory Psalms, of which there are 8: Psalm 35, 52, 55, 58, 59, 79, 109, and 137. An imprecatory psalm is one in which the writer prays that God may afflict his enemies and punish him. We must realize that the feelings of the Psalmists were not necessarily their own feelings of vengeance, but instead they saw their enemies as God's enemies, and they were zealous for God's sake. The words they wrote were not feelings of personal vindictiveness, but their prayers were for God to be vindicated and to judge others because of His great name's sake. The New Testament saint obviously has a different prayer life, and that is why Jesus rebuked James and John for wanting to call fire down from heaven Luke 9:51-56. As New Testament believers, we have a fuller understanding of the Word of God. We know that God in the end will judge each one of us, and wicked men will receive what is due them. One man says "As long as men were in the Old Testament state of revelation, and the example of the blessed Saviour had not yet been given and His blessed words were not yet known, it would be unreasonable to expect these saints to rise to levels that do justice to New Testament thinking."

You might be wondering, "Is it wrong then to pray these prayers?" It is not necessarily wrong for us to pray for God to take vengeance or to plead our cause, or to plead for God's justice to be done. But you and I must be careful that our motives are truly pure when we pray. I confess that several years ago, I prayed Psalm 109 when my husband and I were deeply hurt. It was an extremely hurtful and confusing time for me. But my motives were not purely for God's sake, even though some of them were. Many of my motives were because of my personal hurts. I wanted those who had hurt me to pay for what they had done. I also wanted my acquaintances to know we were innocent. Yet, my godly husband kept reminding me, "Susan, God will vindicate us." He was right, as that is the mind of Christ. Scripture says in Romans 12:19-21, "Beloved, do not avenge yourselves, but rather give place to wrath; for it is written, 'Vengeance is Mine, I will repay,' says the Lord. Therefore if your enemy is hungry, feed him; if he is thirsty, give him a drink; for in so doing you will heap coals of fire on his head. Do not be overcome by evil, but overcome evil with good." So, with God's help, that's what I began to do, and it truly was profitable, even though it was also very difficult.

We cannot be sure what historic occasion was behind this prayer in Psalm 109. We do know that David was being pursued unjustly by his enemies. This psalm may have been written as a result of the injustices of Saul, Doeg, Ahithopel, Shimei, Absalom, or others, or all the above. As you know, David did have a lot of enemies. This psalm is also

Messianic in type as it depicts Christ's sufferings as well.

I have divided this Psalm into four sections: *David's complaints regarding his enemies* (vv. 1-5); *David's cry for vengeance against his enemies* (vv. 6-15); *David's cause for hating his enemies* (vv. 16-20); *David's confidence in the Lord in spite of his enemies* (vv. 21-31).

Let's look first at David's complaints concerning his enemies in verses 1 through 5.

David's Complaints Regarding His Enemies
Psalm 109:1-5

Do not keep silent,
O God of my praise!
2For the mouth of the wicked and the mouth of the deceitful
Have opened against me;
They have spoken against me with a lying tongue.
3They have also surrounded me with words of hatred,
And fought against me without a cause.
4In return for my love they are my accusers,
But I give myself to prayer.
5Thus they have rewarded me evil for good,
And hatred for my love.
(Psalm 109:1-5)

The first thing that David asks God to do is *do not keep silent*. David doesn't understand why God isn't doing something about the situation. Isn't that the way it is for us when we are unjustly attacked? Do something Lord, and do it now! Vindicate me now, oh Lord! Yet, even amidst all the vicious, unjust attacks by his enemies, David still calls God, the *God of my praise.* David trusts in a Sovereign God who is worthy of all his praise. Then David lists four complaints he has about his enemies. 1. *They have spoken against me with a lying tongue.* They had accused David of things which were not true. This happened in the case of Saul, who accused David of trying to take his life. Yet, this was untrue, as David had tried to save Saul's life. 2. *They have also surrounded me with words of hatred.* David felt surrounded with hatred from his enemies: Shimei, Saul, Ahithopel, Absalom, and it was coming from all directions. 3. *They have fought against me without a cause.* Saul, we know, was guilty of this many times. In 1 Samuel 26:18, David says to Saul: "what have I done, or what evil is in my hand?" 4. *They have rewarded me evil for good.* Saul was guilty of this when he tried to kill David after David played his harp to aid in removing an evil spirit from Saul. How would you like to have a javelin thrown at you for doing good to someone? What does David do in response? David says, *But,* in contrast to his enemies who are engaging in slander and vengeful attacks, *I give myself to prayer.* This literally means "but I am wholly prayer;" I do nothing during their attacks on me but pray for them. That is not an easy thing to do when you are repaid evil for good, is it? Our temptation might be to take vengeance, and to let all our friends know just how we have been wronged. But the righteous response is to turn to the Lord. We have an account in 1 Samuel 30, when the Amalekites had invaded Ziklag and had taken David's wives and sons and daughters captive, where we see David weeping along with the people who were with him, (their families being taken also). In fact, it says they wept until they had no more power to weep. The people wanted to stone David, and it says that he was distressed. It was a stressful time for David. So, what did he do? The text tells us that David encouraged Himself in the Lord his God! That's what David is saying here as well. "I will seek the Lord in all my troubles." There was a time when I was going through a lot of personal attacks, and my soul was very distraught, and this verse was the one the Lord brought to my mind often. "Susan, encourage yourself in the Lord." It was a wonderful reminder and a wonderful refreshment to wholly give myself to prayer and to trust in God.

David's Cry for Vengeance Against His Enemies
Psalm 109:6-15

David now turns from his complaints concerning his enemies, to crying out for vengeance against his enemies in verses 6 through 15. Now these are pretty strong prayers against his enemies—eighteen of them to be exact.

> Set a wicked man over him,
> And let an accuser stand at his right hand.
> When he is judged, let him be found guilty,
> And let his prayer become sin.
> Let his days be few,
> And let another take his office.
> Let his children be fatherless,
> And his wife a widow.
> Let his children continually be vagabonds, and beg;
> Let them seek their bread also from their desolate places.
> Let the creditor seize all that he has,
> And let strangers plunder his labor.
> Let there be none to extend mercy to him,
> Nor let there be any to favor his fatherless children.
> Let his posterity be cut off,
> And in the generation following let their name be blotted out.
> Let the iniquity of his fathers be remembered before the LORD,
> And let not the sin of his mother be blotted out.

> Let them be continually before the LORD,
> That He may cut off the memory of them from the earth;
> (Psalm 109:6-15)

Now you might have read the above passage and said, "Wow, these are some pretty wicked prayers!" There really are not, in light of the Mosaic Law. It was not wrong for David to desire that those who were his enemies—and God's enemies—be punished for their sin. These were not malicious prayers, but rather a call for justice according to the Mosaic Law. The first cry against his enemies is 1. *Set a wicked man over him.* In other words, let a wicked man judge him. When taken to the court of law, let it be a wicked man that will punish him for what he has done. 2. *Let an accuser stand at his right hand.* In a court of justice the accuser stood at the accused person's right hand. Satan is rendered in the Hebrew *adversary.* So David is saying, may an adversary, an accuser, betray him. May some-one accuse him, just as he had falsely accused David. 3. *When he is judged, let him be found guilty.* That is, when he goes on trial, may he be found guilty. We should pray for justice to be done to the wicked. In our land, it certainly is the wicked who go unpunished. 4. *Let his prayer become sin.* Here we have the idea that is found in Proverb 28:9, "One who turns away his ear from hearing the law, even his prayer is an abomination." God does not hear the prayers of the wicked. 5. *Let his days be few.* Psalm 55:23 says "Bloody and deceitful men shall not live out half their days." Proverb 10:27 says "The fear of the Lord prolongs days, but the years of the wicked shall be shortened." This prayer is also not considered a prayer of unrighteousness. Why would one desire that a murderer or traitor be allowed to live? According to the Old Testament law, it was a life for a life and a tooth for a tooth (Exodus 21:24). 6. *Let another take his office*. Again, this is not an evil prayer. Why would a God-fearing person desire an ungodly person in a place of leadership? All we have to do is to look at Old Testament History to see that ungodly kings lead the nation in ungodliness. And righteous kings got rid of, or tried to get rid of, ungodliness. This is an interesting prayer in light of the Psalm being Messianic in type as well. Remember in Acts 1:20, after Judas went out and hung himself, that is exactly what the apostles did; they appointed another to take his office as one of the 12 and the lot fell on Matthias. 7. *Let his children be fatherless*. When someone commits a crime, and has to pay for it through death or prison, that is what happens—his children become fatherless. 8. *And his wife a widow*. This is the same as above. There is no malice intended against his wife, but simply the just result of his sin. 9. *Let his children continually be vagabonds, and beg*. This means that their children would be found seeking their bread out of desolate places, which would describe the wild roots or fruits which would barely keep them alive. Again, could be a result of children who have their sole provider, their father, taken from them. 10. *Let the creditor seize all that he has*. This would be the usurer, the one from whom he had borrowed money. Let him lay a snare, or trap, to get all that he has, which is exactly what extortionists did. They say it would be better to be a fly in the web of a spider than to fall into the hands of an extortionist. That would not be difficult, if indeed death or prison did remove the man. Then the usurer could definitely prey on a defenseless widow. 11. *Let strangers plunder his labor*. This would entail plundering his land, stealing his crops, and leaving him destitute. 12. *Let there be none to extend mercy to him*. Let there be no one to draw out kindness to him. David is asking that his neighbors would remain passive toward his enemy, and not lend any mercy or help. 13. *Nor let there be any to favor his fatherless children.* Let not one show mercy to them either. This would be a natural result, as many times children suffer for the sins of their parents. We see this is Psalm 51, after David committed adultery with Bathsheba. There were consequences of his sin: the rape of Tamar by his son Amnon and the murder of Amnon by David's other son, Absolam. Children were not punished for the sins of their parents, but would feel the impact of their parents' sins. We would do well as moms to keep that in mind. Numbers 14:18 says, "The LORD is longsuffering and abundant in mercy, forgiving iniquity and transgression; but He by no means clears the guilty, visiting the iniquity of the fathers on the children to the third and fourth generation." 14. *Let his posterity be cut off.* To have a family name was regarded as one of the greatest and most desirable blessings for the Jew. So this would be a disgrace. If he has children let them die without offspring. And not only the current generation, but, 15. *The generation following, let their name be blotted out.* Let them be erased from the master roll. If you've read Chronicles, you've read those master roles. So and so begot so and so and so and so. Proverbs 10:7 states, "The memory of the righteous is blessed, but the name of the wicked will rot." 16. *Let the iniquity of his fathers be remembered before the LORD.* 17. *Let not the sin of his mother be blotted out*, (verses 14, 16 and 17 really go together). In other words, let the sins of his parents be visited on him. Spurgeon says "Children do procure punishment upon their parent's sins, and are often themselves the means of such punishment. A bad son brings to mind his father's bad points of character, and likewise a daughter. They say he takes after his father, or there is little wonder, when you consider what her mother was."[32] 18. *Let them be*

32 Spurgeon, Charles- *The Treasury of David*—Hendrickson Publishers- page 441.

continually before the Lord. Let their sins never pass from God's mind, (so that God may cut them off from the earth).

Now those are 18 heavy prayers—whew! Did God answer any of these prayers against his enemies? It certainly appears that He did. Absalom, we know, died young, as his hair got caught in a tree and Joab killed him. His sons died early in life as well. Ahithophel, we know committed suicide. David's son, Solomon, had Shimei executed. Saul, we know, was killed in battle along with his son Jonathan, David's beloved friend and companion. Also, Saul's other two sons, Abinadab and Melchishua were killed. Now, you might be asking, "Why in the world would David pray such prayers for his enemies? What is his reason for such hatred?" Well, let's see, as we consider David's cause for hating his enemies, in verses 16-20. There are 5 reasons listed here.

David's Cause for Hating His Enemies
Psalm 109:16-20

> Because he did not remember to show mercy,
> But persecuted the poor and needy man,
> That he might even slay the broken in heart.
> 17 As he loved cursing, so let it come to him;
> As he did not delight in blessing, so let it be far from him.
> 18 As he clothed himself with cursing as with his garment,
> So let it enter his body like water,
> And like oil into his bones.
> 19 Let it be to him like the garment which covers him,
> And for a belt with which he girds himself continually.
> 20 Let this be the LORD'S reward to my accusers,
> And to those who speak evil against my person.
> (Psalm 109:16-20)

1. *Because he did not remember to show mercy*. None of David's enemies showed mercy to him—Saul, Absolam, Ahitophel, etc. 2. They *persecuted the poor and the needy*. Over and over they persecuted him. 3. *That he might even slay the broken in heart*. Many times Saul pursued David with the intent to kill him. Don't you think this broke David's heart? 4. *He clothed himself with cursin*g. This seems to be a reference to Shimei. In 2 Samuel 16:7 we read the following: "Also Shimei said thus when he cursed: 'Come out! Come out! You bloodthirsty man, you rogue!'" David wants Shemei's cursing to come back to him, and for him to be clothed with cursing as a garment. Let it cling to him like a garment, he says in verse 19. David goes on to say: and *like oil into his bones*. Oil is said to penetrate not only into the tissues, but also into his very bones and marrow. And even like a girdle David says in verse 19. The girdle or the waistcloth was even more inseparable from the wearer than his cloak or wrap. Let it be constantly with him like a girdle. Let this be the reward of my adversaries. Remember the Mosaic Law in Deuteronomy 19? Do unto them as they thought to do to you. 5. They *speak evil against my person*. These are all righteous reasons for David to be angry with his enemies. When we consider what David's enemies did to him, it helps us to understand the imprecatory psalms. David is not just praying these prayers because he has gotten his feelings hurt or because someone forgot his birthday or didn't look at him the right way, or was insensitive to his needs. These reasons would describe perhaps why some of us would pray these kinds of prayers. But these were righteous causes which caused David to pray this way. David was grieved for the Lord's sake. Psalm 139: 21, 22 says, "Do I not hate them, O LORD, who hate You? And do I not loathe those who rise up against You? I hate them with perfect hatred;

I count them my enemies." I am glad David does not leave us with these prayers, but instead, in verses 21-31, he leaves us with his confidence in the Lord in spite of his enemies.

David's Confidence in the Lord in Spite of His Enemies Psalm 109:21-31

But You, O GOD the Lord,
Deal with me for Your name's sake;
Because Your mercy is good, deliver me.
22For I am poor and needy,
And my heart is wounded within me.
23I am gone like a shadow when it lengthens;
I am shaken off like a locust.
24My knees are weak through fasting,
And my flesh is feeble from lack of fatness.
25I also have become a reproach to them;
When they look at me, they shake their heads.
26Help me, O LORD my God!
Oh, save me according to Your mercy,
27That they may know that this is Your hand—
That You, LORD, have done it!
28Let them curse, but You bless;
When they arise, let them be ashamed,
But let Your servant rejoice.
29Let my accusers be clothed with shame,
And let them cover themselves with their own disgrace as with a mantle.
30I will greatly praise the LORD with my mouth;
Yes, I will praise Him among the multitude.
31For He shall stand at the right hand of the poor,
To save him from those who condemn him.
(Psalm 109:21-31)

David's confidence in the Lord, even though his enemies are wicked, is mainly due to the fact that David knows the

Lord is merciful, as he mentions in verse 21 and verse 26. In contrast to his enemies who showed no mercy, God was merciful. From verse 21 we can see the motives for David's prayers are for the Lord's sake. Are those your motives in praying?

David ends his prayer with confidence in the Lord and he manifests it by praising the Lord in verse 30. Even though his enemies have treated him wickedly, yet he will greatly praise the Lord with his mouth and with the multitude (in the congregation). This would probably be in the sanctuary. The words *greatly praised* are not used anywhere else in the Psalms. They are indicative of a strong feeling of thankfulness. David must have needed to express great praise because of his great suffering from his enemies. There is a lesson for us here: The more difficult the trial, the more we should praise.

David ends his prayer in verse 31 with confidence that God would indeed deliver him. David couldn't help himself but God could. He could save David. It is interesting that David talks about God standing at the right hand of the poor and, in verse 6, he asks for an adversary to stand at the right hand of the enemy. Just as David wished the accuser would stand at the right hand of his enemies, accusing them, David also knew that God would be at his right hand defending him justly. God will always come to the assistance of the poor and needy. Psalm 12:5 states: "For the oppression of the poor, for the sighing of the needy, now I will arise," says the LORD; "I will set him in the safety for which he yearns." Or consider Psalm 113:7, "He raises the poor out of the dust, and lifts the needy out of the ash heap." So David ends his prayer with a note of confidence in His God in spite of his enemies.

Are you feeling a little persecuted this day? Has someone been speaking lies or words of hatred about you? Is there anyone that is being contentious with you without cause? Has anyone paid you back with evil for the good you did to them? Has anyone been unmerciful toward you lately? If you answered yes to any of these questions, you can take comfort in the fact that others have gone through the same struggles. David did; our Savior did. And Christ has promised a way of escape. What is that escape? According to Psalm 109, it is to give yourself wholly to prayer and to greatly praise the Lord. In fact, there are two words for praise in verse 30. The second one is *halal*; it has the idea of radiance, praising, glorifying. The first one, however, is the Hebrew word *yadah*, which has more of the idea of praise which leads to the giving of thanks. David could end on that note of praising God and even thanking Him in the midst of such awful circumstances. He could pray, and he could do that with thanksgiving. Let us encourage our hearts with the words Paul left to the church at Philippi in Philippians 4:6,7: "Do not fret or have any anxiety about anything, but in every circumstance and in everything by prayer and petition, with thanksgiving continue to make your wants known to God. And God's peace which transcends all understanding shall garrison and mount guard over your hearts and minds in Christ Jesus." (Amplified Version)

Questions to Consider

A Prayer of Vengeance

Psalm 109

1. Read Psalm 109. (a) How does David's cry for vengeance toward his enemies compare with what the Lord said on the Sermon on the Mount in Matthew 5:38-45? (b) How do you reconcile this?

2. (a) What was the punishment for a false witness according to the Mosaic Law in Deuteronomy 19:15-21? (b) How does this help you to understand David's prayers for his enemies in Psalm 109?

3. Read 2 Kings 1. (a) What did Elijah desire for his enemies? (b) Did it happen? (c) How does this reconcile with what Jesus said in Luke 9:51-56?

4. David says in Psalm 109:2, 3 that his enemies spoke wickedly, spoke lies, and spoke words of hatred about him. (a) In the following passages, who is speaking against David and what are they saying? 1 Samuel 22:6-16; 2 Samuel 15:1-12; and 2 Samuel 16:8-14. (b) How do you think this would affect David? (c) How would it affect you?

5. (a) Who in the following verses sought to "persecute the poor and needy man, that he might even slay the broken in heart" (Psalm 109:16)? 1 Samuel 18:10,11; 1 Samuel 19:1, 10, 11; 20:31; 23:8, 14, 25; 24:2; 2 Samuel 17:1,2. (b) What was David's response to these things according to 1 Samuel 26:1-20? (c) What does this teach you about David, the man after God's own heart? (d) What can you learn for your own life when you are persecuted?

6. (a) When you are being attacked by your enemies, what is usually your first response? (b) Is it godly? (c) What *should* be our response according to 1 Peter 2:21-23? (d) What are some other Biblical responses you could cling to when going through persecution?

7. In looking over Psalm 109, would you say that these are prayers we should pray for our enemies? Why or why not?

8. Write a prayer request for someone whom you sense is your enemy. (Try to focus on a prayer request that is not vengeful, but one that overcomes evil with good.)

Chapter 17

A Prayer of Praise

Psalm 145

We have come to the final chapter and the final lesson of *With the Master On Our Knees*. It is my prayer that each of you are now enjoying a deeper and more meaningful prayer life. In our study we have looked at Jehoshaphat's prayer when facing what seemed to be the impossible; Solomon's prayer for wisdom; the Lord's prayer before the cross; a prayer of repentance; a prayer of vengeance; prayers when depressed; prayers in the wilderness; prayer from a broken heart; the Lord's model of prayer; prayers of those who fasted; prayers of those with sick children; a prayer from a young man; the prayer of the first martyr; and the prayer of the 10 lepers. But, as we come to our final study of *With the Master On Our Knees*, I thought it would be appropriate for us to end with a prayer of praise, a prayer which focuses on God and God alone. Psalm 145 is a simple, yet profound prayer of praise for who God is. Let's look at this prayer.

> I will extol You, my God, O King;
> And I will bless Your name forever and ever.
> [2]Every day I will bless You,
> And I will praise Your name forever and ever.
> [3]Great is the LORD, and greatly to be praised;
> And His greatness is unsearchable.
> [4]One generation shall praise Your works to another,
> And shall declare Your mighty acts.

5I will meditate on the glorious splendor of Your majesty,
And on Your wondrous works.
6Men shall speak of the might of Your awesome acts,
And I will declare Your greatness.
7They shall utter the memory of Your great goodness,
And shall sing of Your righteousness.
8The LORD is gracious and full of compassion,
Slow to anger and great in mercy.
9The LORD is good to all,
And His tender mercies are over all His works.
10All Your works shall praise You, O LORD,
And Your saints shall bless You.
11They shall speak of the glory of Your kingdom,
And talk of Your power,
12To make known to the sons of men His mighty acts,
And the glorious majesty of His kingdom.
13Your kingdom is an everlasting kingdom,
And Your dominion endures throughout all generations
14The LORD upholds all who fall,
And raises up all who are bowed down.
15The eyes of all look expectantly to You,
And You give them their food in due season.
16You open Your hand
And satisfy the desire of every living thing.
17The LORD is righteous in all His ways
Gracious in all His works.
18The LORD is near to all who call upon Him,
To all who call upon Him in truth.
19He will fulfill the desire of those who fear Him;
He also will hear their cry and save them.
20The LORD preserves all who love Him,
But all the wicked He will destroy.
21My mouth shall speak the praise of the LORD,
And all flesh shall bless His holy name
Forever and ever.
(Psalm 145:1-22)

This prayer was written by David. The historic occasion is unknown, but it was probably written toward the end of David's life. David seems to be reflecting on the wonderful attributes of His God throughout his lifetime, and cannot help but praise His God. Psalm 145 is called a psalm of praise, and it is the only psalm with this inscription. The word *praise* is mentioned five times in this psalm. It is a psalm which has a tone of devoted worship, and so it is certainly a great ending to the Davidic psalms. This Psalm is also alphabetical, in that each verse begins with a letter of the Hebrew alphabet. There are 22 letters in the Hebrew alphabet, and the only letter which is omitted in this psalm is Nun—n. It is possible that this letter was left out on purpose, so that the psalm could neatly be divided into three stanzas, with seven verses in each stanza. This psalm really does not lend itself to divisions—I know some of you like that—but even Spurgeon says, "This Psalm does not have any marked divisions, but is one and indivisible."[33]

The Hebrews said that whoever would utter this Psalm thrice a day (3 times a day for you Non-King Jamers) would be declared happy. In the old Jewish synagogue, this psalm was assigned to be used twice in the morning service and once in the evening service. So let's begin with our study of Psalm 145 and see why we might do well to utter this Psalm 3 times a day! David begins his prayer of praise by saying:

> I will extol You, my God, O King;
> And I will bless Your name forever and ever.
> (Psalm 145:1)

Even though David was *King* of Israel, he recognized

33 Charles Spurgeon. *The Treasury of David*—Hendrickson Publishers-Volume III. page 375.

that God was the only true *King*. He is the King of Kings! David says that he will *extol You,* which means I will lift You up; I will lift up your name so that it can be heard. Now this entire psalm would be in vain if it were not for a two letter word that David uses—*my*. Apart from a personal relationship with God, David could not praise Him. God was *his* God, and *his* King. This is a personal relationship that David recognized was for all eternity, as evidenced by his next words, *I will bless Your name forever and ever*. David didn't wonder and doubt about the covenant he had made with his God. He would praise Him forever and ever, and throughout eternity. Can you echo with King David: *I will bless your name forever*? Not only will David bless God forever in eternity, but he will bless him every day as seen in verse 2.

> Every day I will bless You,
> And I will praise Your name forever and ever.
> (Psalm 145:2)

This verse is very similar to a verse in another Davidic psalm. In Psalm 34:1 David says, "I will bless the LORD at all times; his praise shall continually be in my mouth." Psalm 34 was not written at a great time in David's life, but rather when he was fleeing Saul, and yet he could say he would bless the Lord continually. The 21st century Christian's psalm of praise I am afraid would sound something like this: "On Sunday morning will I bless thee." But David says *every day* will I bless You. I will bless You when you take my newborn son; I will bless You when my son Absalom is killed; I will bless You when Shimei casts curses at me; I will bless You when Ahithophel, my dearest friend, betrays me. I will bless you everyday. As Job said to his wife after he had had just a *few* bad days, "Shall we indeed accept good from God, and shall we not accept adversity?" (Job 2:10). Shall we not bless the Lord everyday? Let me stop and ask a question. Do we receive blessings from God every day? Then shouldn't we bless Him everyday? The answer is yes, we should. What kind of a God would be worthy of that kind of praise even when things are going so well? A *great* God, as verse 3 says—that's what kind of God!

> Great is the LORD, and greatly to be praised;
> And His greatness is unsearchable.
> (Psalm 145:3)

David says that God is so great that His greatness is unsearchable. This literally reads, and *of His greatness there is no search*. I love that! Romans 11:33, 34 says, "Oh, the depth of the riches both of the wisdom and knowledge of God! How *unsearchable* are His judgments and His ways past finding out! For who has known the mind of the Lord? Or who has become His counselor?" (emphasis mine). Ephesians 3:8 talks about the unsearchable riches of Christ. Man cannot even begin to search God's greatness. We can search a lot of things, and many of us do on the internet, but not even the internet can give us the facts on the unsearchable greatness of God! No one has plumbed its depths. Because of God's unsearchable greatness, David desires to pass those truths on to his children, as seen in verse 4.

> One generation shall praise Your works to another,
> And shall declare Your mighty acts.
> (Psalm 145:4)

This verse demonstrates the principle of Scripture whereby we are commanded to pass things down to our children. Do your children and grandchildren hear you praising the Lord for all He has done? What legacies are you passing down to your children? What kind of mom will they remember? Will they remember a mother who is always complaining, arguing, and unhappy, or one who is full of joy and thanksgiving, giving praise to God for all He has done? David desires that he pass down to the next generation the praises of God's wonderful works and mighty acts. All this contemplation of God's great and mighty works causes David to shout out with words of praise—he cannot keep silent.

> I will meditate on the glorious splendor of Your majesty,
> And on Your wondrous works.
> (Psalm 145:5)

David says he will meditate on God's majesty and the wondrous works of God. These would be those works that are distinguished, extraordinary, and miraculous. These are the works that only God can perform. Do we choose to meditate on God's attributes or do we meditate on things that distract from the glorious majesty and works of our God? David is not the only one who will praise God; others will join David in this praise as stated in verse 6.

> Men shall speak of the might of Your awesome acts,
> And I will declare Your greatness.
>
> (Psalm 145:6)

What does David mean by *awesome acts*? What are these? In all probability, these included the plagues in Egypt; the overthrowing of Pharaoh and his host in the Red Sea; the earth swallowing up the Sons of Korah. Why should David speak of these things? It would remind him of the awesome power of God in the performing of these acts. This would cause David to declare His greatness! Men also will speak of two more of God's attributes.

> They shall utter the memory of Your great goodness,
> And shall sing of Your righteousness.
> (Psalm 145:7)

The word *utter* means to sputter forth, as from a bubbling, overflowing fountain. Do you ever feel that way when desiring to give praise to God for His great goodness to you? I remember years ago when my mother-in-law embraced Christ. We thought she would never see the light. When she made that decision to give her life to God, we made so many calls. It was a sputtering forth, overflowing fountain, at the goodness of God! Not only will men speak of His goodness, but they will also sing of God's righteousness. David says, they shall sing hymns of praise for thy righteous dealings with them. When your heart is overflowing with praise, do you ever catch yourself breaking out in song? I have a dear friend who is always singing. She wakes up singing and goes to bed singing. I even remember asking her husband one time how he lives with such a woman? She is a constant reminder to me to praise the Lord in song! David now adds four more attributes of God to his prayer of praise in the next verse.

> The LORD is gracious and full of compassion,
> Slow to anger and great in mercy.
> (Psalm 145:8)

David says *the Lord is gracious*. This is undeserved favor that God bestows. He is not just compassionate, but David says He is *full of compassion*. He has pity on his children, just as a father has pity on his children. This reminds me of the daughter of Pharaoh when she saw baby Moses floating in the ark on the river. The Bible tells us in Exodus 2:6, "And when she had opened it, she saw the child, and behold, the baby wept. So she had compassion on him, and said, 'This is one of the Hebrews' children.'" That compassion led to action. She didn't just say, "Oh, isn't that a cute baby," and let him float on down the river. She got him out of there, and sent for a Hebrew woman to nurse the child (See Exodus 2:7-9). She took care of him. God is like that. He is compassionate, but more than Pharaoh's daughter, He is perfect in His compassion, and He is full of compassion. He also is *slow to anger*, which means He is long of anger. Anger refers to the breathing part of the body, the nose, the nostril or face. By the act of breathing, emotions can be expressed. In anger the nose dilates and breathing becomes more intense. This anger is expressed in the flaring of the nostrils. God is slow to get angry, unlike much of humanity, which is quick to fly off the handle. Sometimes even running errands can be hazardous, as people have become increasingly angry on the roads! He also is *great in mercy*. His mercy is great, just like his goodness in verse 7. David certainly knew that God's mercy was great. He deserved death, according to the Old Testament law, after his adultery with Bathsheba, and yet God spared his life (2 Samuel 2:12, 13). There was also another time as well in David's life when he numbered the Israelites and Judah, and he knew he had greatly sinned against the Lord. Gad the prophet gave him three choices: seven years of famine, three months of pursuit by his enemies, or three days of pestilence. David answered Gad by saying, "I am in great distress. Please let me fall into the hand of the LORD, for His *mercies* are very great; but do not let me fall into the hand of man." David is looking over his life and reflecting on the mercy of God that has been shown to him. Many times David deserved the wrath of God, just like we do, and yet God showed great mercy. Not only are His mercies great, but in verse 9 David reflects on another attribute of God—His goodness!

> The LORD is good to all,
> And His tender mercies are over all His works.
> (Psalm 145:9)

Notice that *the Lord is good to all*, and that *His tender mercies are over all His works*. *Tender mercies* is one Hebrew word, and it expresses the tender pity, the yearning compassion of a parent. God is good to all His creation and all His creatures. He sends rain on the just and the unjust according to Matthew 5:45. Not only do men give praise to God, but so do His works.

> All Your works shall praise You, O LORD,
> And Your saints shall bless You.
> (Psalm 145:10)

Psalm 148 is a good example where all creation is called upon to praise the Lord. Also, in the New Testament, in Luke 19, we read that Jesus was riding into Jerusalem on a donkey, and it says the disciples began to rejoice and praise God with a loud voice for all the mighty works that they had seen. Some of the Pharisees, not liking that, told Jesus to rebuke them. Jesus replied, "I tell you that if these should keep silent, the stones would immediately cry out" (Luke 19:40). Not only do His works praise Him, but David says *Your saints shall bless You*. *Saints* would include all those who have gone before us in heaven now, the angels, as well as all on earth who are holy ones. What will the saints and His works praise God for anyway? The answer is found in verses 11 and 12.

> They shall speak of the glory of Your kingdom,
> And talk of Your power.
> (Psalm 145:11)

Is this a topic you've had lately with your friends, your family, or at church—God's kingdom and His power? We will talk about a lot of topics: children, weather, sports, the latest news, but when did you have a talk about the glory of the kingdom, where God rules and reigns? If you don't talk about it now, you will in heaven according to Revelation 11:15-17: "Then the seventh angel sounded: And there were loud voices in heaven, saying, 'The kingdoms of this world have become the kingdoms of our Lord and of His Christ, and He shall reign forever and ever!' And the twenty-four elders who sat before God on their thrones fell on their faces and worshiped God, saying: 'We give You thanks, O Lord God Almighty, the One who is and who was and who is to come, because You have taken Your great power and reigned.'" The saints will do this:

> To make known to the sons of men His mighty acts,
> And the glorious majesty of His kingdom.
> (Psalm 145:12)

The phrase *sons of men* means a child or a boy. The idea here is that we should desire to tell children about the power of God, and the glorious majesty of His Kingdom. This is very similar to verse 4. There are those who don't know of the kingdom and what is to come, and we should have a desire to share with them. It is not just any kingdom that compels us to share. It is a very special kind of kingdom. What kind of a kingdom is it? Verse 13 tells us!

> Your kingdom is an everlasting kingdom,
> And Your dominion endures throughout all generations.
> (Psalm 145:13)

God's *kingdom* will last forever. What is a *dominion*? It is a rule, reign or government. It is used of God's sovereignty and the scope of His rule. Other kingdoms rise and fall, but the kingdom and reign of our Lord is forever and ever. Nebuchadnezzar says in Daniel 4:3, "How great are His signs, and how mighty His wonders! His kingdom is an everlasting kingdom, and His dominion is from generation to generation." And as we come to verse 14, David is perhaps reflecting at the end of His life on the wonderful attribute of God, the attribute of His strength!

> The LORD upholds all who fall,
> And raises up all who are bowed down.
> (Psalm 145:14)

David says *The Lord upholds all who fall.* The word *fall* is a participle, meaning the falling; they are the ones that are ready to fall. This would be those who have no power to hold themselves up, who have no strength. The next phrase, *and raises up all who are bowed down*, also contains a participle—*raises*. It means is raising. God is continually giving strength to those who are bent under the weight of their burdens. *Bowed down* would include those who are bent down under the duties and cares and trials of life. God can strengthen them so that they do not fall or become crushed under the heavy load. This was certainly true in the life of King David. We could spend a lot of time recounting the numerous times in David's life where he was bowed down and had no strength. How often do we read things in the psalms like, "He only is my rock," "He is my defense," "He is my salvation," "He is my strong habitation," "He is my refuge, my strength?" God was constantly raising up King David when he was ready to fall. By the way, He has done the same for you and me, over and over again. So David now praises God for the provision of his physical needs in the next verse, verse 15.

> The eyes of all look expectantly to You,
> And You give them their food in due season.
> (Psalm 145:15)

The idea is that all creatures are looking to God for their needs. The phrase *due season* means at the right time, or at the proper time. Psalm 104:27 says something similar, "These all wait for You, that You may give them their food in due season." Psalm 147:9 tells us, "He gives to the beast its food, and to the young ravens that cry." Isn't it amazing that the animals look to God and know that He is the sustainer of life, and yet we humans, made in the image of God, look to others at times to meet our needs? He provides not only for our physical needs but even our desires as evidenced in verse 16.

> You open Your hand
> And satisfy the desire of every living thing.
> (Psalm 145:16)

David says of God: *You open Your hand,* which is equated with power or strength. And that hand is said to *satisfy the desire*, not simply what is necessary, of *every living thing*. *Living thing* would include men, birds, fish, beasts, and insects—all living things. Paul states in Acts 14:17, "Nevertheless He did not leave Himself without witness, in that He did good, gave us rain from heaven and fruitful seasons, filling our hearts with food and gladness." It would only be fitting that God would care for those He created. And with that King David praises God for yet another of His wonderful attributes—His righteousness.

> The LORD is righteous in all His ways,
> Gracious in all His works.
> (Psalm 145:17)

In everything the Lord does, David says, He does it right and He does it with holiness. He is totally perfect. He can never be unjust or impure, as that is totally contrary to His nature, to who He is. He wrongs no one—He does what is right. Because he can never be unjust, He is near to those who call upon Him.

> The LORD is near to all who call upon Him,
> To all who call upon Him in truth.
> (Psalm 145:18)

David says call out to the Lord. He will help you! When David was fleeing from Saul he wrote Psalm 34:18, "The LORD is near to those who have a broken heart, and saves such as have a contrite spirit." But you must call on Him *in truth*. *Truth* is sincerity, without hypocrisy. John 4:24 reminds us, "God is Spirit, and those who worship Him must worship in spirit and *truth*." God is interested in truth in the inward man as He is a God of truth. If you call on Him in truth, then something wonderful will happen:

> He will fulfill the desire of those who fear Him;
> He also will hear their cry and save them.
> (Psalm 145:19)

God will hear those who fear him and He will deliver them out of their trouble. Psalm 37:4 reminds us to "Delight yourself also in the LORD, and He shall give you the desires of your heart." Are you desirous of something this day dear one? Then fear the Lord and delight yourself in Him, and the promise is that He will grant those desires. Jesus tells us in Matthew 7:11, "If you then, being evil, know how to give good gifts to your children, how much more will your Father who is in heaven give good things to those who ask Him!" Not only is there a promise of answered prayer for those who fear Him, but there is another wonderful promise in verse 20 for those who love Him.

> The LORD preserves all who love Him,
> But all the wicked He will destroy.
> (Psalm 145:20)

The word *love* in the Hebrew is a word which expresses an ardent and vehement inclination of the mind and a tenderness of affection at the same time. If you feel that way about God, then His promise is that He will keep you, watch over you and defend you. You might say, why did David have to go and ruin a perfectly good psalm about God's wondrous attributes by putting the next phrase in there? *But all the wicked will He destroy*, which, by the way, expresses utter ruin and extermination. David included this because God's justice is another one of His attributes, just like His goodness, His mercy, His greatness, and all the other attributes we have looked at. It is part of who He is and another reason why David praises Him. Exodus 34:7 says of God, that He is "keeping mercy for thousands, forgiving iniquity and transgression and sin, *by no means clearing the guilty,* visiting the iniquity of the fathers upon the children and the children's children to the third and the fourth generation." What if God decided not to destroy the wicked? We would be spending our eternity with wicked people and wickedness. By now I hope we are all as excited and thrilled as David is in this psalm of praise and can echo the last verse of this psalm with him. David ends the same way he began it, with a determination to praise the Lord.

> My mouth shall speak the praise of the LORD,
> And all flesh shall bless His holy name
> Forever and ever.
> (Psalm 145:21)

Not only will David praise the Lord, but he also calls upon all flesh to bless His name forever and ever! *Holy name* means the name of His holiness. It is similar to the last verse in the Psalter, Psalm 150:6, "Let everything that has breath praise the LORD. Praise the LORD!" What a wonderful song of praise to the great and awesome God we serve. Perhaps the Hebrews had a great idea saying it three times a day. Do you think if you quoted Psalm 145 three times a day it would change your outlook on life?

As one man said, "Let the song begin and there shall be no end to it. It shall go on for ever and a day, as the old folks used to say. If there were two for-evers or 22 for-evers, they ought to be spent in the praises of the ever-living, ever-blessing, ever-blessed Jehovah."[34] As we close this lesson, and as we close this book, let's stand and praise our God with this prayer of praise!

> *I will extol You, my God, O King*
> *And I will bless Your name forever and ever.*
> *Every day I will bless You,*
> *And I will praise Your name forever and ever.*
> *Great is the LORD, and greatly to be praised;*
> *And His greatness is unsearchable.*
> *One generation shall praise Your works to another,*

34 Charles Spurgeon. *The Treasury of David*-Hendrickson Publishers-Volume III. page 382.

And shall declare Your mighty acts.
I will meditate on the glorious splendor of Your majesty,
And on Your wondrous works.
Men shall speak of the might of Your awesome acts,
And I will declare Your greatness.
They shall utter the memory of Your great goodness,
And shall sing of Your righteousness.
The LORD is gracious and full of compassion,
Slow to anger and great in mercy.
The LORD is good to all,
And His tender mercies are over all His works.
All Your works shall praise You, O LORD,
And Your saints shall bless You.
They shall speak of the glory of Your kingdom,
And talk of Your power,
To make known to the sons of men His mighty acts,
And the glorious majesty of His kingdom.
Your kingdom is an everlasting kingdom,
And Your dominion endures throughout all generations
The LORD upholds all who fall,
And raises up all who are bowed down.
The eyes of all look expectantly to You,
And You give them their food in due season.
You open Your hand
And satisfy the desire of every living thing.
The LORD is righteous in all His ways
Gracious in all His works.
The LORD is near to all who call upon Him,
To all who call upon Him in truth.
He will fulfill the desire of those who fear Him;
He also will hear their cry and save them.

The LORD preserves all who love Him,
But all the wicked He will destroy.
My mouth shall speak the praise of the LORD,
And all flesh shall bless His holy name
Forever and ever.
Psalm 145:1-22

Questions to Consider

A Prayer of Praise

Psalm 145

1. (a) Read Psalm 145 and list all the attributes of God. (b) Are any of these new to you?

2. (a) Using a Bible Dictionary (or some other help), look up these attributes of God and write down their definitions. (b) How does this help you better understand who God is? (Note: If you don't have any Biblical helps, use a regular dictionary. The meaning may not be as rich, but it will do!)

3. In thinking back over David's life, how were these attributes of God manifested toward him? Scan 1 and 2 Samuel for help.

4. (a) According to the following passages, what things were shared from generation to generation? Exodus 12:25-28; Exodus 13:11-16; Deuteronomy 6:6-9; Joshua 4:19-24; Psalm 44:1-3; Psalm 71:18; Psalm 78:1-7. (b) Why was this so important? (c) What are you passing down to your children regarding the works and mighty acts of God? (See Psalm 145:4)

5. David says in Psalm 145:5 that he *will* speak of the glorious honor of God's majesty and declare His wondrous works. Determine this week to speak to at least two people of God's majesty and mighty works, and come prepared to share how God used that to bless your life.

6. (a) Looking back at question number one, how has God manifested these attributes in your life? (b) Have you stopped to praise Him? If not, do so now!

7. (a) After meditating on the attributes of God, which one stands out as especially lacking in your own life? (b) How can you become more like Him? Please write it down in the form of a prayer request.

About the Author

Susan Heck, and her husband Doug have been married for over 40 years. She has been involved in Women's Ministries for over 30 years. This includes teaching Bible Studies, counseling, and leading Ladies with the Master women's ministry at Grace Community Church in Tulsa, Oklahoma. (www.gccoftulsa.net)

Susan is a certified counselor with the Association of Certified Biblical Counselors (ACBC, formerly NANC). She is the author of "With The Master" Bible Study Series for women. Previously published books in that series are,

- With the Master Shepherding the Sheep:
  A Ladies' Bible Study of 1 Timothy
- With the Master on the Mount:
  A Ladies' Bible Study of the Sermon on the Mount
- With the Master in the School of Tested Faith:
  A Ladies' Bible Study of the Epistle of James
- With the Master in Heavenly Places:
  A Ladies' Bible Study on Ephesians
- With the Master on our Knees:
  A Ladies' Bible Study on Prayer
- With the Master in Fullness of Joy:
  A Ladies' Bible Study on the Book of Phillipians
- With the Master Before the Mirror of God's Word:
  A Ladies' Bible Study on First John

She is also the author of five published booklets:

- Putting Off Life Dominating Sins
- A Call to Scripture Memory
- A Call to Discipleship
- Assurance: Twenty Tests for God's Children
- The Liberating Gospel: A Call to Salvation

Susan's teaching ministry is an outgrowth of her memorization work on the Bible. She has personally memorized 23 books of the New Testament word-for-word (The Gospel of Matthew, The Gospel of John, Romans, Second Corinthians, Galatians, Ephesians, Philippians, Colossians, First and Second Thessalonians, First and Second Timothy, Titus, Philemon, Hebrews, James, First and Second Peter, and First, Second, and Third John, Jude, Revelation), one book of the Old Testament (Jonah), and several other portions of Scripture.

Susan and her husband have two grown children and seven grandchildren. Both children and their spouses are in full-time ministry. Because of the enthusiasm of ladies who attended Susan's Bible studies, she has been invited to speak to ladies' groups both nationally and internationally. (www.withthemaster.org)